IMAGES
of America

DORCHESTER COUNTY

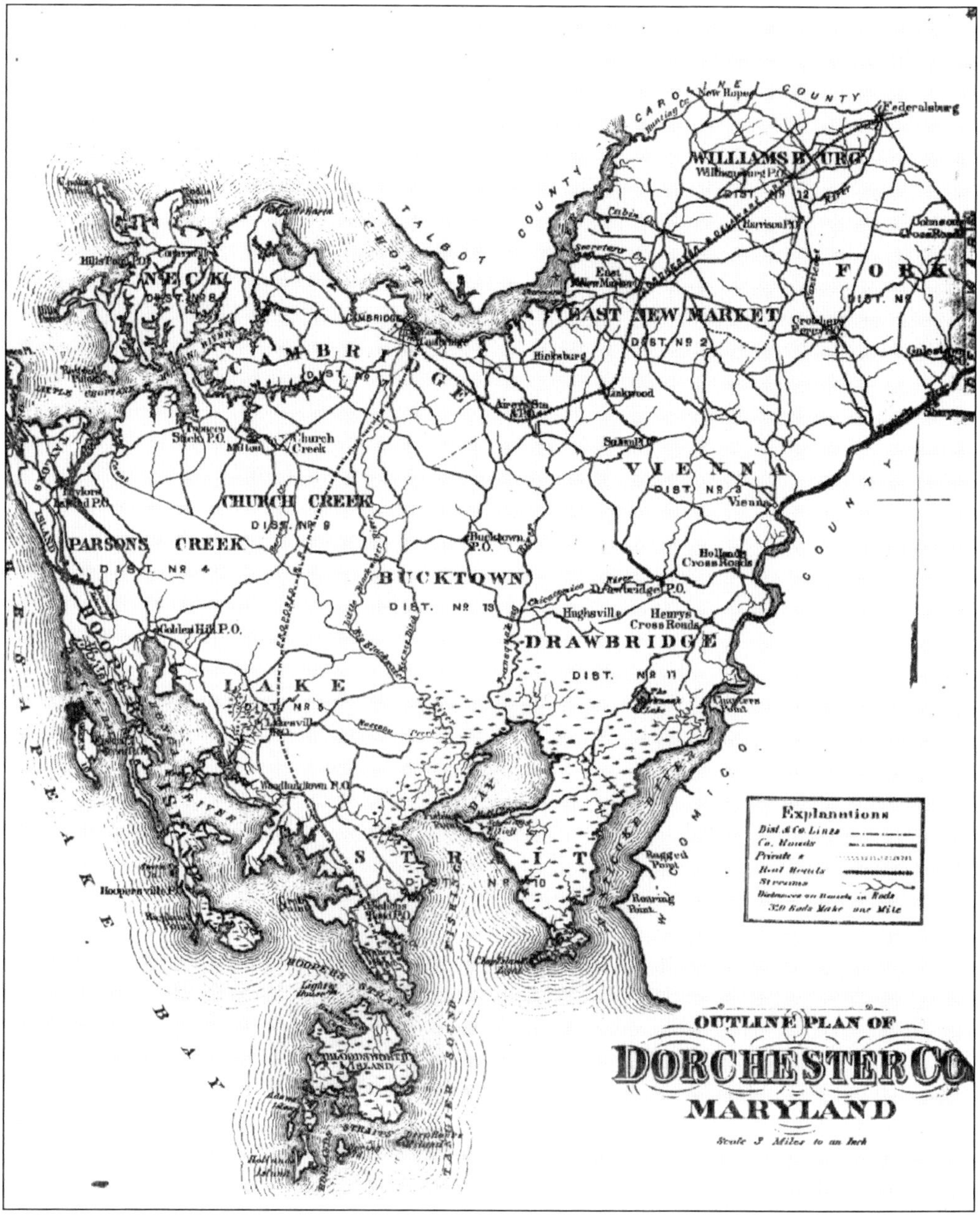

This map appeared in *An Illustrated Atlas of Talbot & Dorchester Counties, Maryland* and had been compiled, drawn, and published from actual surveys by Lake, Griffing, and Stevenson of Philadelphia, Pennsylvania in 1877. Noteworthy on this 1877 map is the absence of a bridge across the Choptank River to carry the old Vienna-Cambridge turnpike farther northward. It would be another 60 years before the Emerson Harrington Bridge spanned the river. The Dorchester and Delaware Railroad came down from Seaford across Caroline County and stopped at Williamsburg, New Market, Linkwood, Aireys, Thompson, and Cambridge. The proposed track shown from Cambridge south to Crapo never materialized.

IMAGES
of America

DORCHESTER COUNTY

A.M. Foley and Gloria Johnson-Mansfield

ARCADIA
PUBLISHING

ISBN 978-0-7385-1472-7

Published by Arcadia Publishing
Charleston, South Carolina

Printed in the United States of America

Library of Congress Catalog Card Number: 2002109232

For all general information contact Arcadia Publishing at:
Telephone 843-853-2070
Fax 843-853-0044
E-mail sales@arcadiapublishing.com
For customer service and orders:
Toll-Free 1-888-313-2665

Visit us on the Internet at www.arcadiapublishing.com

Every effort has been made to respect and trace copyrights and check facts prior to publication. However, in some instances, this proved impossible. If notified of any omissions or errors, we will be pleased to correct future editions.

Contents

ACKNOWLEDGMENTS

The authors want to apologize up front for the noteworthy people, events, and locales of Dorchester County not in these pages or not receiving the coverage they merit. With the format available, only a snapshot of such a large and varied county could be attempted. Taken together with the earlier *Images of America: Cambridge*, perhaps the picture presented here will serve to whet appetites for delving further into family and community history.

We're especially indebted to Jean Jenkins, curator, and the Dorchester County Historical Society and the staff housing their collection and that of the Dorchester County Libraries in Cambridge and Hurlock.

Others who have so generously shared their knowledge and personal collections and family treasurers were Pamela J. Abbott, Dawn Barnett, Fernando Barroso, Anna L. Blocker, Lance Bramble, Norma Lee Brinsfield, Laura Bromwell, Elizabeth Chase, Lena Collins, Oliver Collins, Flossie Conway, Ruth Hurley Dawson, Ann and Leolin Dockins and the Thompsontown Civic Association, Judy Bratten Dukes, Edward H. Nabb Research Center for Delmarva History and Culture, Calvert Evans, Shelda Truitt Fitzhugh, Mary Lee Foxwell, Neal Frampton, Claude Gootee, Rev. Enez S. Grubb, Rev. Leon B. Hall Sr., Sam and Betty Harrison, John E. Jacob, Dorothy Thomas Jensen, Lois Lane, Carol LeVarn McCabe, James and Shirley McCready, Kay N. McElvey Ph.D., Joe and Jennie Norton, Sheriff Phillip and June McKelvey, Mrs. Frederick C. Malkus Jr., Melvin Marine, Hilda Lee Marshall, Mark Marshall, Debbie Marvel, Pat Merrit, Millie's Roadhouse, Shriver and Magdalene Mills, Debra Moxey, Margaret Powell, Russell Powell, Dale Price, Peggy R. Saunders, Gene Spear, Lynn Stubbs, Mary Thompson, Freddie Waller, Debbie Wheedleton, Sylvia Brannock Windsor, and Jean Woolston. A special thanks goes to our own family members and to Dr. Gianni DeV-Hayes.

Especially helpful reference resources were:

Burton, R. Lee, Jr. *Canneries of the Eastern Shore*. Centreville MD: Tidewater, 1986.

Bourne, Michael. "Historic Homes Survey." February 1967.

Foley, A.M. and Freddie Waller. *Elliott's Island: The Land That Time Forgot*. Elliott MD: Dogwood Ridge Books, 1999.

Footner, Geoffrey M. *Tidewater Triumph*. Mystic, CT: Mystic Seaport Museum, Inc., 1998.

Forman, H. Chandlee. *Old Buildings, Gardens, and Furniture in Tidewater Maryland*. Cambridge MD: Tidewater, 1967.

Johnson-Mansfield, Gloria and A.M. Foley. *Cambridge*. Charleston SC: Arcadia, 2002.

McElvey, Kay Najiyyah, Ph.D. *Early Black Dorchester*. Ann Arbor MI: UMI, 1990

Mowbray, Calvin W. *First Dorchester Families*, vol 1. Cambridge MD, 1984.

Osborn, Albert. *John Fletcher Hurst*. NY: Eaton and Mains 1905.

INTRODUCTION

According to legend and to ancient painted-bark pictographs, the land that became Dorchester County was originally settled by people of the Lenni Lenape tribe. Over time, they developed communities along waterways that facilitated the travel and trade they loved. Game abounded in the forests and in the marshes. Fin and shellfish were readily available from Chesapeake Bay and its tributaries. Europeans settling on the western shore of Chesapeake Bay saw towering forests to the east, luring newcomers who possessed the same adventurous spirit and love of trade as the natives.

Lord Baltimore, proprietor of Maryland, wanted settlers to block encroachment from his rivals in Virginia. A Catholic himself, he granted freedom of religion to all settlers, the first religious tolerance in any colony. Land was granted to all who sailed for Maryland, with added allotments for every family member and servant in the party. Inevitably, conflicts arose with American natives. By 1669, a county of approximately 500 settlers was established. It was called Dorset and a sheriff was appointed whose natural sympathies were for his European brethren. Large tracts reserved for native peoples on the Choptank and Nanticoke Rivers passed to ever-advancing Europeans. The Native Americans either merged and adapted to a new way of life or migrated northward carrying the bones of their ancestors, knowing they would not return.

Many from Dorchester's oldest settlements on Taylors and Hoopers Island and along its waterways joined Gen. George Washington's Continental Army when English rule became intolerable. At home, the militia struggled to repel attacks by British forces and the mercenary picaroons they employed, a struggle to be repeated in 1812.

John Henry (1750–1798) was born on the Nanticoke River, educated at Princeton and Middle Temple, London, and served after the Revolution as Maryland's first United States senator before being elected the 10th governor of Maryland in 1797. No portrait of Governor Henry is known to exist, and even the precise location of his birthplace, Weston, is disputed. Weston was his father's plantation below Lewis Wharf, whose manor was razed by the British during the Revolution while Henry served in the Continental Congress. John Henry was elected to public office throughout his short life, from the time he completed his education until forced by ill health to resign the governorship.

Another future governor entered public life a few miles above Weston, in Vienna. Thomas Holliday Hicks (1798–1865) was Maryland's governor when the Civil War erupted. The county population by 1860 was 20,461, of whom 11,654 were white. Of the 8,807 blacks enumerated that year, 4,684 were freemen and 4,123 enslaved. Like many large landowners, Hicks's father owned slaves. The governor, however, resisted pressure to allow the general assembly to vote on the issue of secession. Other governors from Dorchester were Charles Goldsborough, Henry

Lloyd, Phillips Lee Goldsborough, and Emerson C. Harrington. Gov. Thomas King Carroll, who was from Somerset County, settled on the Choptank River after leaving Annapolis.

The forests that first caught the eye of settlers harbored many varieties of creatures. Fur trading was important then and continues to be in south Dorchester, although diminished recently because of controversy over the ancient practice. Along with fur traders and lumbermen, shipbuilders gravitated to the timber-rich county. Small craft were fashioned in the Native American manner, hewn from logs, and called canoes (*kun'* ers). More sophisticated Dorchester-built craft included everything from a 1814 "Baltimore" Clipper, *Catch Me Who Can*, built by John C. Tyler, to James Richardson's 1978 *Dove*, a replica of the pinnace that first brought settlers to Maryland.

Inland, the 1869 arrival of the Dorchester and Delaware Railroad and telegraph lines tied Dorchester County to markets in the north and west. Technical advances created a booming oyster canning industry in Cambridge that spread up and down river, then branched into vegetable canning. Tomatoes and produce built canning dynasties of such families as Phillips, Webster, Simmons, and others. With commerce freed by trains from waterways, hamlets and towns developed inland along the rail line.

In the Spanish-American War, eyewitnesses swore it was Hal Barber and the Ninth Cavalry, not Theodore Roosevelt and his Rough Riders, who were first up San Juan Hill. Barber, the son of Rev. Theodore Barber of Trinity Church in Cambridge, was a lieutenant commanding the African-American unit, later a major. Other locals saw military service a few years later, when Company C of the Maryland National Guard was deployed to Texas to repel raids by Francisco "Pancho" Villa, then federalized again and shipped to France in World War I. In World War II, locals served from Pearl Harbor to the Battle of the Bulge, with large numbers taking part in landings at Normandy and in the Pacific. Korea and Vietnam again saw men and women from Dorchester County answering the call.

Many of the islands whose inhabitants suffered British raids and occupation in the 1700s and 1812 are no longer inhabited. Islands now unpopulated include Hollands, Spring, Applegarth, Bloodsworth, Grays, Greens, Guinea, Snake, Clay, Barrren, James, Langralls, and Axies Islands. Relentless natural forces drove people from many of these islands, where ancestors withstood enemy assaults. Several Dorchester islands connected to fast land by scenic back roads and bridges are still inhabited and there are nine municipalities in the county—Brookview, Cambridge, Church Creek, East New Market, Eldorado, Galestown, Hurlock, Secretary, and Vienna—all worth a visit. The main thoroughfare in the county, of course, is Route 50, its Dorchester County portion dedicated to the memory of Harriet Tubman, "Moses of Her People."

One

EARLY DAYS

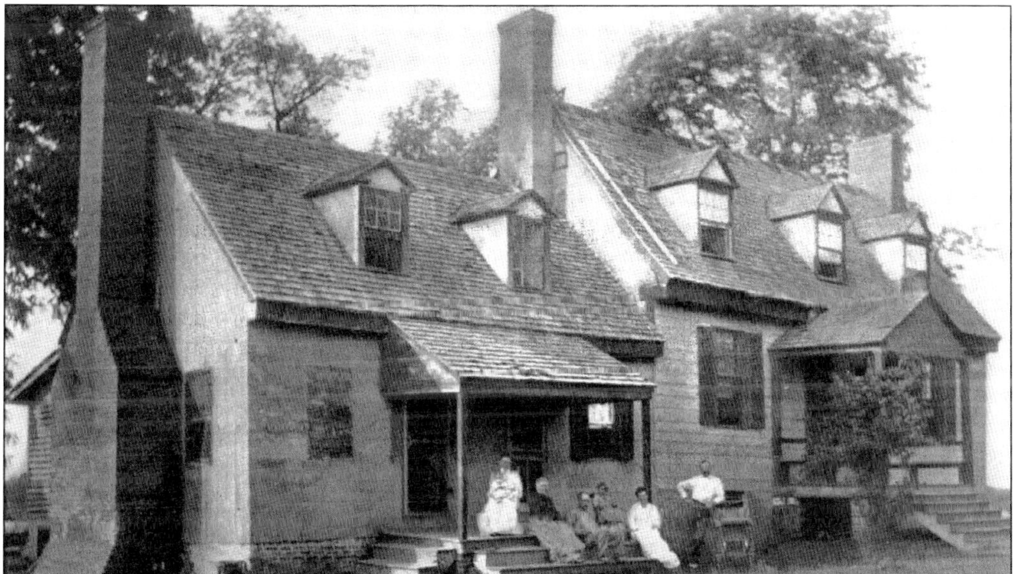

In 1704, several years after accepting appointment to arbitrate differences between European settlers and Choptank River natives, Thomas Ennals traded 6,000 pounds of tobacco, 40 pounds of sterling, and 320 rough cloaks called "match coats" in exchange for 4,660 acres that had been reserved for the native people. Pictured here in 1904 is the manor house of Piney Neck, later called Bonnie Brook. Bonnie Brook occupied a portion of former Ennals land that has long since been subdivided.

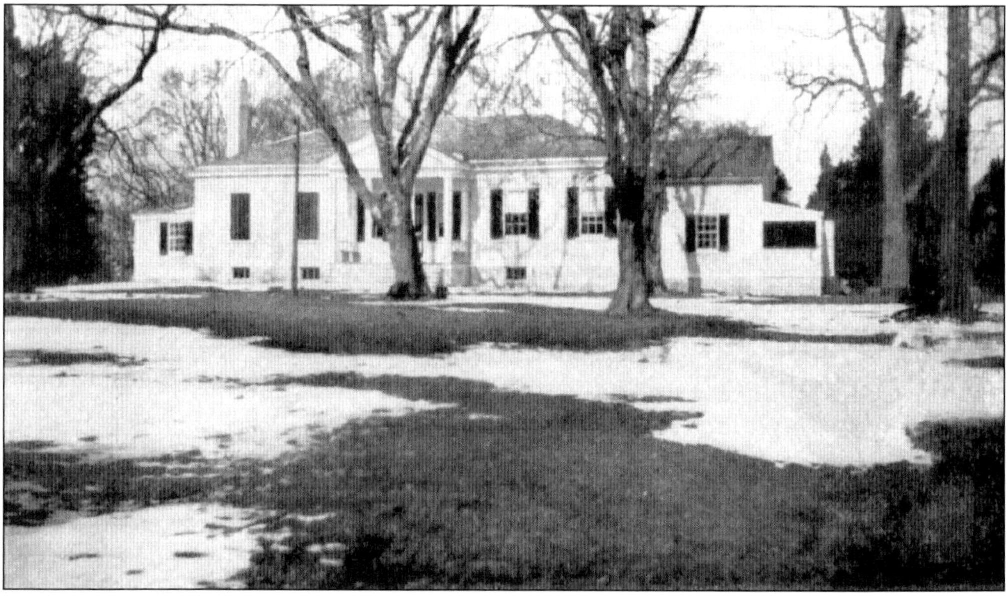

Eldon occupied a portion of the land purchased by John Ennals in 1704. It later became famed for its ancient boxwood garden. The house at Eldon was destroyed by an accidental fire, and the Elks Lodge now occupies the site. Beside Bonnie Brook and Eldon, other portions of Ennals's purchase along the Choptank evolved into Shoal Creek, Whitehall, Weir or Ware Neck, and Fairview.

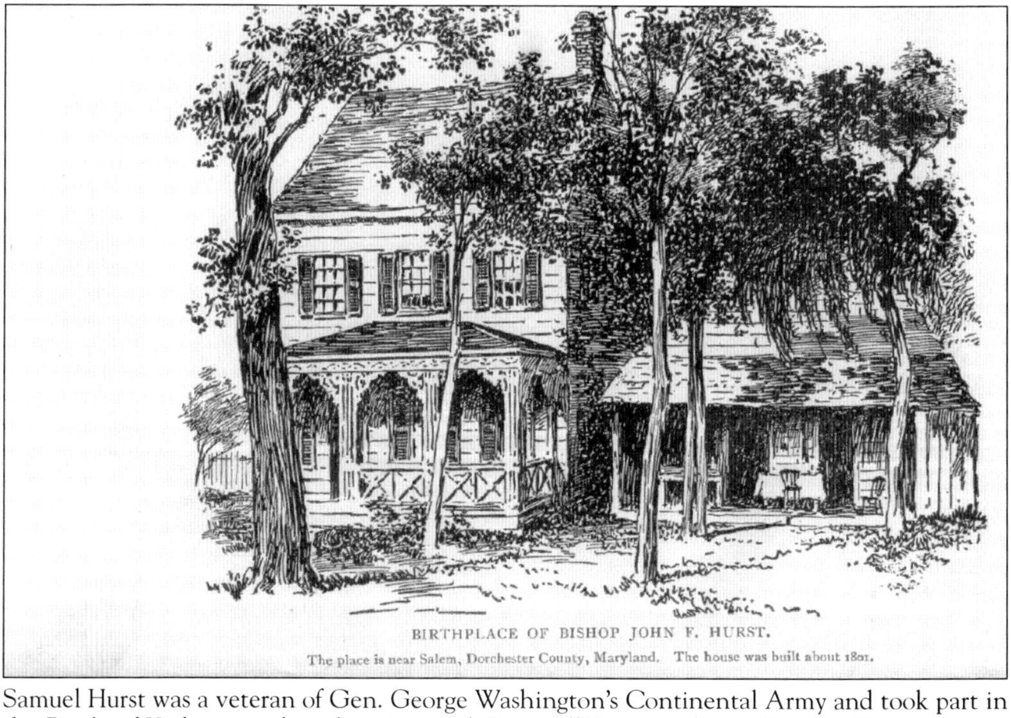

BIRTHPLACE OF BISHOP JOHN F. HURST.

The place is near Salem, Dorchester County, Maryland. The house was built about 1801.

Samuel Hurst was a veteran of Gen. George Washington's Continental Army and took part in the Battle of Yorktown, where he witnessed Cornwallis's surrender ending the Revolutionary War. Returning to Dorchester County, he settled on a farm near Salem, which was passed to his son Elijah in 1824. In this farmhouse in 1834, Elijah's son John Fletcher Hurst was born.

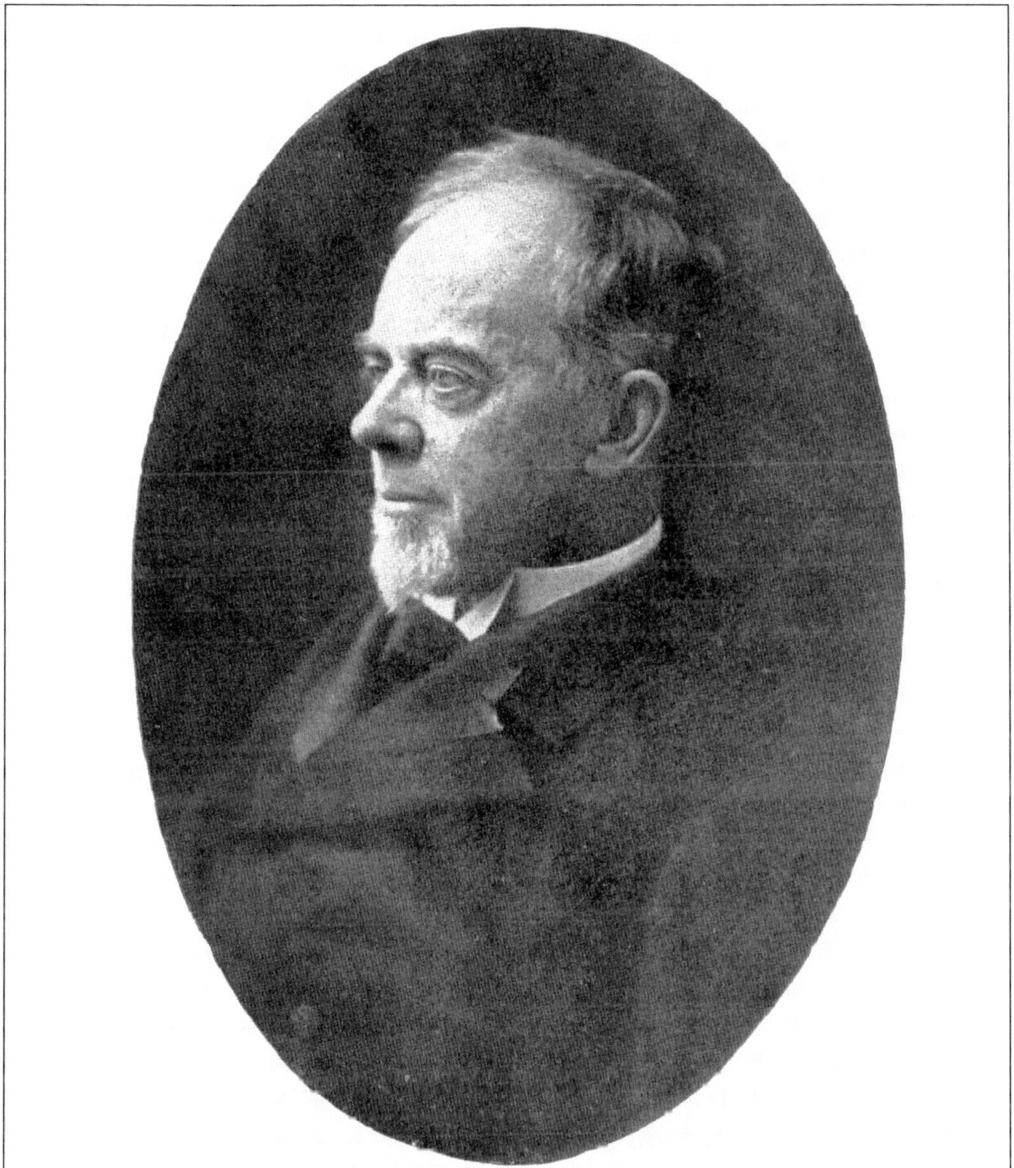

From photograph by G. C. Cox, 1896.

John Fletcher Hurst (1807–1880) was born near Salem and moved at age four, when his father Elijah bought Piney Neck, a 250-acre farm across the creek from Samuel Hurst. Despite being asthmatic, John attended Cambridge Academy, usually walking for miles, occasionally having to lie down to wait for his breath and strength to return. Elijah's last surviving son, John, was destined to be a farmer, but one day became so engrossed in a book while watering the horses that they strayed off, unnoticed. "John," Elijah said, "there's no use of you staying around here. You'll never make a farmer. Pack your trunk and go to school." John Hurst completed his classical education at Dickinson College, where his Cambridge pastor wrote, "I have not the shadow of a doubt upon my mind the Lord will make a useful man of you, both in the church and in the world." John became Bishop Hurst, saved Drew University from the scandalous financial ruin of Daniel Drew, "The Wolf of Wall Street," and proceeded to found American University in Washington D.C.

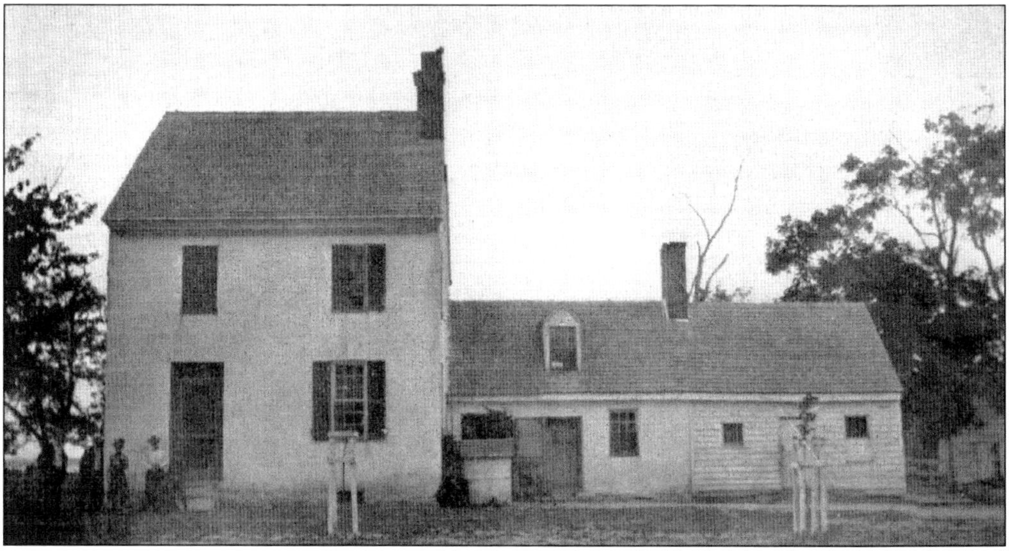

Weir Neck farm was purchased by Revolutionary War veteran Samuel Hurst around 1809. It was located just east of Cambridge on what came to be called Hurst's Creek, previously known as Cavithey Willis's Creek. Samuel's son Elijah later moved from his farm in Salem to Bonnie Brook, across Hurst Creek from Weir Neck, where he raised John Fletcher Hurst, a future bishop. Bishop Hurst owned Weir Neck, above, from 1839 to 1863.

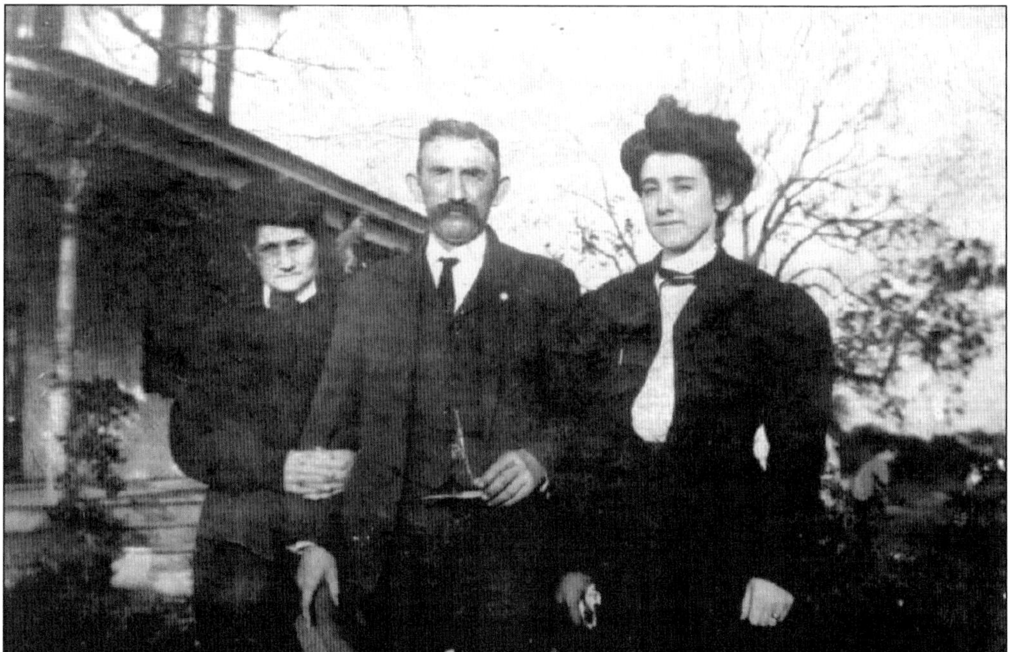

Bishop John Fletcher Hurst sold Weir Neck farm to Charles Henry Seward, who left it to his son-in-law and daughter, James Phillips and Sarah Cornelia Seward Handley. The Handleys are pictured here at Weir Neck with their daughter Nellie Clyde Handley, a pioneering photographer who stepped in front of the camera on this day around 1910.

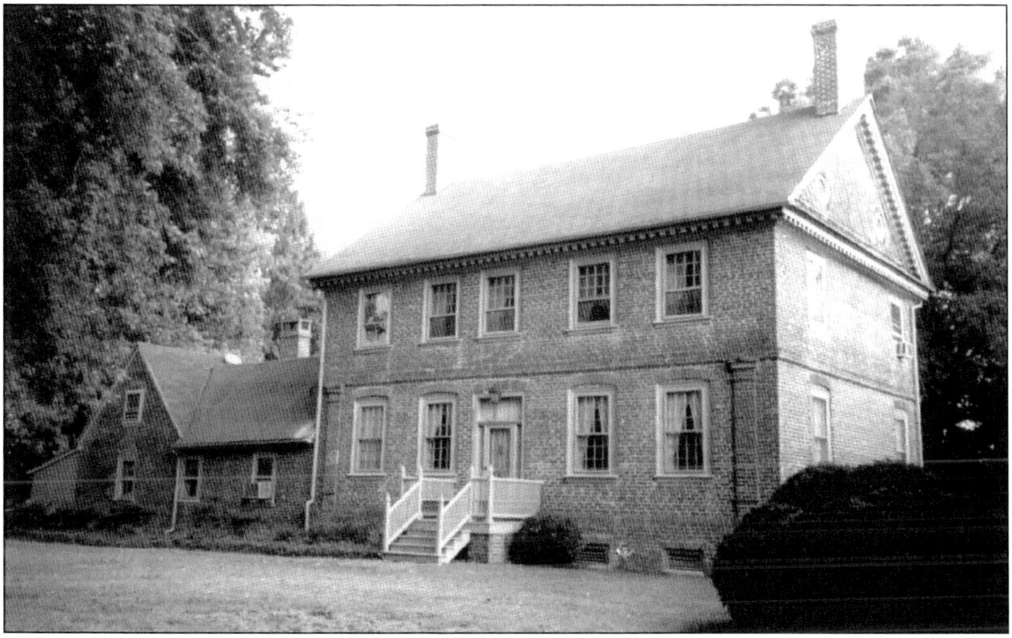

The Battle of the Boyne is still disputed in Northern Ireland, but James O'Sullivane left for Maryland after King James's setback. Here, his descendant James Sullivane prospered during the American Revolution and is credited with building Friendship Hall in (East) New Market. On the Register of Historic Places, along with much of East New Market, Sullivane's Friendship Hall reputedly included every amenity for gracious entertaining, including its own racecourse.

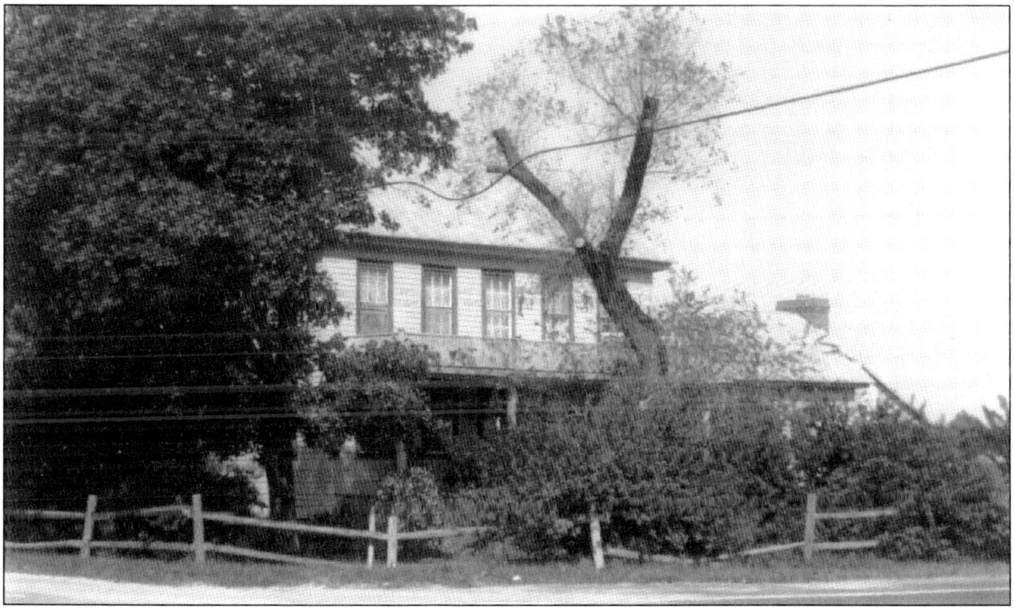

Joe Johnson ran a tavern on the Mason-Dixon Line at the junction of Dorchester, Caroline, and Sussex Counties, now Reliance. His mother-in-law Patty Cannon lived across the road. The county seats were so distant that Joe and Patty's gang terrorized the region throughout the early 1800s, murdering travelers and kidnapping freemen to sell into slavery. Patty was finally charged with murder, but Joe fled and was never found.

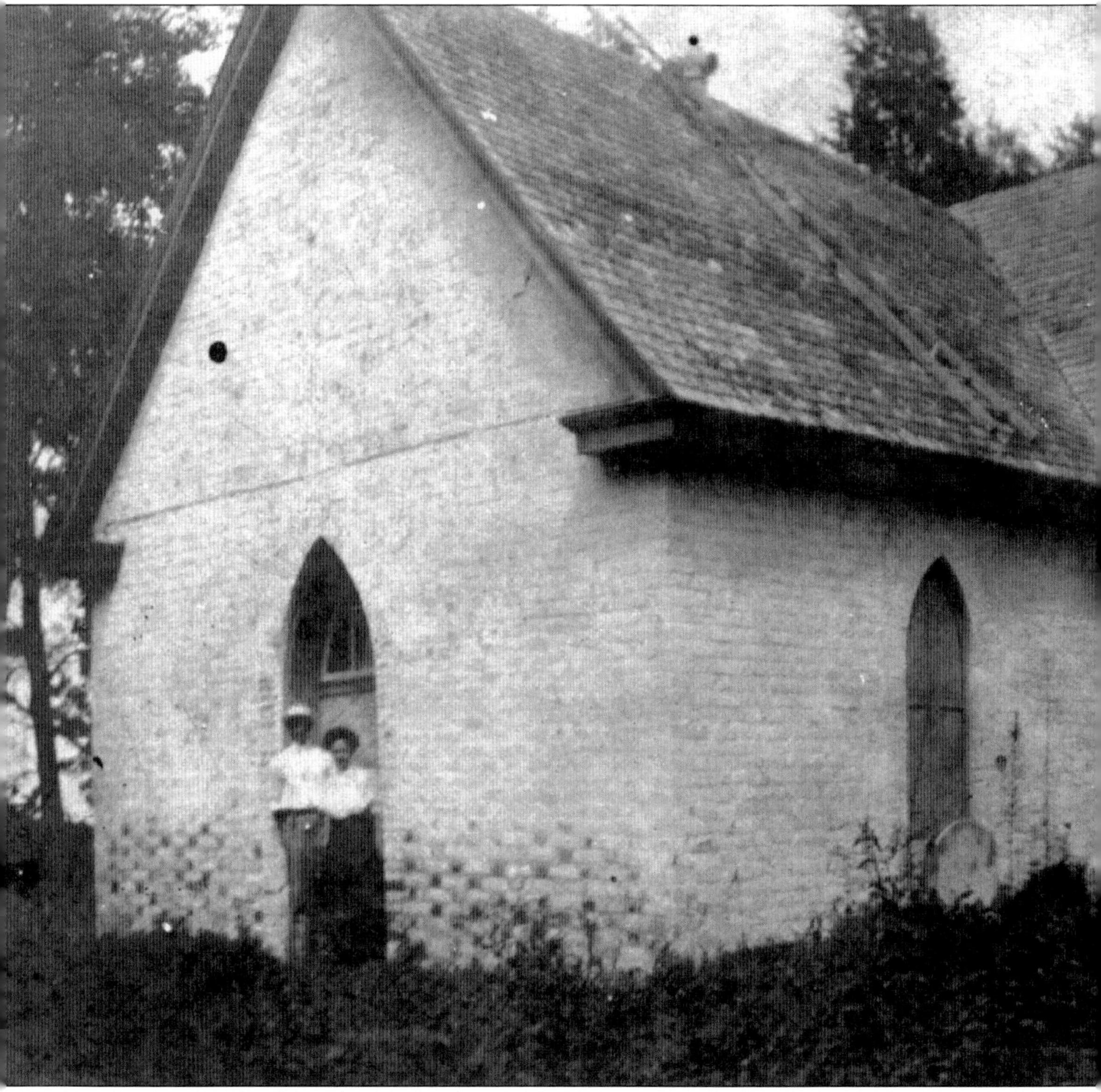

Trinity Church of Dorchester Parish, pictured in 1908 with Rev. and Mrs. Roy Jones in its doorway, originated in the late 1600s. "The Old Church," as it was known, suffered periodic neglect, even enduring use as a sheep and cattle enclosure, before regaining its present state of grace. Early in the 1900s, local preservationists joined to finance the maintenance of the church and upkeep of the grounds. Then, between 1953 and 1960, Col. and Mrs. Edgar Garbish decided to sponsor complete restoration of the venerable structure in memory of her parents, Mr. and Mrs. Walter P. Chrysler. In the Williamsburg manner, and not without controversy, additions were removed, even a vestry room dating to the mid-1700s. The original church was then taken apart brick by numbered brick, and reassembled around steel framing. Meticulous care was taken that every fixture was appropriate to the original. Historic figures rest in its shaded grove at Church Creek, including a number of Revolutionary War veterans, Maryland governor Thomas King Carroll, and his daughter Anna Ella Carroll, who was a military strategist and advisor to President Abraham Lincoln.

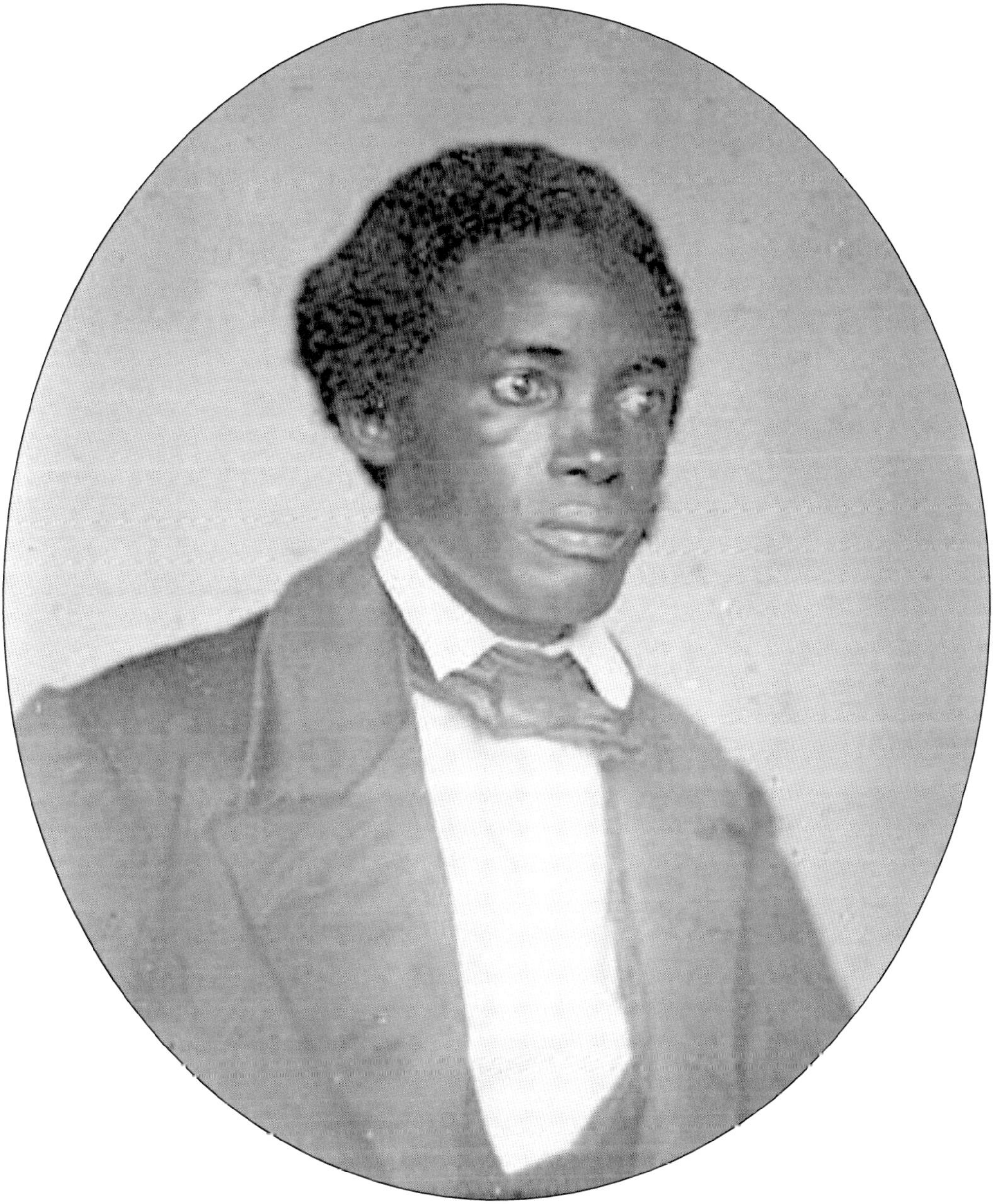

Stephen Allen Benson (1816–1865), pictured here in a daguerreotype taken shortly before his death, was born a freeman in Dorchester County. When he was six, his family emigrated to Liberia on the African coast in a resettlement movement sponsored by the American Colonization Society, a white-sponsored movement of mixed motives. The settlers initially met resistance from native Africans. Stephen and four brothers and sisters were captured and carried off in an attack in which his father was wounded and one brother killed. By 1842, a government similar to early American development was taking shape. Stephen Benson won a seat on the Colonial Council and served as a judge from 1847 until his election as the Republic of Liberia's first vice president in 1853. Benson advanced to serve as Liberia's second president for eight years from 1856 to 1864. He spoke several indigenous languages. After leaving office, he returned to his coffee plantation in Grand Bassa County, where he died in 1865.

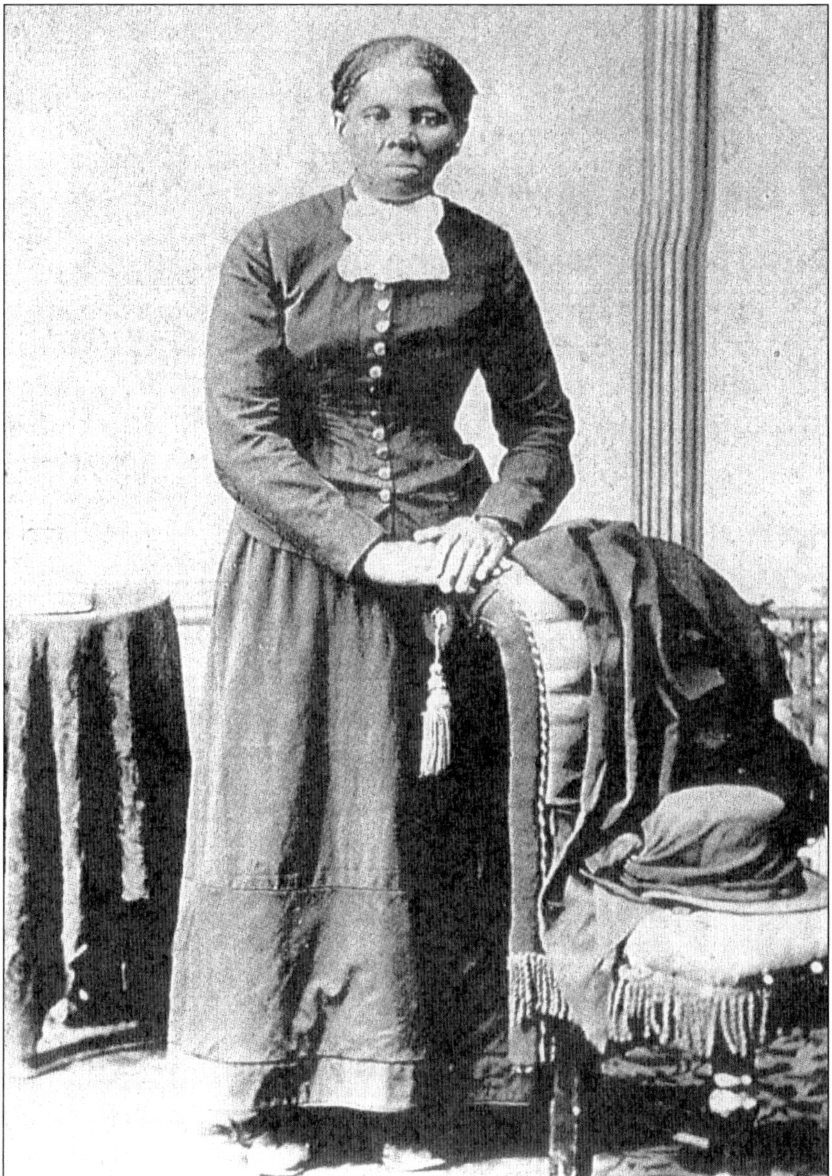

Harriet Tubman (c. 1820–1913), a woman of inestimable courage, was born near Bucktown and fled north to freedom in 1849. She cooked at a resort hotel at Cape May, New Jersey saving to aid those she planned to free. Risking all, she returned to south numerous times, prodding with her pistol those who lost courage and protecting the secrecy of the Underground Railway network and its travelers. Famed abolitionist Frederick Douglass, addressing Tubman, wrote, "The difference between us is very marked. Most that I have done and suffered in the service of our cause has been in public, and I have received much encouragement. . . . You, on the other hand, have labored in a private way. . . . I have had the applause of the crowd . . . while the most that you have done has been witnessed by a few trembling, scarred and foot-sore bondmen and women, whom you have led out of the house of bondage, and whose heartfelt 'God bless you' has been your only reward." Harriet told a fellow conductor that she returned "only where God sent." Her tombstone reads, "Servant of God, well done."

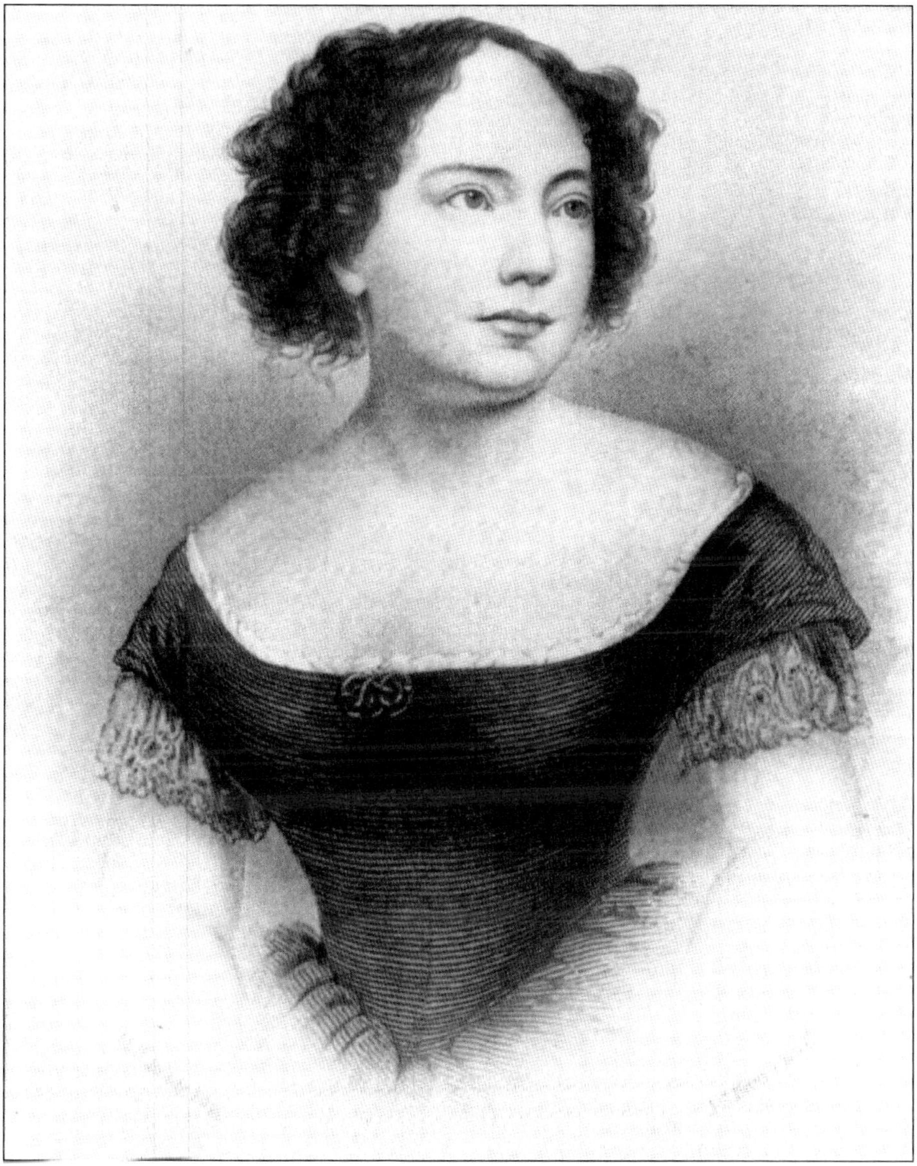

Anna Ella Carroll (1815–1894), though not a Dorchester resident, lies in Old Trinity Churchyard alongside her mother and her father, Thomas King Carroll, who moved to Castle Haven from Somerset County after serving as governor in 1830 and 1831. Anna was the eldest of eight and educated in politics and law by her father. She was a Whig Party and anti-slavery activist, though born into a slave-owning society. Upon Abraham Lincoln's election in 1860, she freed her own slaves and espoused the Union cause. When the Civil War erupted, she refocused her writings and travel from politics to military strategy. Lincoln sent her to the western front to assess Union efforts, and she is credited with devising the plan executed by Ulysses Grant. A Congressional bill was introduced to award her a pension equal to a major general, but the bill mysteriously disappeared. Her role as a civilian and a woman military advisor embarrassed some, but an 1864 painting of Lincoln with his Cabinet signing the Emancipation Proclamation includes an empty chair at the table, by a folder and maps such as she carried.

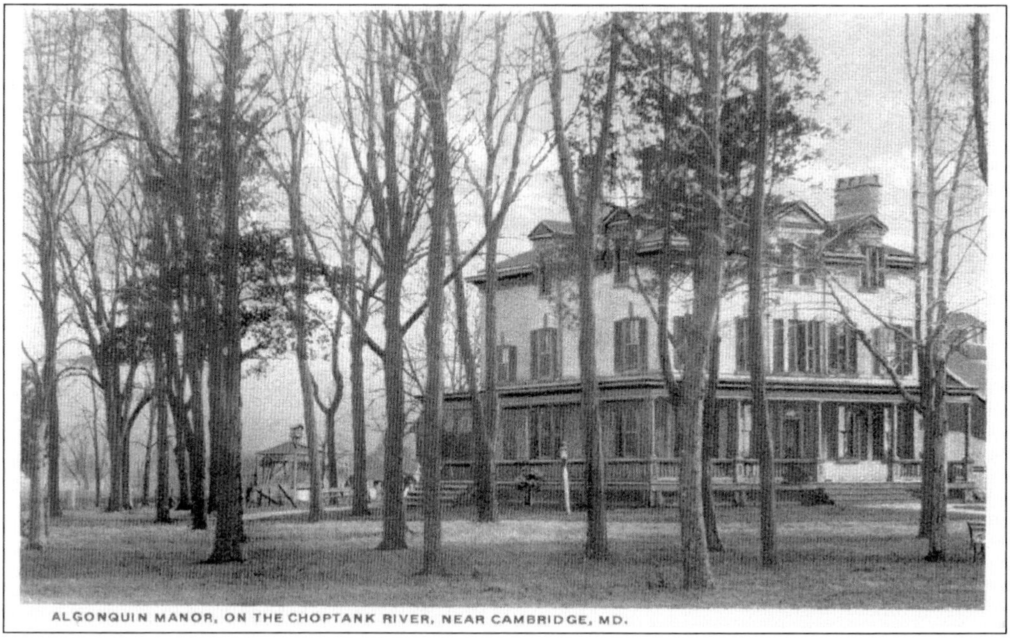

The house at Algonquin, formerly Sandy Hill, was built around 1895 for the Joseph Mundy family. The original Choptank River native people belonged to the Algonquin language group and had a village on this site. Beautiful ceremonial relics were unearthed here in the 1920s from the high, sandy riverbank—a bank accumulated over thousands of years from northwest winds blowing down the Choptank River.

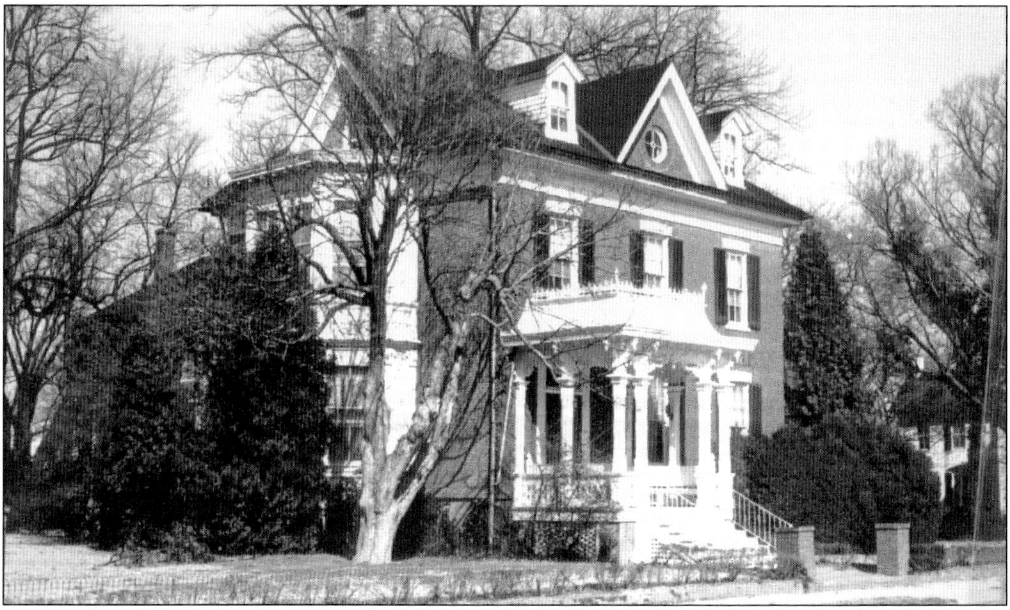

One hundred years ago, passengers and freight headed for the Cambridge steamboat wharf rumbled past the houses on historic brick-paved High Street. This house at 111 High Street was built much earlier, in 1840, before a channel was dredged in the Choptank River to admit steamers to Long Wharf. Maryland governor Phillips Lee Goldsborough (1865–1946) was reportedly born in this Federal/Greek Revival–style house.

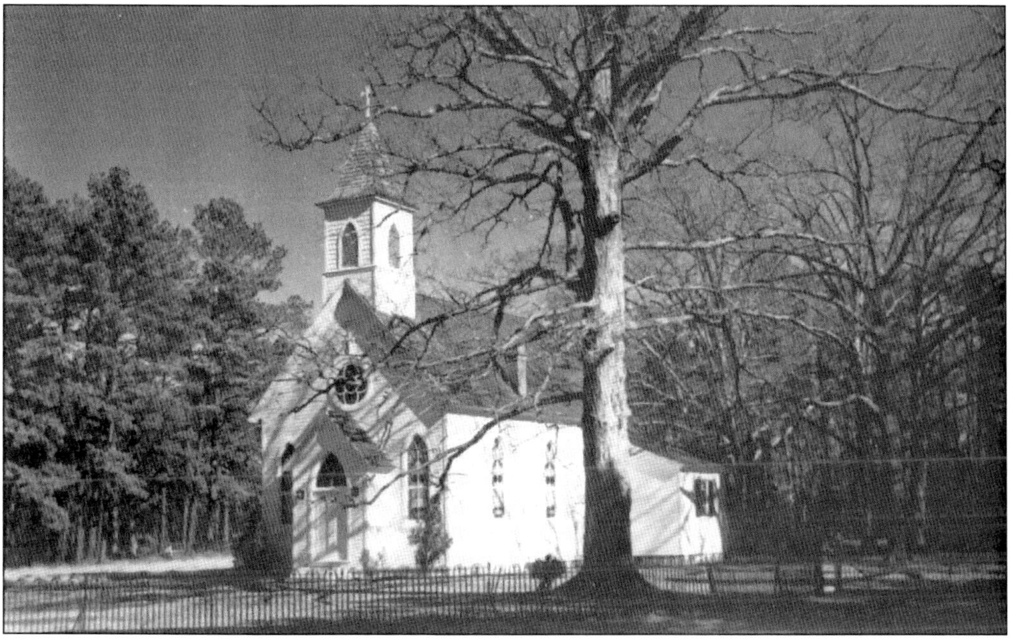

St. Mary Star of the Sea was built in 1872 in Meekins Neck. A lovely country-Gothic church, it replaced a smaller chapel across the road. The earlier St. Mary's or Tubman Chapel, built on land donated in 1769 by Richard Tubman II of nearby St. Giles Field, was originally served by Jesuit priests sailing twice yearly across Chesapeake Bay from St. Mary's County to what was called "Ye Isles of Dorset."

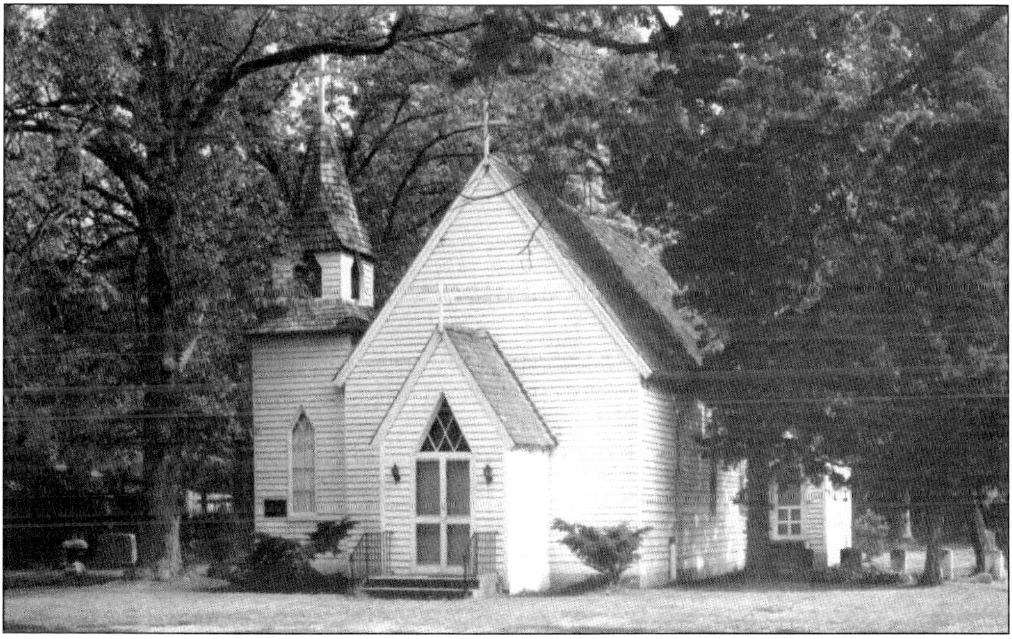

Rev. Theodore P. Barber, a Great Choptank Parish rector, undertook to replace an earlier Chapel of Ease in the Neck District. He made his decision one Sunday when he had to hold his service outdoors because of the overflowing congregation in a small schoolhouse. His vision of "a very simple chapel of wood" was realized as St. John's Chapel in Cornersville.

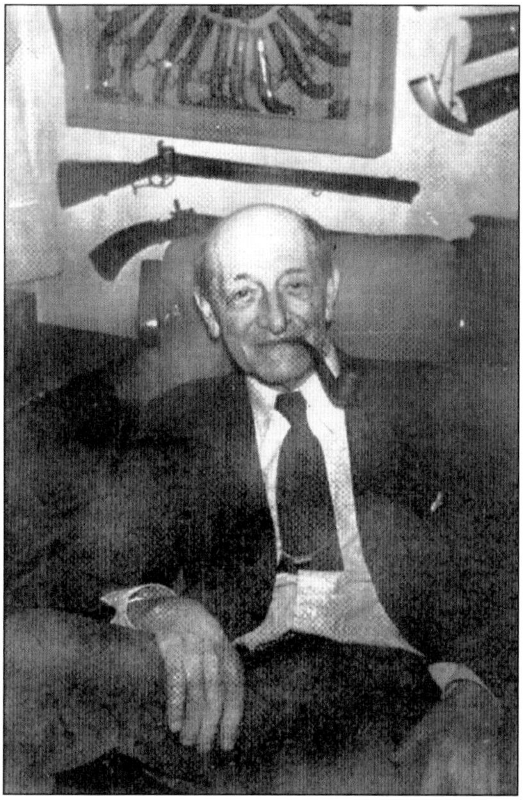

As a youngster Francis Breuil (1870–1940) haunted Philadelphia wharves, fascinated with old weapons. He shipped at 17, sailing twice around the world in a square-rigger. An army scout during the Spanish-American War, he then prospected for silver out west. Around 1900, the government rid arsenals of flintlocks and Civil War muskets, and he added to his collection. Because of its location where salt air would not harm his collection, Rehobeth attracted him.

Rehobeth was a 2,350-acre estate granted to John Lee of Virginia. The historic house suffered severe fire damage in 1916, before John Breuil purchased and painstakingly restored it. The location across Marshyhope Creek from bogs allowed him to test fire his weapons, including the Battle of Gettysburg cannon on his lawn. The interior was once arrayed chronologically with Chinese firesticks, matchlocks, blunderbusses, Revolutionary War pieces, and Captain Bligh's pistols, all in working order.

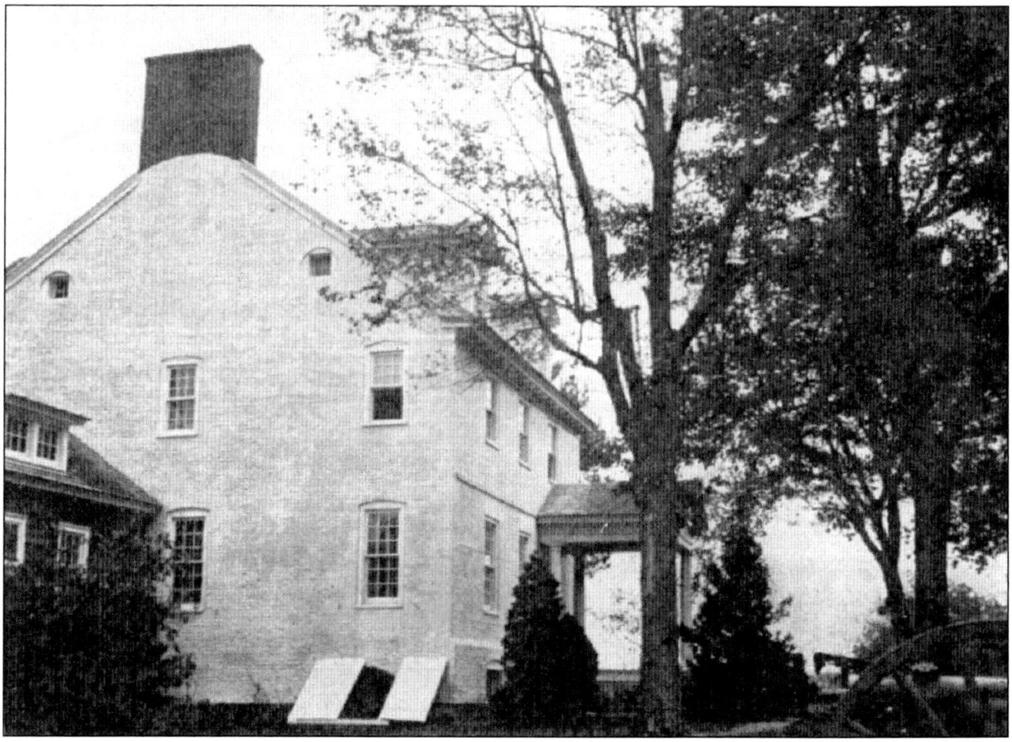

James W. McCready was a prominent Cambridge clothier who operated a haberdashery on Poplar Street. Downstairs were stylish menswear and shoes, some of his own design. Upstairs he carried work clothes for oystermen like his maternal grandfather, Levin McNamara of Elliott Island, who raised him after his own father's death. The McCreadys bought and summered at Jarvis Hill in 1910 and later lived there, where his son James is pictured here.

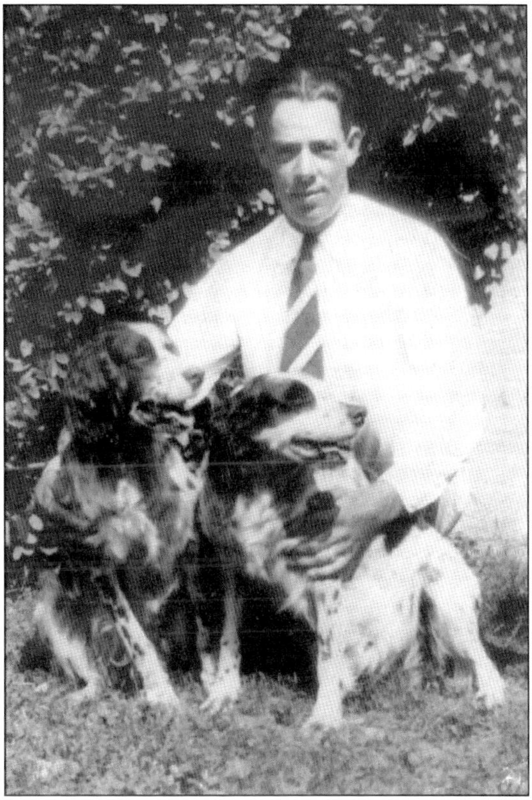

Jarvis Hill Farm was part of extensive lands wrested from native inhabitants by French Huguenot Anthony LeCompte, an early Dorchester settler. The house, built in the mid-1700s, stood on the highest ground in the Neck District, from before the American Revolution until the late 1900s. The land, and later the house, remained in the LeCompte family for two centuries. The frame and brick dwelling was studied by architectural historians.

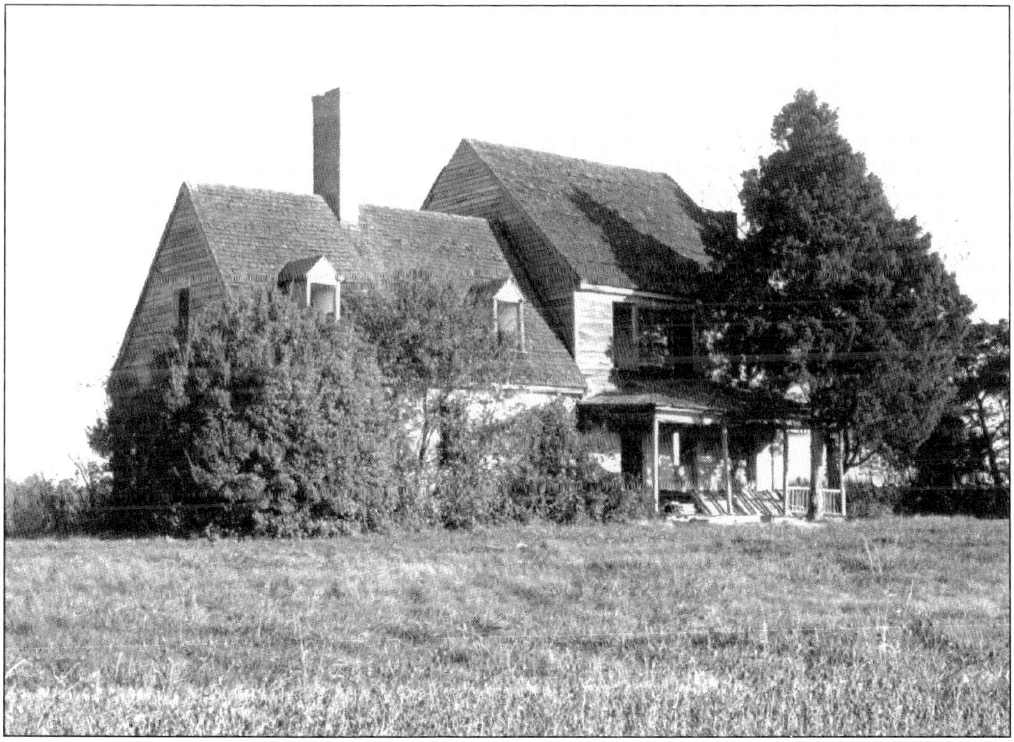

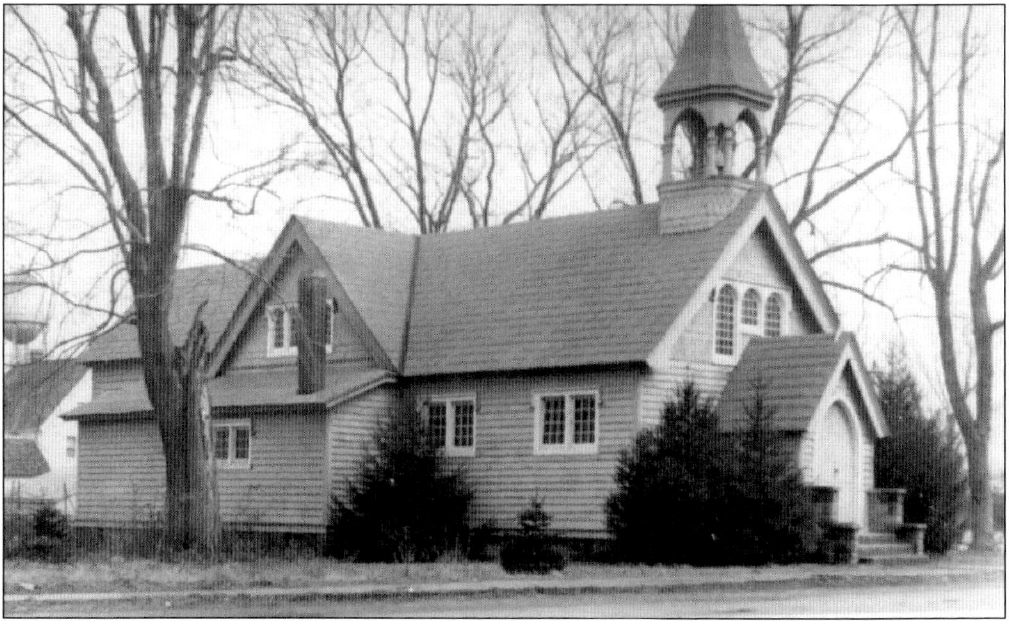

St. Paul's congregation in Vienna traces back to 1709, when Great Choptank Parish built a chapel of imported brick north of town. To serve people of the Nanticoke area, Rector Thomas Howell came from Cambridge to conduct services one Sunday each month. The present St. Paul's was designed by New York architect W. Harley Wood and was built in 1895 to replace a frame church on Race Street.

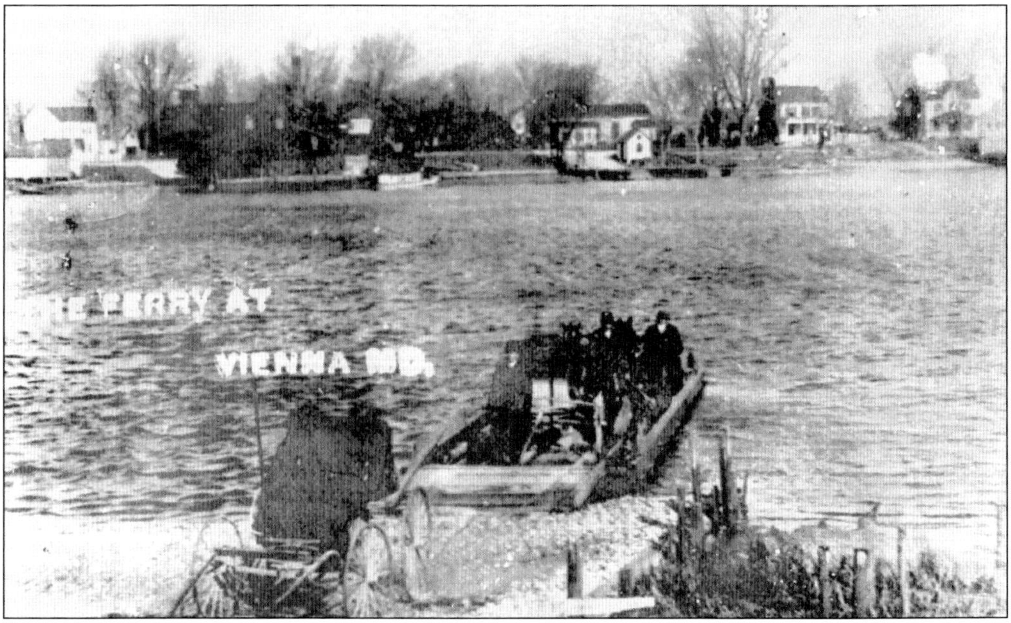

Ferries across the Choptank and Nanticoke Rivers were authorized 100 years prior to Independence. Crossings points, like this Vienna ferry, were essential to the water-laced county's development. A wooden bridge replaced the ferry for a time but fell into disuse and the ferry was re-established. Laid out in 1706, Vienna retains a federal customs house that operated from 1791 to 1866, as well as the ferry collector's house.

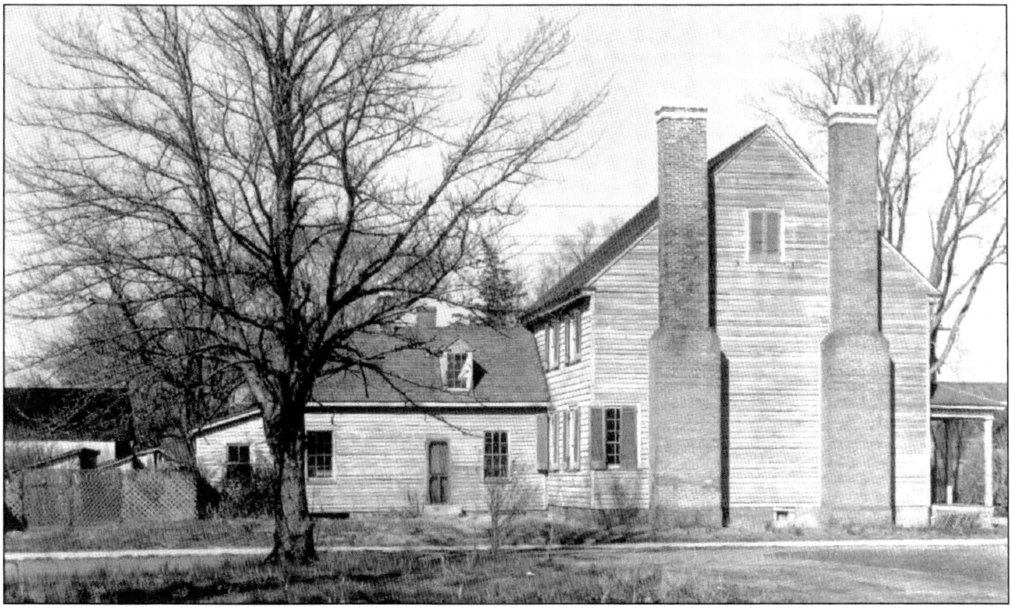

Thomas Holliday Hicks (1798–1865), the son of a large planter and slave owner, was born near East New Market and lived in Vienna on the corner of Water and Church Streets while in trade from 1820 to 1840. He served as Maryland's governor and is credited with saving Maryland for the Union at the outbreak of the Civil War. His former residence is considered the most sophisticated Federal-style house in Vienna.

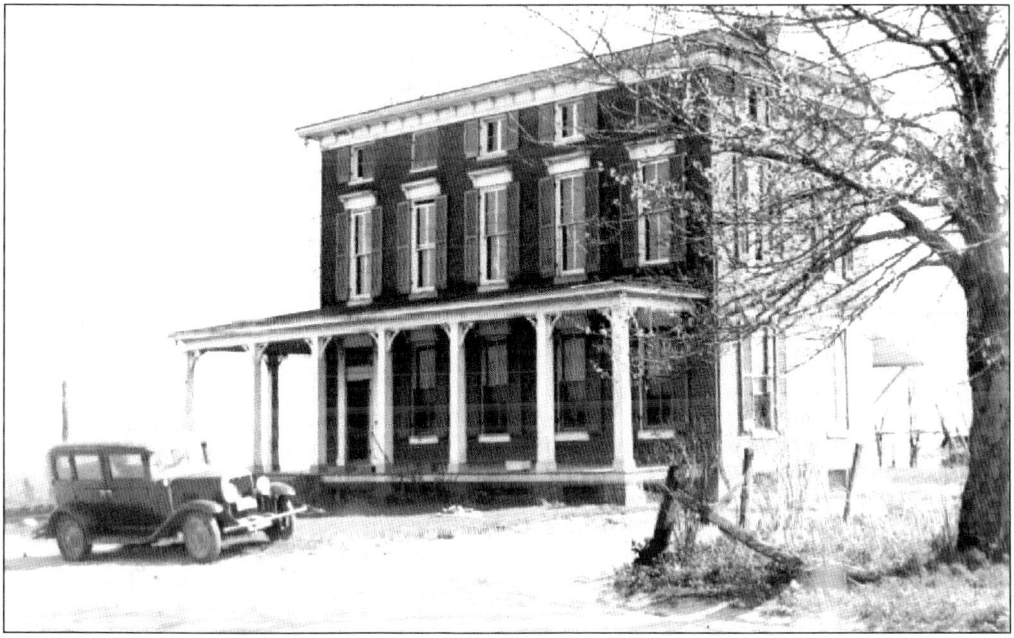

Vienna was surrounded by forests and had enough shipyards to draw the British enemy upriver repeatedly during the American Revolution and War of 1812. For many years, the town had only one brick house. The Civil War had exposed deep divisions between the townsfolk themselves. While Governor Hicks was keeping Maryland in the Union, across the street from his former residence Capt. James Lewis built "something the damn Yankees can't burn."

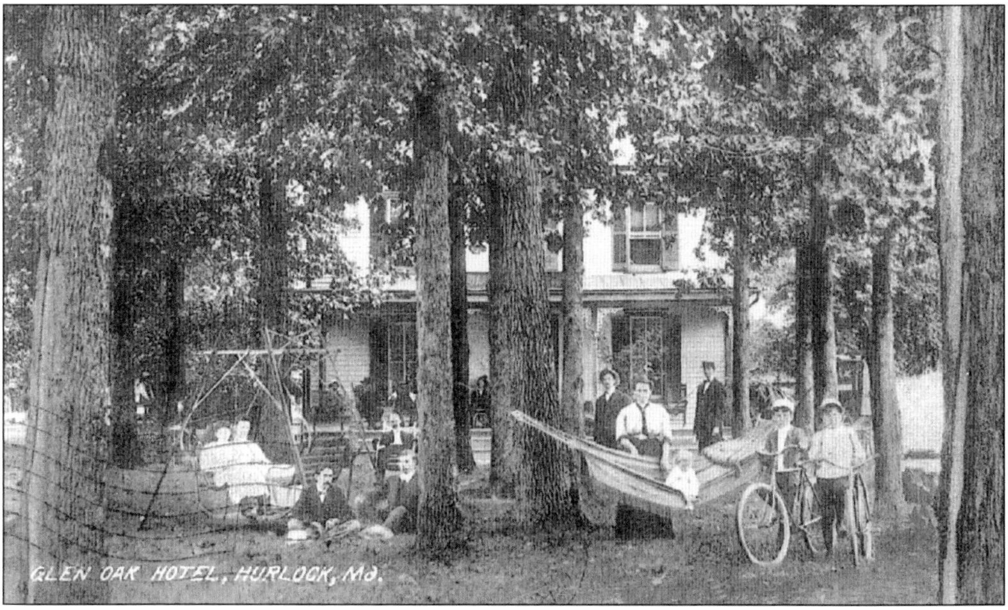

Listed on the National Register of Historic Places, Glen Oak Hotel was built in Hurlock after the railroad began bringing traveling salesman, or "drummers," to town. A drummer rented a rig from W.C. Bradley's Carriage Repository, serviced the stores that operated at most crossroads, and, with any luck, was back in time for a fine supper at the hotel. Pictured here in 1906, Glen Oak is now an apartment house.

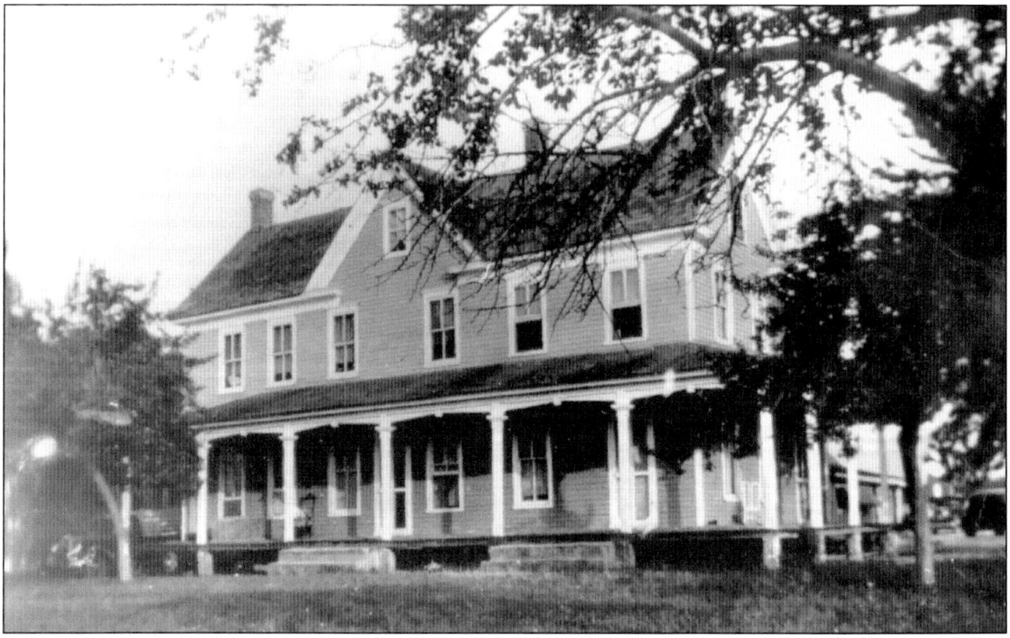

In the steamboat era, Yates Colony Hotel served salesmen and excursionists arriving at Cabin Creek. The three-story hotel included a wrap-around porch, banquet room, large hall, and a circular staircase from England. The Era family came to Dorchester from Czechoslovakia, and the hotel building was later bought by George J. and Elizabeth Era as an ideal location to raise their 11 children. It burned in the 1960s.

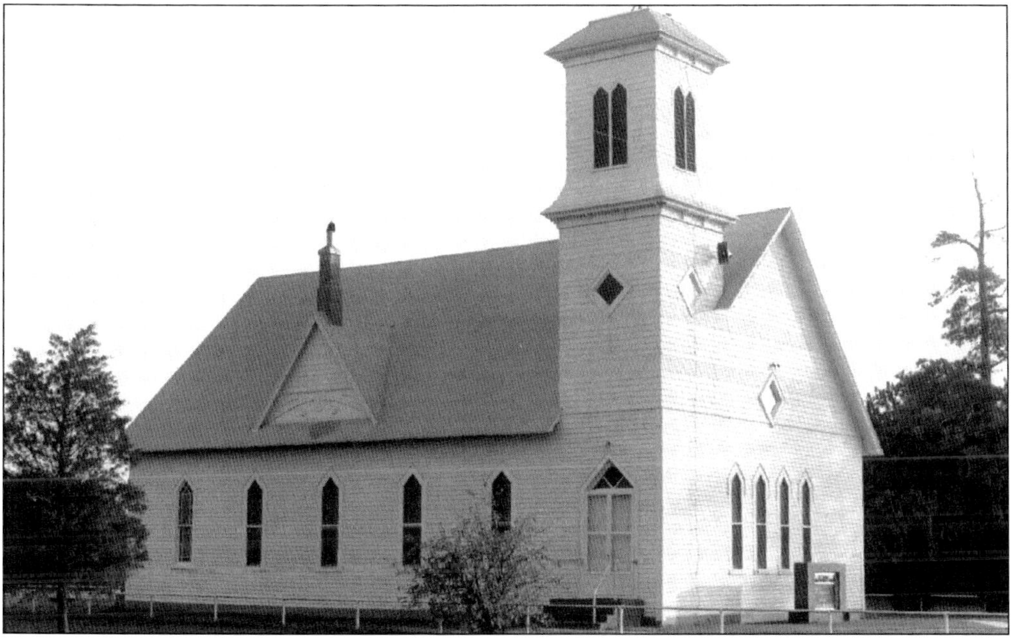

St. Thomas U.M. Church at Bishop's Head is known as "The Mother Church of the Delaware-Peninsula Conference." The largest structure in the area, the church has stood well over 100 years in testament to the faith of the community, as well as to the building skills of its members, many of whom were boat builders.

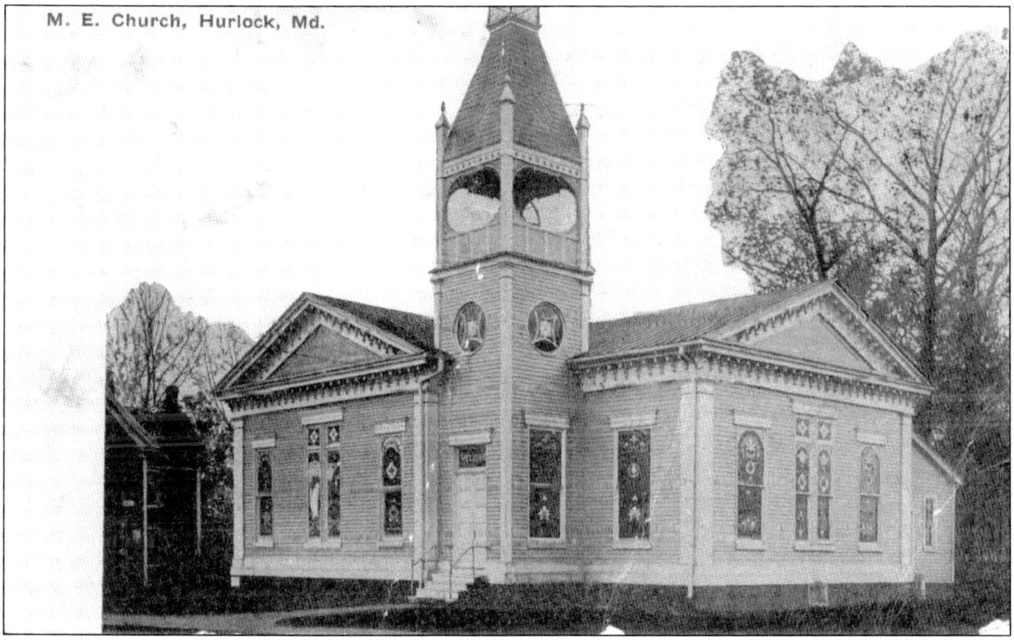

Washington Church of Hurlock, pictured on an early 1900s postcard, pre-dates the town itself. The first church was originally built in 1801, at the dawn of Methodism in Dorchester County, in a grove by the site of Washington Cemetery. In 1888, the congregation relocated into the village as the railroad spurred continued growth. In 1969 the church was renamed Unity Washington U.M. Church to incorporate the Grove Circuit.

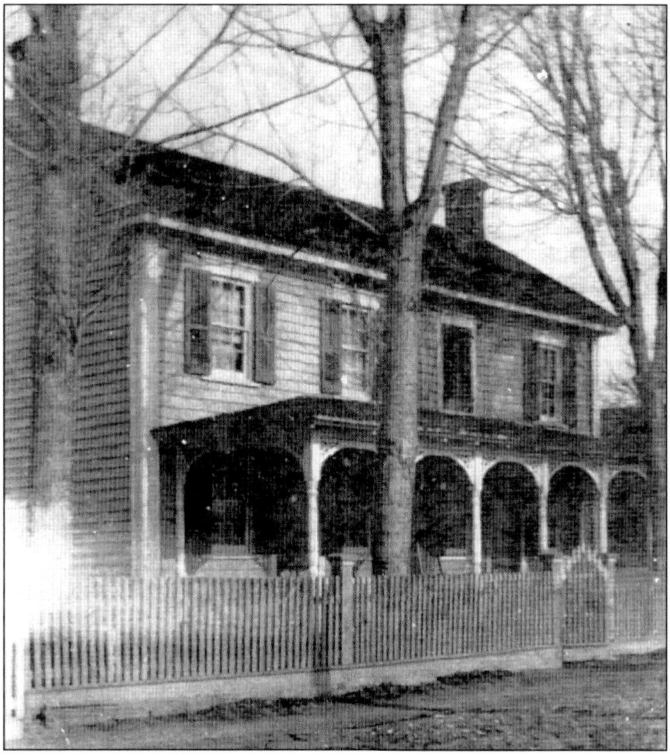

Around 1700, Black Walnut Island on Fishing Bay's eastern shore passed to Archibald Gray. It was thereafter known as Gray's Island. The Gray family endured and prospered for over 200 years on their island. This house burned around 1950 after the last family members had either died or moved. Today, only the graveyard remains on the island, but genealogists have identified over 5,000 descendants of Gray's Island.

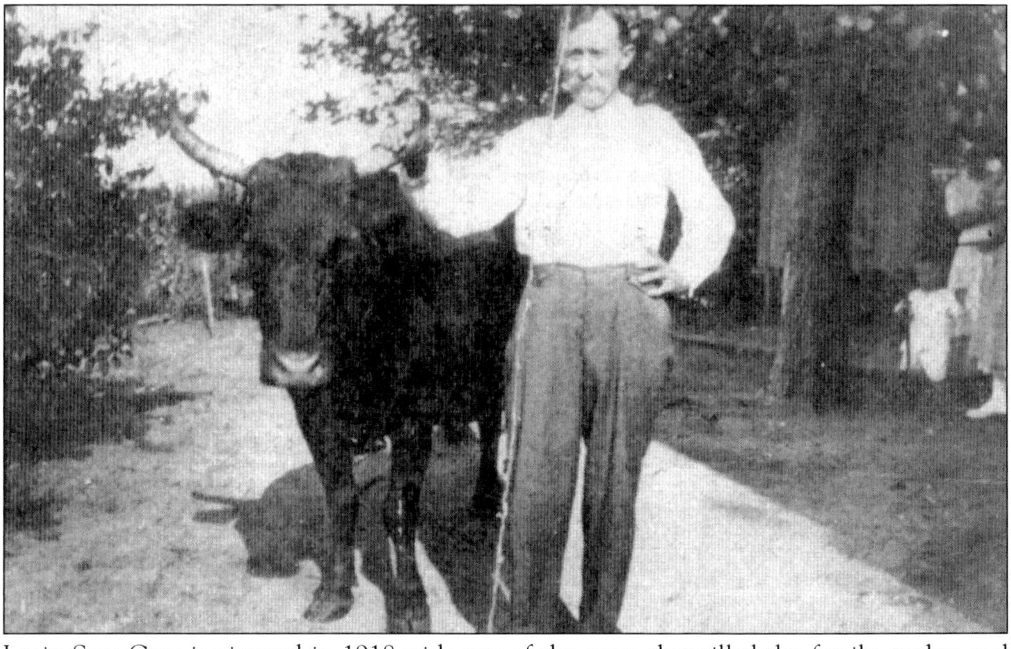

Levin Spry Gray is pictured in 1918 with one of the oxen that tilled the family garden and mowed marsh hay. Captain Spry's brother, Captain Sam, owned two of the finest bugeyes ever to sail, the *Margaret A. Travers* and the *Mocking Bird*. Oysterbeds of the pioneering Grays were not only among the first cultivated on bottom leased from the state, but they were also said to produce Maryland's most flavorful oysters.

Two

As Time Goes By

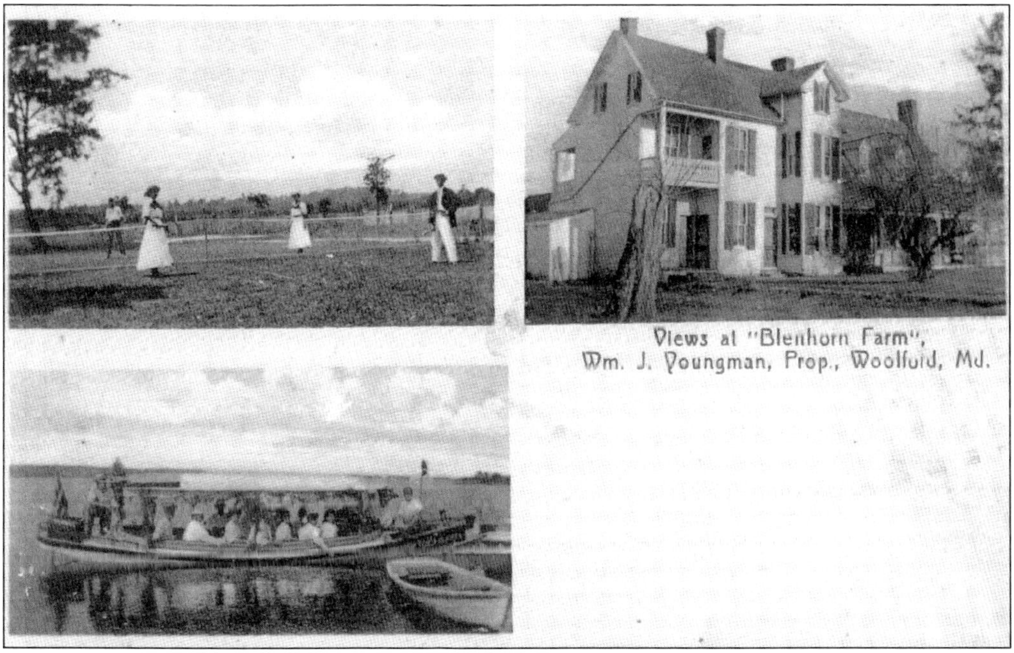

Illustrative of an ongoing trend, this early 1900s postcard depicts lawn tennis and yachting on the Choptank at Blenhorn Farm in Woolford. Blenhorn Farm was under the sway of William J. Youngman during the early 1900s. Before it passed into Mr. Youngman's hands, 1890s letterheads advertised "Blenhorn Farm, T. Guy Woolford, Proprietor, Breeder of Thoroughbred Hogs. Sty Pigs a Specialty."

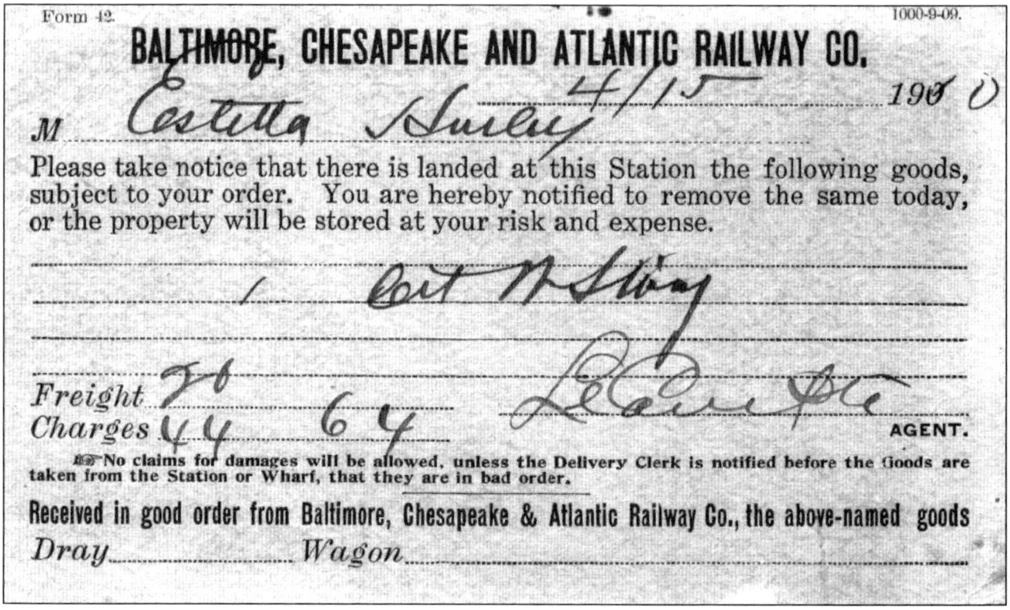

Form 42. 1000-9-09.

BALTIMORE, CHESAPEAKE AND ATLANTIC RAILWAY CO.

4/15 1910

M Estella Hurley

Please take notice that there is landed at this Station the following goods, subject to your order. You are hereby notified to remove the same today, or the property will be stored at your risk and expense.

Freight
Charges

AGENT.

No claims for damages will be allowed, unless the Delivery Clerk is notified before the Goods are taken from the Station or Wharf, that they are in bad order.

Received in good order from Baltimore, Chesapeake & Atlantic Railway Co., the above-named goods

Dray .... *Wagon* ....

This notice from the Baltimore, Chesapeake, and Atlantic Railway was sent in 1910 to Mrs. Estelle Hurley in Vienna notifying her that her goods had arrived at the station. Some said the BC&A on trains stood for "black coal and ashes." By the time summer excursionists reached Ocean City on the BC&A, they were covered with soot blown in through the train windows.

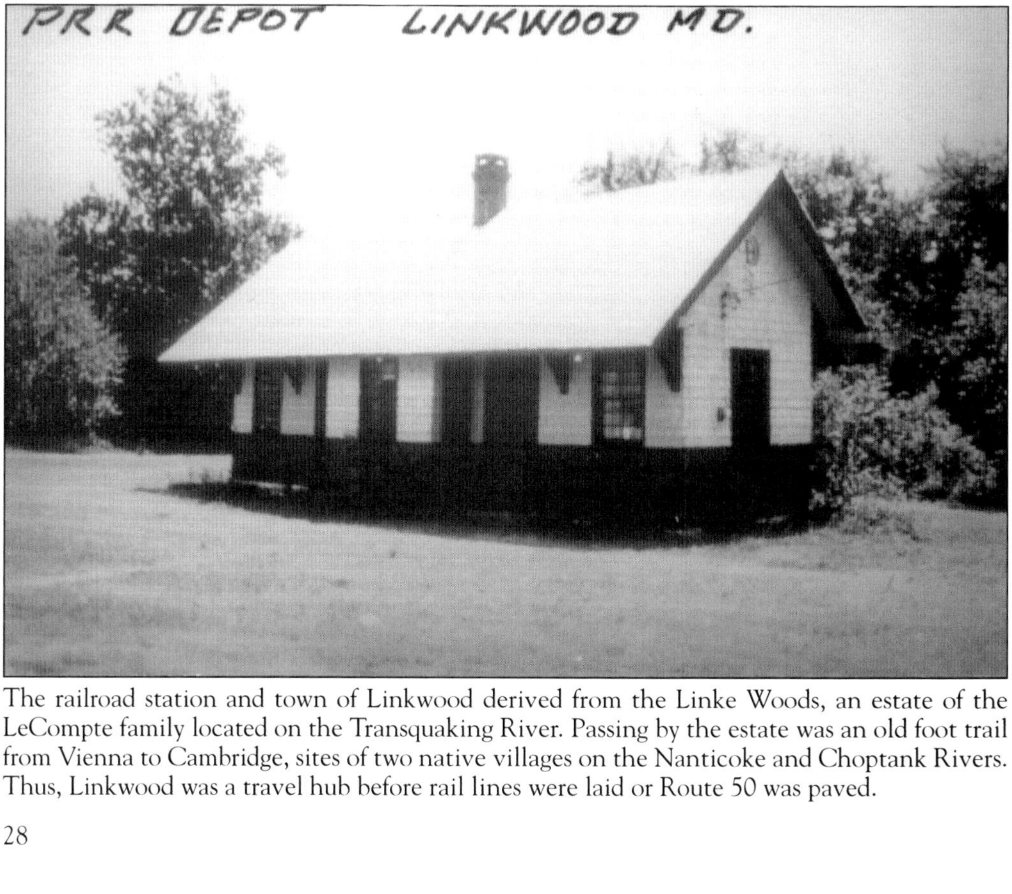

The railroad station and town of Linkwood derived from the Linke Woods, an estate of the LeCompte family located on the Transquaking River. Passing by the estate was an old foot trail from Vienna to Cambridge, sites of two native villages on the Nanticoke and Choptank Rivers. Thus, Linkwood was a travel hub before rail lines were laid or Route 50 was paved.

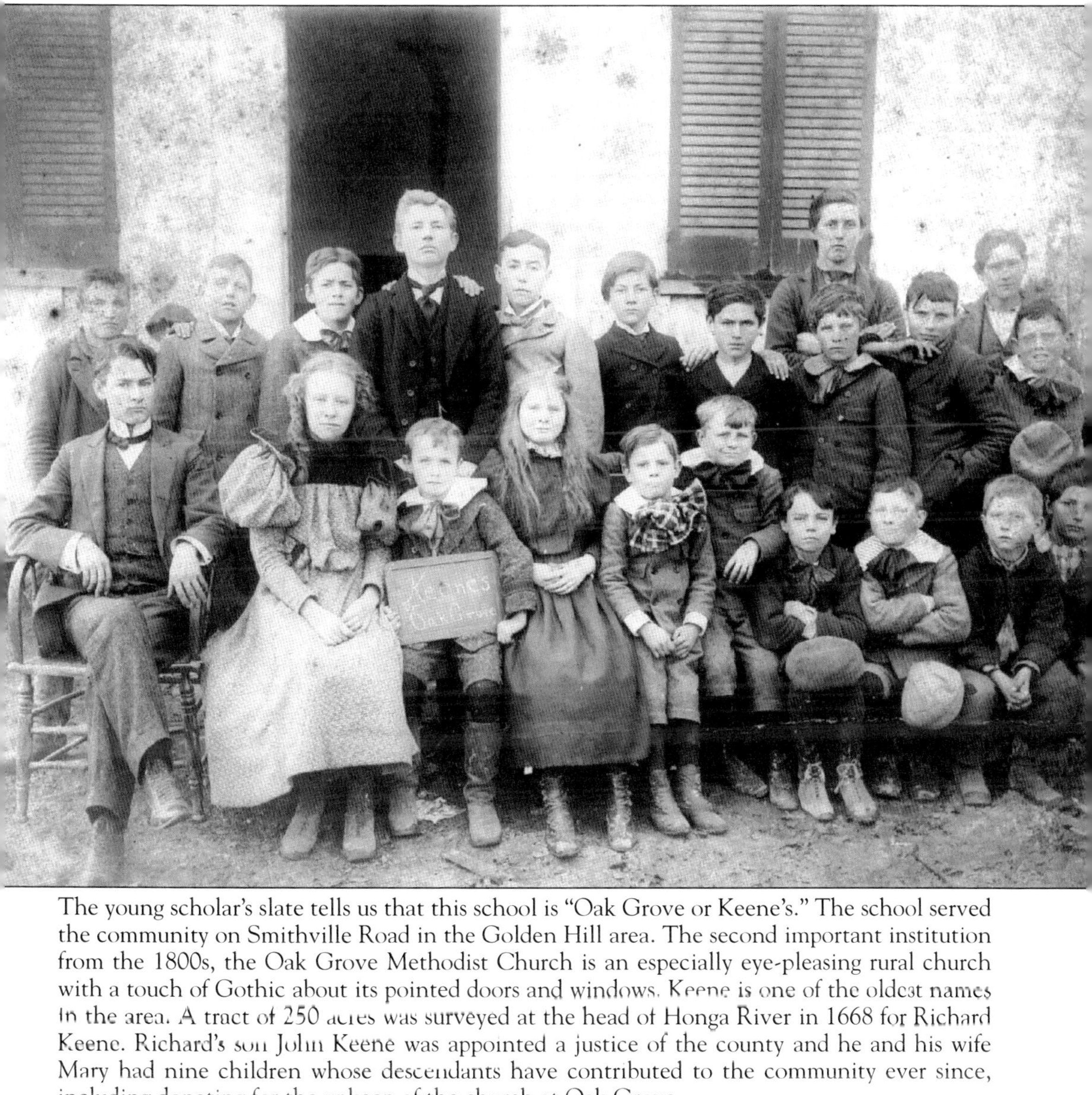

The young scholar's slate tells us that this school is "Oak Grove or Keene's." The school served the community on Smithville Road in the Golden Hill area. The second important institution from the 1800s, the Oak Grove Methodist Church is an especially eye-pleasing rural church with a touch of Gothic about its pointed doors and windows. Keene is one of the oldest names in the area. A tract of 250 acres was surveyed at the head of Honga River in 1668 for Richard Keene. Richard's son John Keene was appointed a justice of the county and he and his wife Mary had nine children whose descendants have contributed to the community ever since, including donating for the upkeep of the church at Oak Grove.

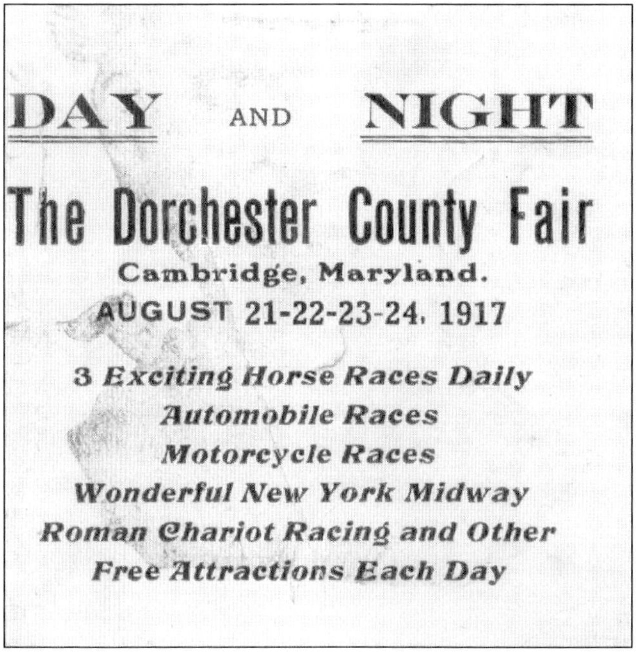

The Dorchester County Fairground on the old road to Church Creek saw plenty of excitement in 1917. Later, during World War II, the fairground held a camp for German prisoners of war. Captives deemed non-threatening worked on farms and in canneries during the severe manpower shortage created by the wartime draft. Many POWs were farmers and undoubtedly preferred captivity on the Eastern Shore to service on the Eastern Front.

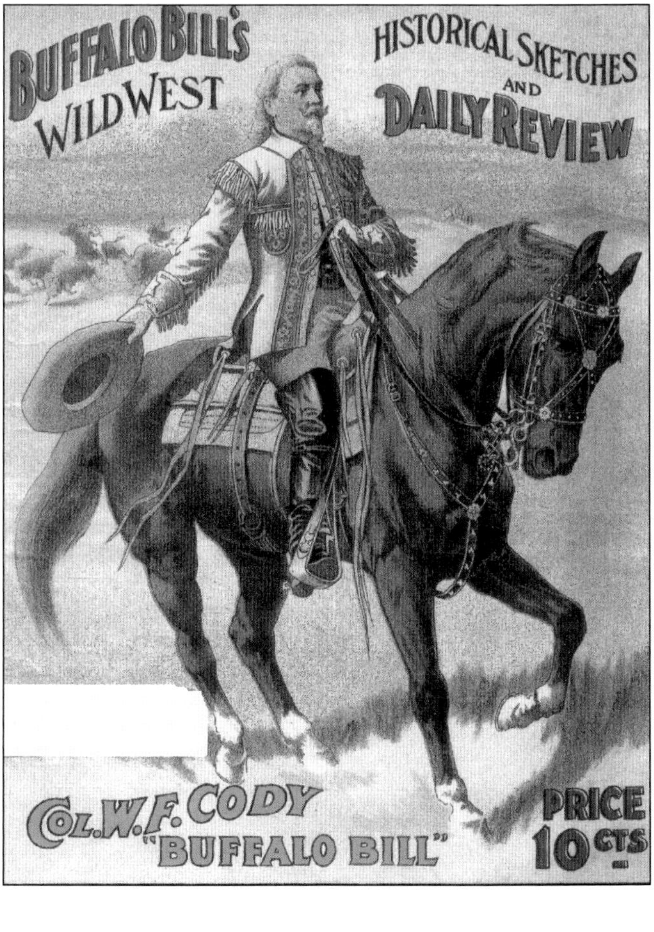

In "store talk" at Charles J. Foley's North Platte, Nebraska store, William F. Cody (1846–1917) chided the mayor for having no Fourth of July celebration planned for 1882. Therefore, the mayor named Cody event chairman. Cody created a celebration that became the basis of modern rodeo and of his internationally successful Wild West Show. This show traveled with 800 people, 120 horses, and 18 buffalo. Cody came to Cambridge around the turn of the 20th century.

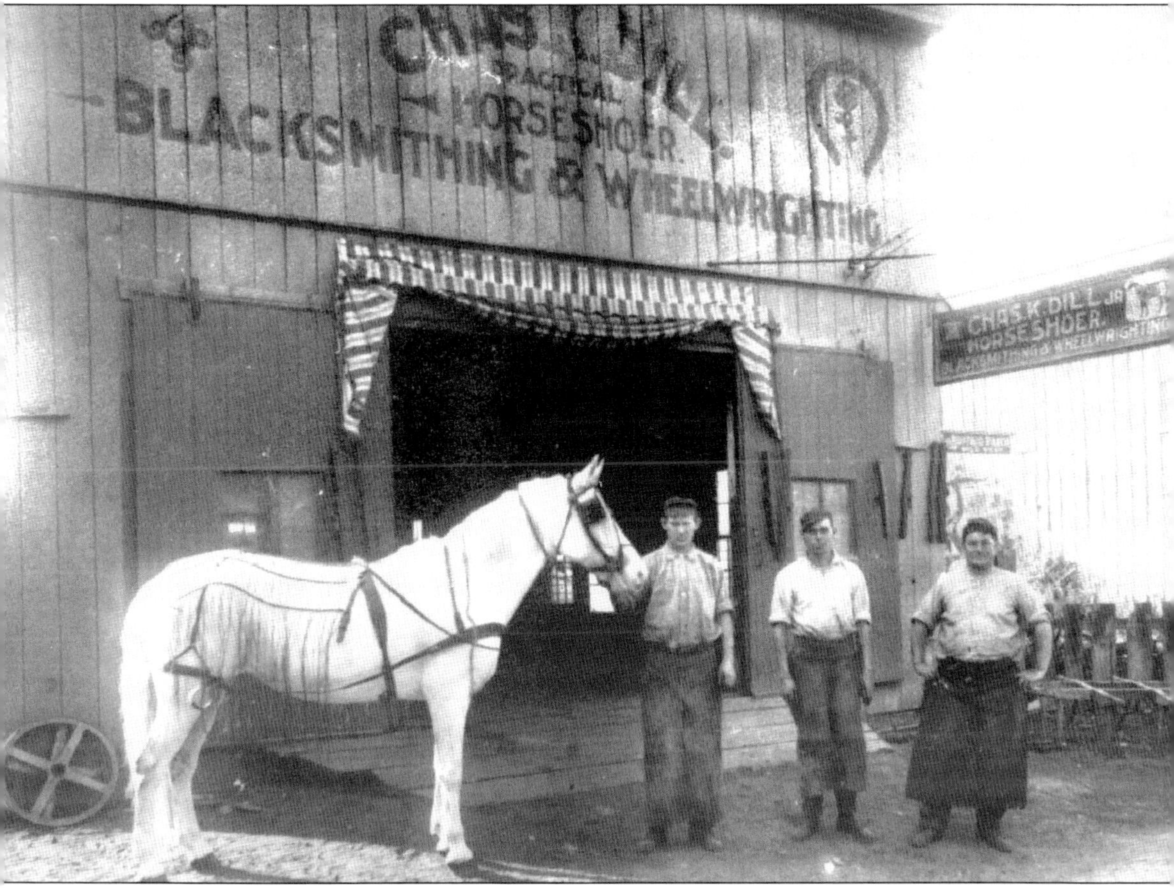

Charles K. Dill stands outside his blacksmith and wheelwright shop early in the 1900s with Moonlight, Annie Oakley's horse who was injured during a show at the fairgrounds and left in Dill's care. Moonlight's covering protects him from flies. Many blacksmiths also operated livery stables. In addition to shoeing horses, their work fashioning and repairing implements was crucial to the trades of shipbuilders, dredgers, and farmers. Among the blacksmiths operating around Cambridge at that time were C. Allen Tyler, blacksmith and wheelwright; J.W. Christopher, blacksmith and wheelwright; and Capt. Milford Phillips and S.E. Holland and Son's, who specialized in "shipsmithing" and dredge building, and were also blacksmiths. Every community had someone handy at the forge. Many boatbuilders found it easier to fashion their own marine hardware rather than describe their needs to a smith.

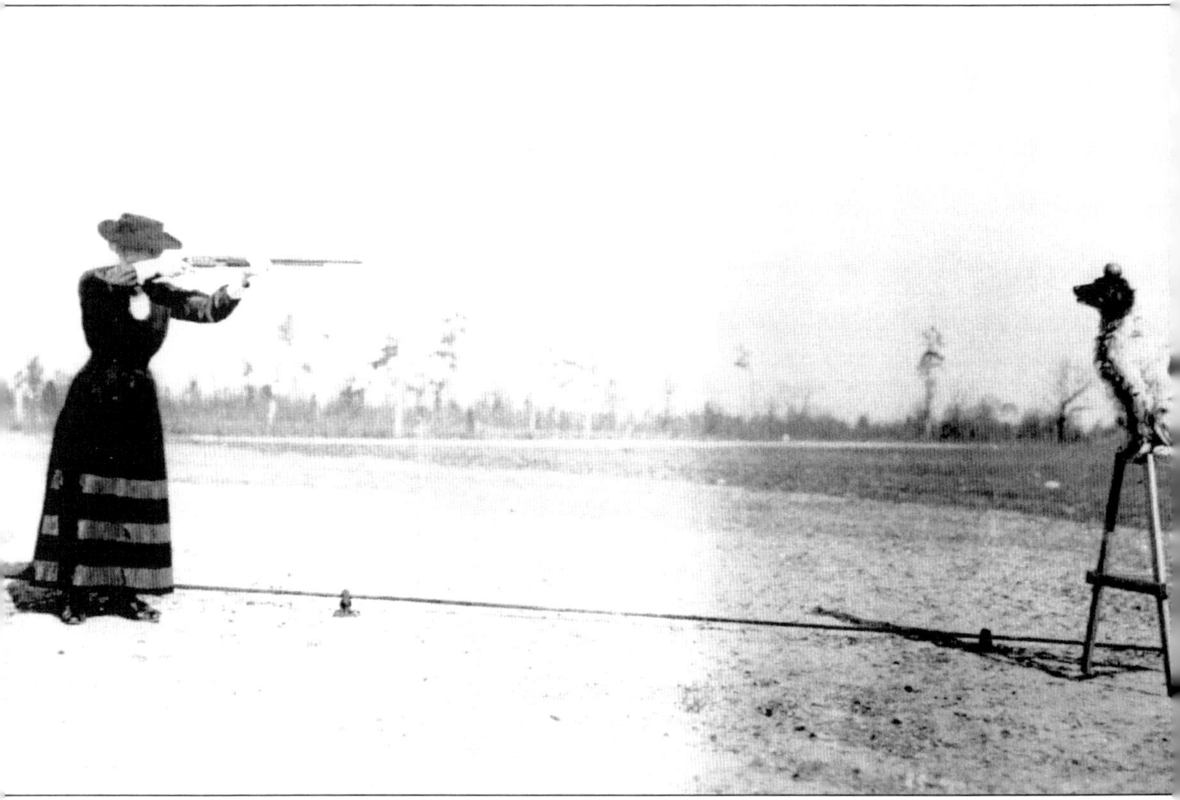

Annie Oakley came to Dorchester County with Buffalo Bill Cody's Wild West Show around the turn of the 20th century. She and her husband, Frank Butler, so enjoyed their visit that they designed and built a home on the Choptank River, where they relaxed between tours with their dog, Dave. Annie Oakley, a petite woman who made her own costumes, was such a natural shot she hardly needed to aim. Many of her exhibition shots were made with her back turned as she looked in a mirror at her target. Skeptics thought no woman could be such a sharpshooter and said there was trickery involved in her exhibitions. Obviously, Dave was no skeptic. He would sit trustingly as Annie played William Tell and shot an apple or potato from his head. Annie occasionally gave exhibitions at the fairgrounds outside Cambridge after settling there.

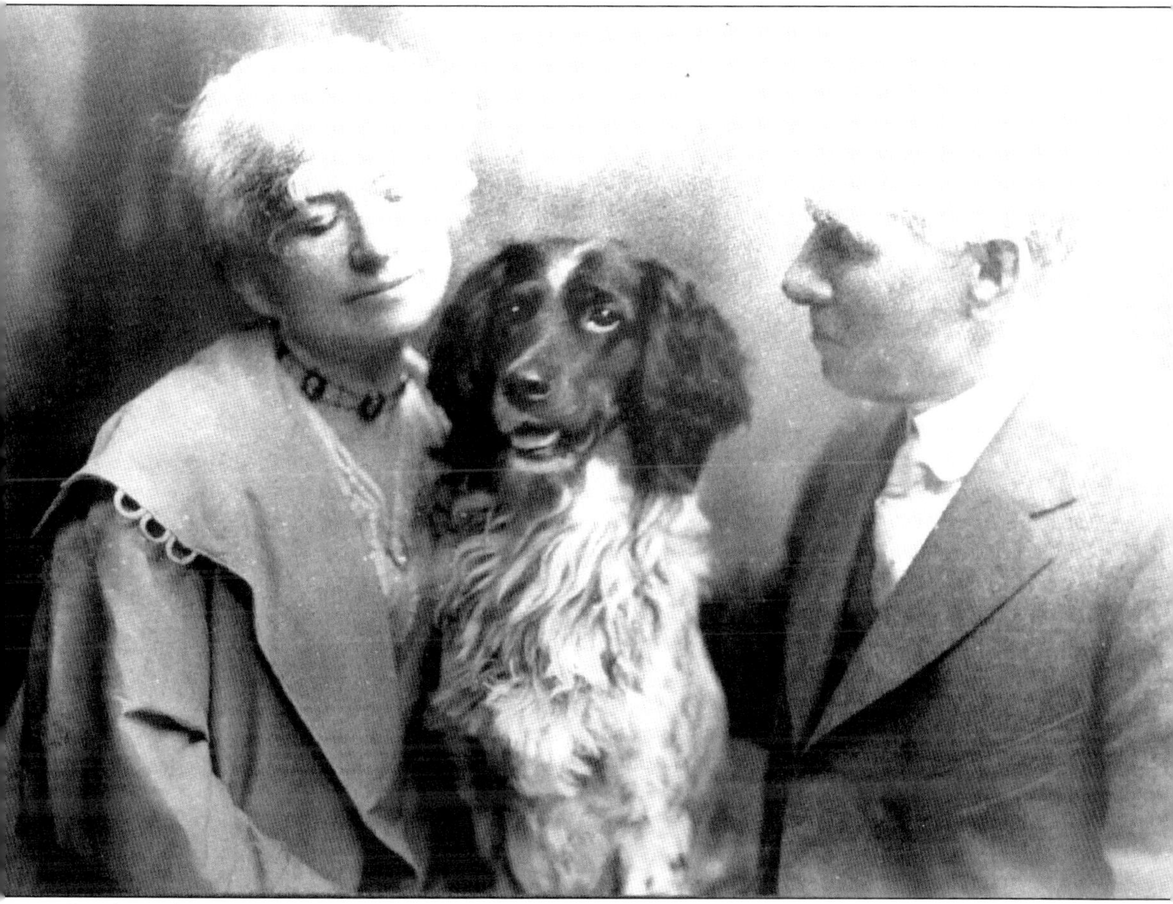

Frank Butler and Annie Oakley gaze fondly at Dave in this photo. During their residence in Cambridge, they were rarely pictured without him. Annie was so fond of animals that her hair turned white overnight after a train carrying Buffalo Bill's Wild West Show crashed one night and several horses were killed. In the Irving Berlin musical "Annie Get Your Gun," Frank Butler and Annie Oakley are portrayed as forever competing for the upper hand, but this seems to have been dramatic license. The couple lived together so many years out of a trunk that they neglected to include any closets in the design of their Cambridge house. Eventually they were induced to leave Dorchester County for Pinehurst, North Carolina. A hotel seeking to trade on their fame advertised Annie Oakley and Frank Butler as overseeing their shooting range.

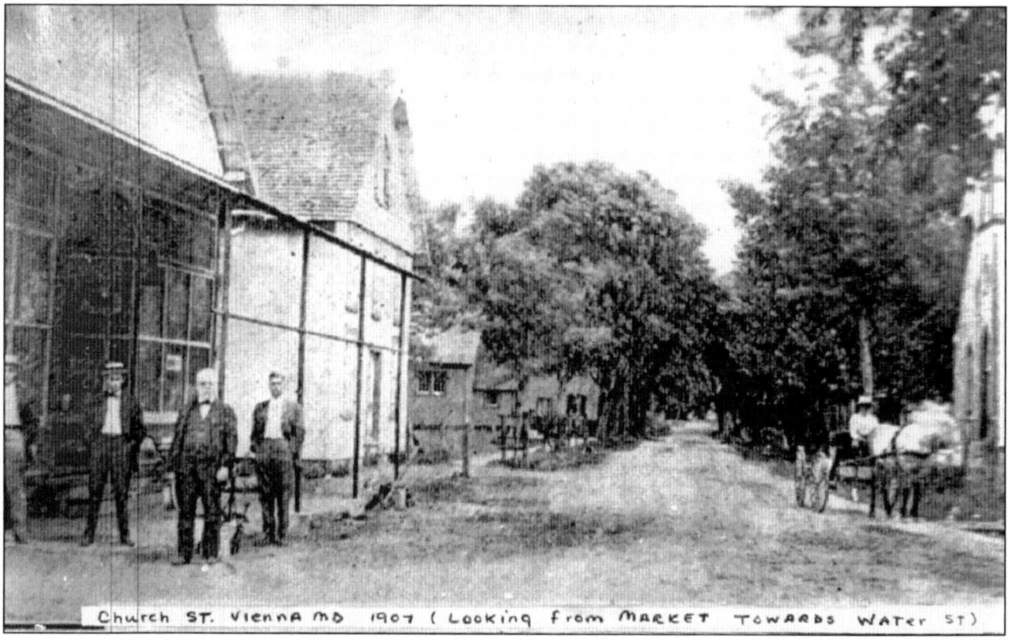

This postcard shows the view of Church Street, Vienna in 1907 as seen from Market Street, looking toward the Nanticoke River. From this point of view, St. Paul's P.E. Church was on the left just beyond the store. On the far corner, on the river at what was Thames Street, is the former residence of Gov. Thomas Holliday Hicks.

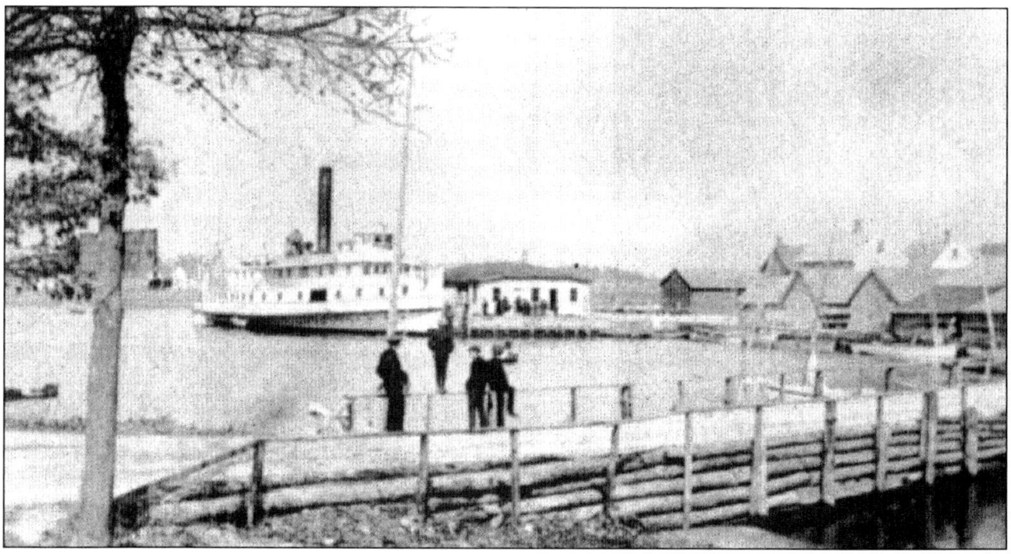

In the 1890s, three different steamboat lines competed for business on the Warwick River. Two hundred years of quiet ended in 1882 when Joseph Cook and his son-in-law Joseph Conkle joined forces to sub-divide part of the old tract "My Lady Sewell's Manor." Soon Secretary boasted an oyster-packing house and vegetable cannery and claimed to ship Baltimore more produce than any other Eastern Shore port.

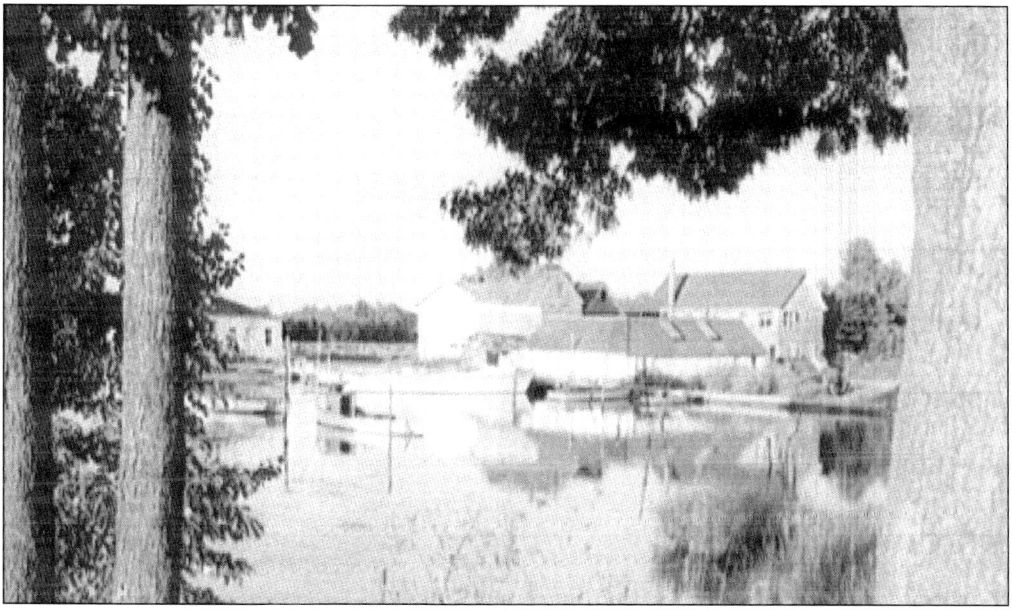

This photograph of Secretary was taken early in the 1930s. The town, which was incorporated in 1900, became a major shipping point for the rich farmlands of North Dorchester. Besides the steamboats, many local oyster boats sailed in the off-season laden with watermelons and other produce. Arriving from Baltimore was fabric for Rosenbloom Garment Factory. The Carroll Rosenbloom family, who owned the Baltimore Colts, had a Secretary shirt factory.

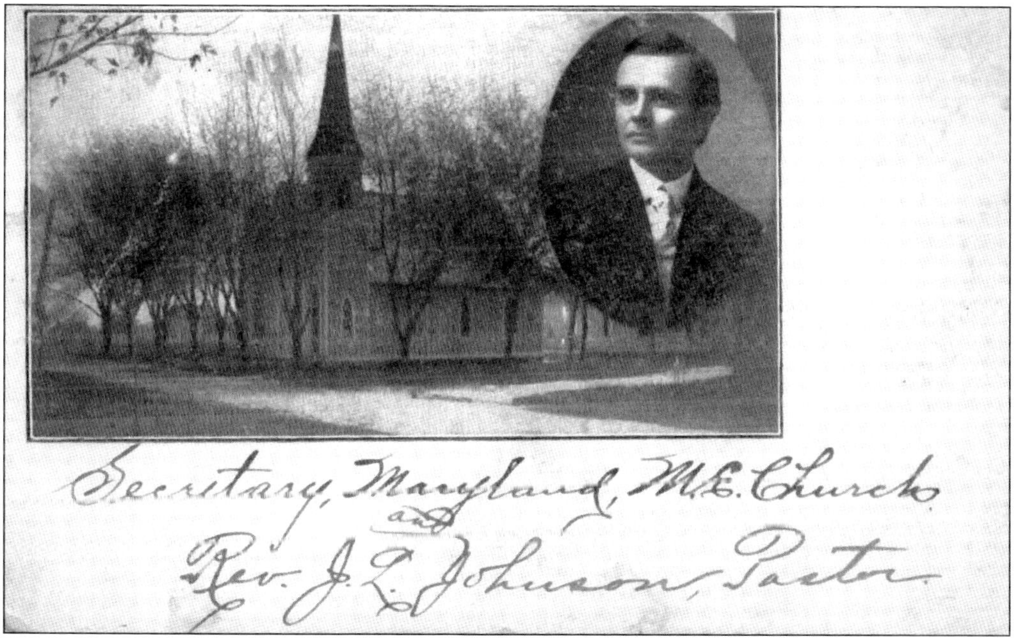

The Secretary M.E. Church was quite new when this postcard was sent on March 8, 1909 and Rev. J.L. Johnson was pastor. As Secretary grew, its first Methodist congregation met in a building at the wharf. This church replaced a small chapel in 1901. The Roman Catholic congregation of Secretary was initially a mission of Saints Peter and Paul of Easton. They built their first church in 1892.

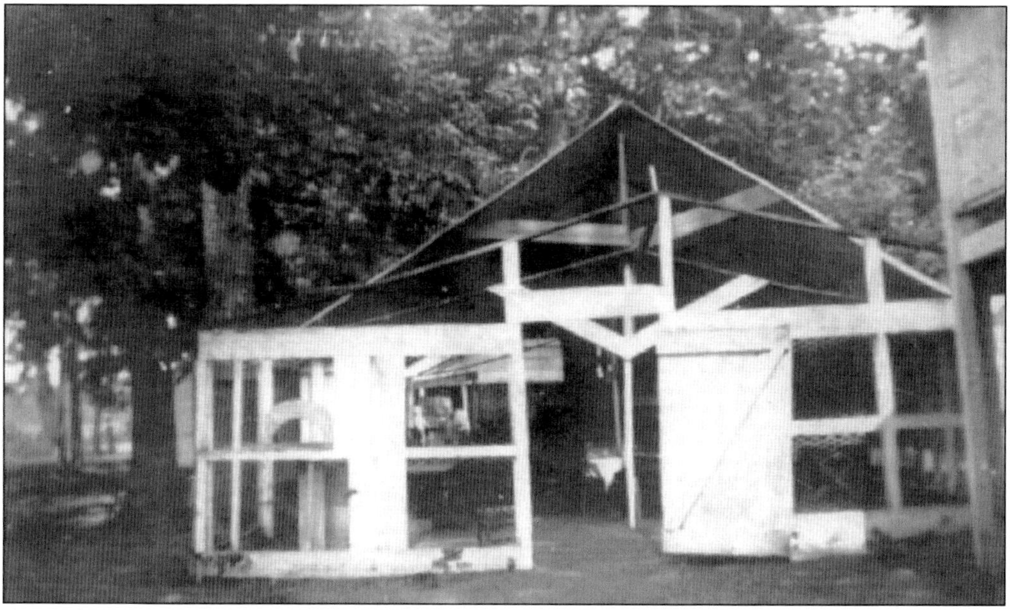

An early visitor wrote in *Lippincott's Magazine* in 1876, "Camp-meetings are in high favor, and in many places, the humbler 'bush-meetings' attract a large attendance. The latter is always held at night, and the slow, dirge-like melodies which float away among the shadows are strangely suggestive of the forest conventiclers of other and long-gone times." This photo shows a cabin for rent at Salem for the 1910 camp meeting.

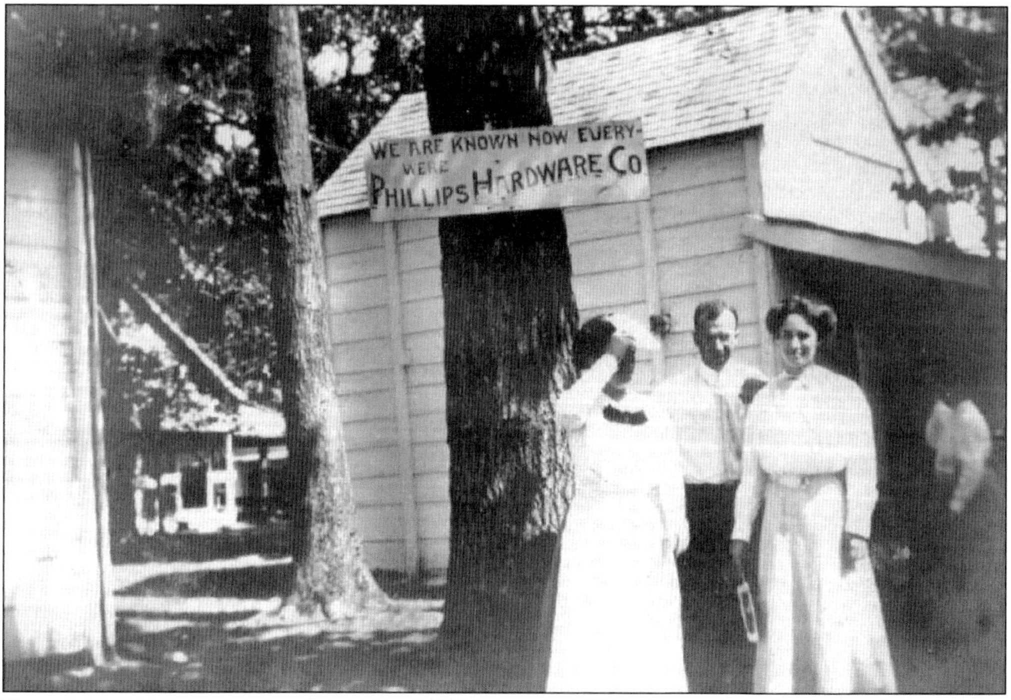

Even at camp meetings, the ubiquitous Phillips companies were in evidence. The sign tacked to this tree outside the cabins at the August 1909 Salem meeting proclaims, "We are known now everywhere—Phillips Hardware Co."

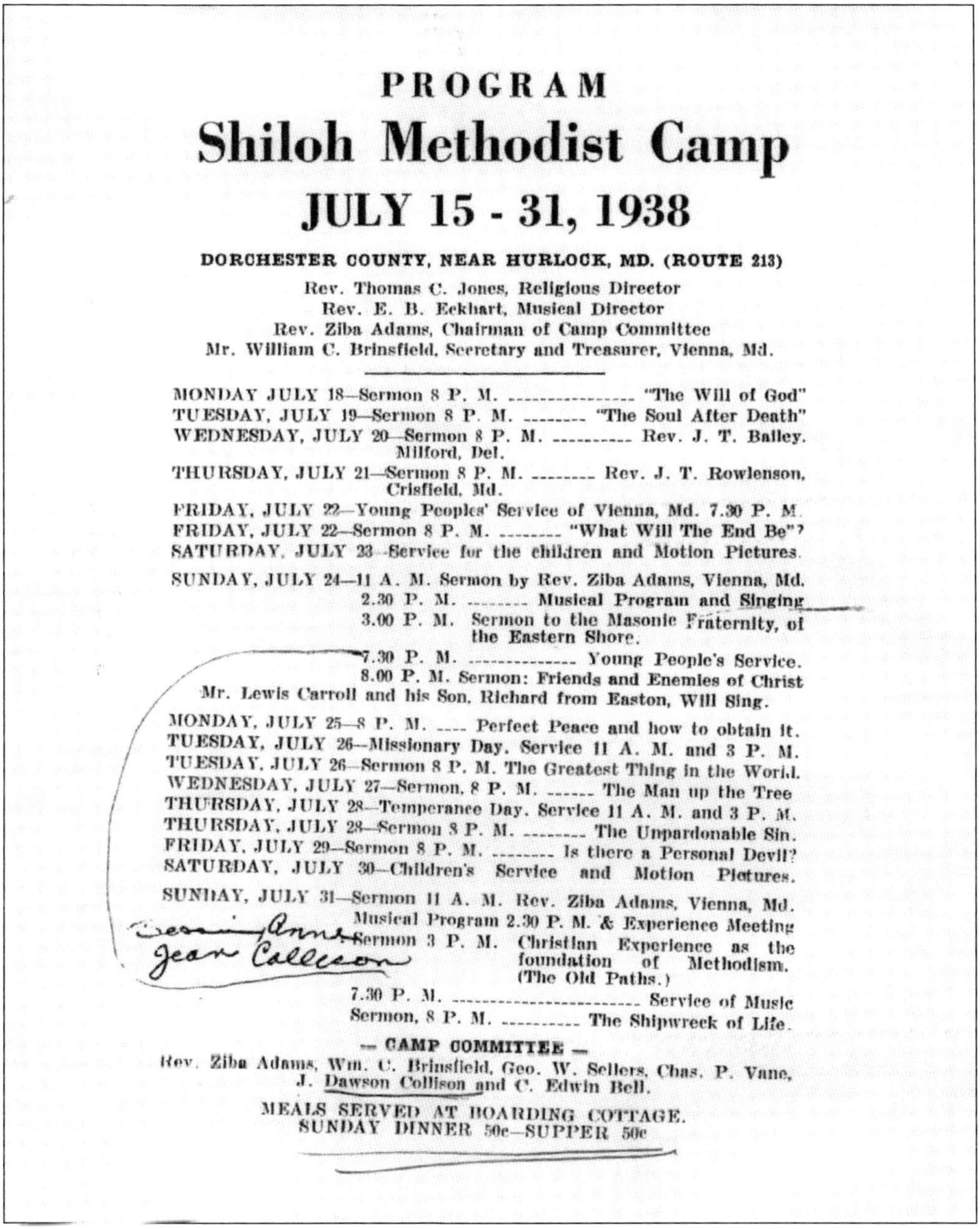

PROGRAM

Shiloh Methodist Camp

JULY 15 - 31, 1938

DORCHESTER COUNTY, NEAR HURLOCK, MD. (ROUTE 213)

Rev. Thomas C. Jones, Religious Director
Rev. E. B. Eckhart, Musical Director
Rev. Ziba Adams, Chairman of Camp Committee
Mr. William C. Brinsfield, Secretary and Treasurer, Vienna, Md.

MONDAY JULY 18—Sermon 8 P. M. ---------------- "The Will of God"
TUESDAY, JULY 19—Sermon 8 P. M. -------- "The Soul After Death"
WEDNESDAY, JULY 20—Sermon 8 P. M. ---------- Rev. J. T. Bailey, Milford, Del.
THURSDAY, JULY 21—Sermon 8 P. M. -------- Rev. J. T. Rowlenson, Crisfield, Md.
FRIDAY, JULY 22—Young Peoples' Service of Vienna, Md. 7.30 P. M.
FRIDAY, JULY 22—Sermon 8 P. M. -------- "What Will The End Be"?
SATURDAY, JULY 23—Service for the children and Motion Pictures.
SUNDAY, JULY 24—11 A. M. Sermon by Rev. Ziba Adams, Vienna, Md.
2.30 P. M. -------- Musical Program and Singing
3.00 P. M. Sermon to the Masonic Fraternity, of the Eastern Shore.
7.30 P. M. -------------- Young People's Service.
8.00 P. M. Sermon: Friends and Enemies of Christ
Mr. Lewis Carroll and his Son, Richard from Easton, Will Sing.
MONDAY, JULY 25—8 P. M. ---- Perfect Peace and how to obtain it.
TUESDAY, JULY 26—Missionary Day. Service 11 A. M. and 3 P. M.
TUESDAY, JULY 26—Sermon 8 P. M. The Greatest Thing in the World.
WEDNESDAY, JULY 27—Sermon, 8 P. M. ------ The Man up the Tree
THURSDAY, JULY 28—Temperance Day. Service 11 A. M. and 3 P. M.
THURSDAY, JULY 28—Sermon 8 P. M. -------- The Unpardonable Sin.
FRIDAY, JULY 29—Sermon 8 P. M. -------- Is there a Personal Devil?
SATURDAY, JULY 30—Children's Service and Motion Pictures.
SUNDAY, JULY 31—Sermon 11 A. M. Rev. Ziba Adams, Vienna, Md.
Musical Program 2.30 P. M. & Experience Meeting
Sermon 3 P. M. Christian Experience as the foundation of Methodism. (The Old Paths.)
7.30 P. M. ---------------------- Service of Music
Sermon, 8 P. M. ---------- The Shipwreck of Life.

— CAMP COMMITTEE —

Rev. Ziba Adams, Wm. C. Brinsfield, Geo. W. Sellers, Chas. P. Vane, J. Dawson Collison and C. Edwin Bell.

MEALS SERVED AT BOARDING COTTAGE.
SUNDAY DINNER 50c—SUPPER 50c

As Methodism spread in the 1800s and congregations outgrew homes and barns, outdoor meetings were often held. Popular locations developed into permanent sites for extended camp meetings, where tabernacles were erected and families built or rented cabins. As roads and automobile travel developed, central inland sites like Salem and Shiloh replaced some popular meeting places formerly reached by boat. The Shiloh meeting in 1938 lasted 16 days and included various preachers, singers, special services for youth, and children's movies. Camp meetings drew the faithful and curious alike and powerful sermons persuaded many to change their ways and step forward to denounce past transgressions.

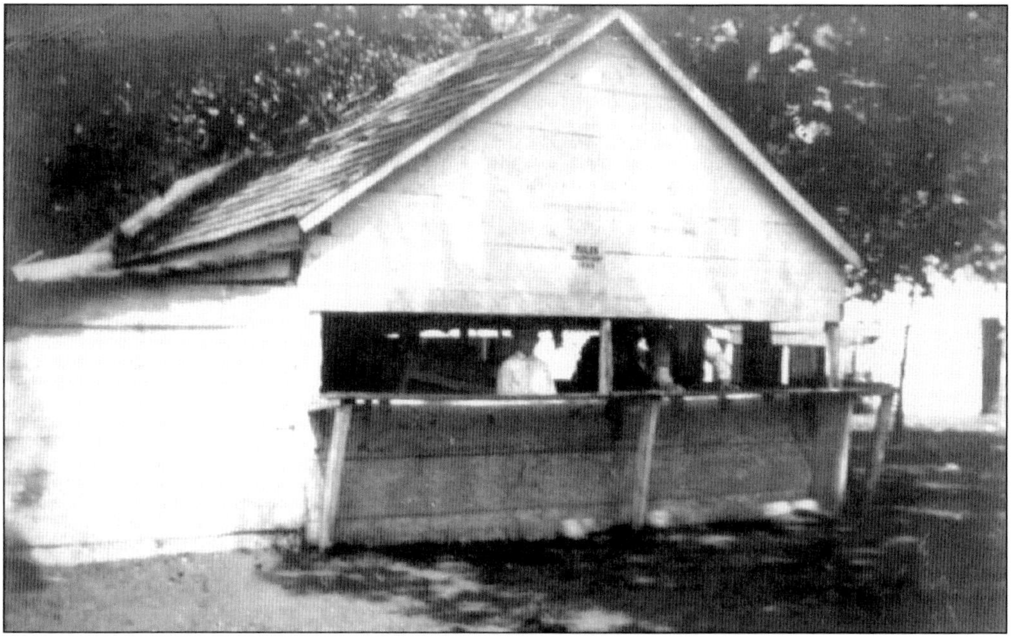

The "boarding tent" and "confectionery" at camp meetings gave mothers a rare chance to dine out. Meetings featuring famous preachers and numerous hymns were lengthy, but meal breaks provided time for visits with friends and relations from other parts of the county. Camp meeting was a much-anticipated annual break from routine chores and an excuse for a new outfit.

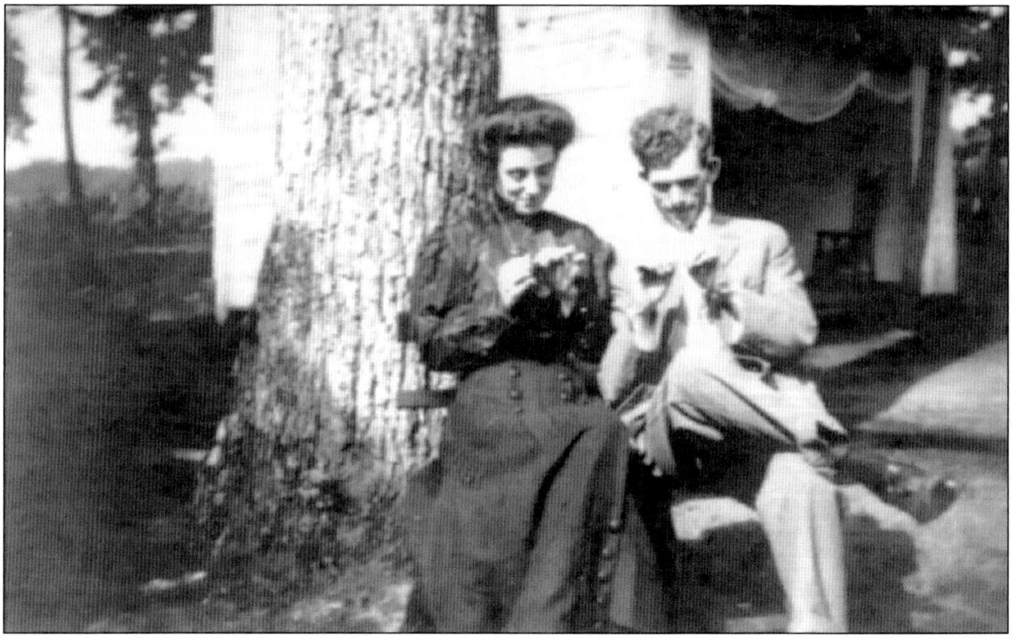

Nellie Clyde Handley and Harry Hubbard enjoy a snack at Salem. The year was 1909 and, along with being an important spiritual event, camp meeting was a social occasion. Between services, a young lady would "promenade" a circular path around the tabernacle with relations or friends under the watchful eye of potential suitors. A gentleman might step forward and offer his arm for her to accept or reject.

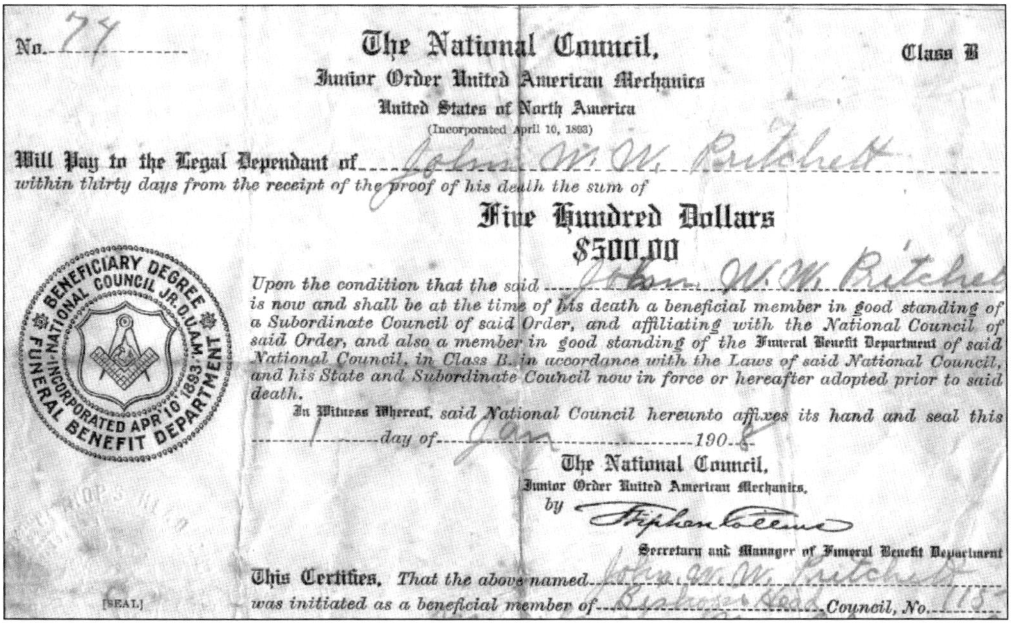
No. 77 **The National Council,** Class B

Junior Order United American Mechanics

United States of North America

(Incorporated April 10, 1893)

Will Pay to the Legal Dependant of John W. W. Pritchett *within thirty days from the receipt of the proof of his death the sum of*

Five Hundred Dollars

$500.00

Upon the condition that the said John W. W. Pritchett *is now and shall be at the time of his death a beneficial member in good standing of a Subordinate Council of said Order, and affiliating with the National Council of said Order, and also a member in good standing of the* Funeral Benefit Department *of said National Council, in Class B, in accordance with the Laws of said National Council, and his State and Subordinate Council now in force or hereafter adopted prior to said death.*

In Witness Whereof, *said National Council hereunto affixes its hand and seal this* 1 *day of* Jan *190*8

The National Council,

Junior Order United American Mechanics,

by Stephen Collins

Secretary and Manager of Funeral Benefit Department

This Certifies, *That the above named* John W. W. Pritchett *was initiated as a beneficial member of* Bishops Head *Council, No.* 115

[SEAL]

The Order United American Mechanics originated in Philadelphia in 1845, a blue collar Masonic-like organization of mechanics and shipwrights. Before Social Security and other government programs, fraternal organizations such as this Bishops Head Council of the Junior OUAM often provided a family's only security. Gentlemen in good standing were eligible for sick and death benefits. The good fellowship they enjoyed at their meetings was a bonus.

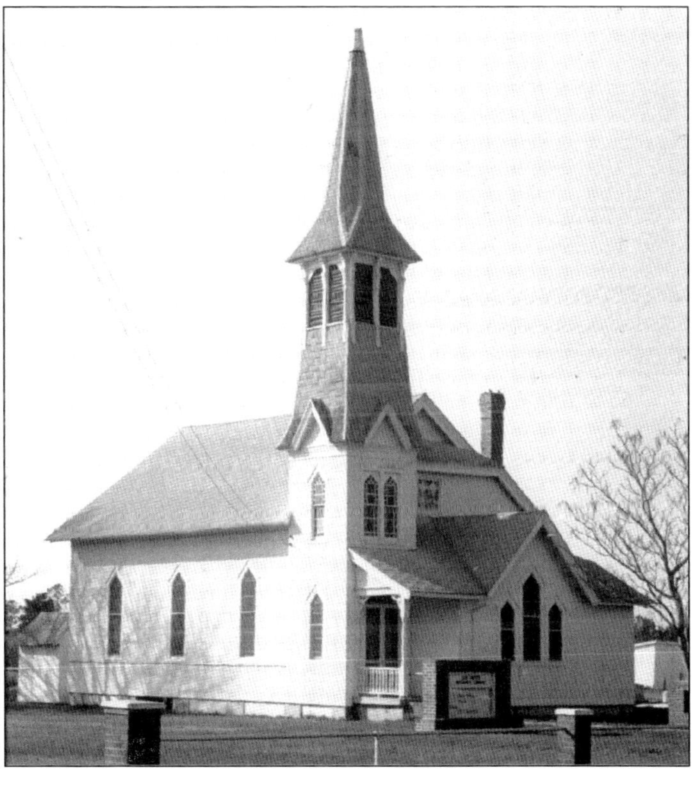

Zion United Methodist Church of Toddville stands as a monument to faith, reaching for heaven above the vast flat, surrounding landscape. The present church was built in 1910, replacing an 1846 structure lost to fire. The history of Methodism in the area, however, goes back farther, to the days when preachers like Joshua Thomas from Deals Island sailed in his log canoe *The Methodist* to communities "down below."

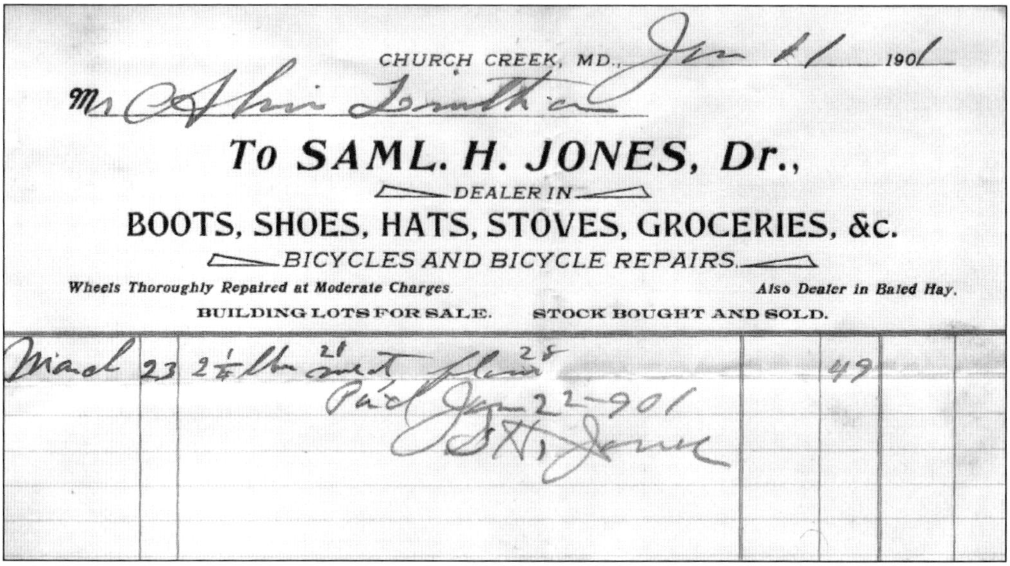

CHURCH CREEK, MD., Jan 11 1901

To SAML. H. JONES, Dr.,

DEALER IN

BOOTS, SHOES, HATS, STOVES, GROCERIES, &c.

BICYCLES AND BICYCLE REPAIRS

Wheels Thoroughly Repaired at Moderate Charges — Also Dealer in Baled Hay.

BUILDING LOTS FOR SALE. — STOCK BOUGHT AND SOLD.

March 23 2½ lbs meat 21 flour 28 — 49

Paid Jan 22-901 S.H. Jones

As early as 1901, Sam Jones could outfit a man from head to toe, sell him a cow or building lot, and send him on his way on a bicycle. This day Sam Jones collected money for two-and-a-half pounds of meat at 21¢, plus 28¢ worth of flour. Dorchester was an early site of bicycle racing and today well over 1,000 people race annually in the Eagleman Triathlon, a qualifier for Hawaii's Ironman.

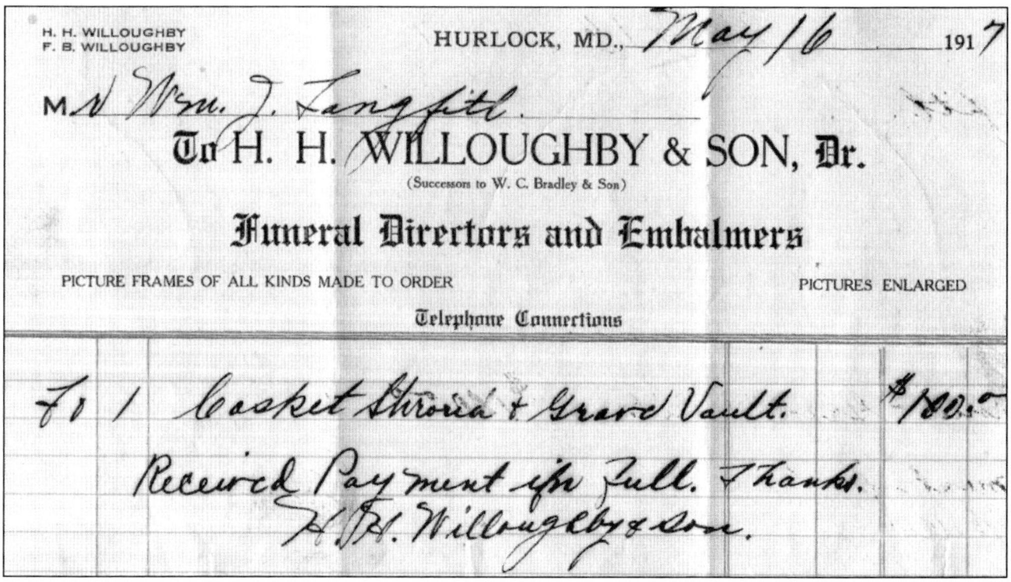

H. H. WILLOUGHBY
F. B. WILLOUGHBY

HURLOCK, MD., May 16 1917

Mr Wm. J. Langfitt.

To H. H. WILLOUGHBY & SON, Dr.

(Successors to W. C. Bradley & Son)

Funeral Directors and Embalmers

PICTURE FRAMES OF ALL KINDS MADE TO ORDER — PICTURES ENLARGED

Telephone Connections

To 1 Casket Shroud & Grave Vault. $180.00

Received Payment in Full. Thanks.
H.H. Willoughby & Son.

H.H. Willoughby and Son succeeded W.C. Bradley, who had operated an undertaking business in conjunction with his "Carriage Repository" in Hurlock. That was before funeral directing became a specialty. Even the Willoughby's had a sideline in the furniture business. When this bill was presented, they still offered "picture frames of all kinds made to order" and "pictures enlarged." Zeller Funeral Home of East New Market succeeded the Willoughbys.

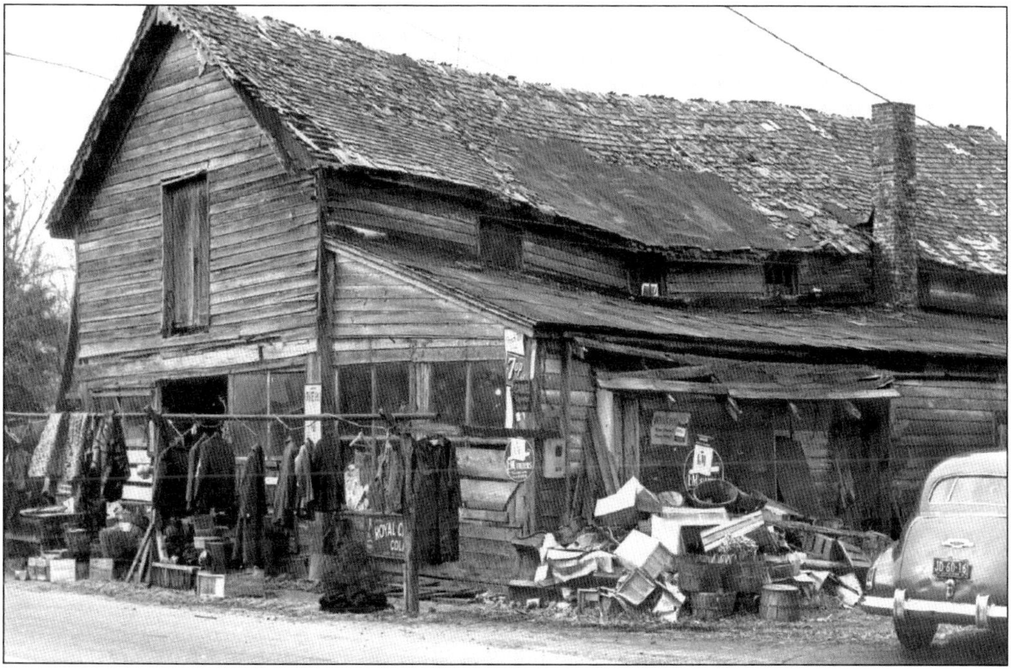

Sam Jones's Church Creek store offered all things imaginable and unimaginable. Inside the rambling building, one walked at one's own risk through a maze of paraphernalia and infestations. Jones prided himself on "The Worst Kept Store in the World," featured in *Look* magazine and on *We the People*, which netted him a three-day, expense-paid trip to New York. Church Creek Volunteer Fire Company now occupies this site, donated by Jones.

Around the time of the Civil War, Benjamin Rhodes operated this store and post office on Marshyhope Creek at Crotchers Ferry, now Brookview. Postmaster Rhodes, who was known to carry cash, was murdered by a local man, Cyrus Stack, on December 20, 1869. In the 1930s, when this picture was taken, Thomas Collison owned the store. The couple on the left is James Dawson and Ruby Rhodes Collison.

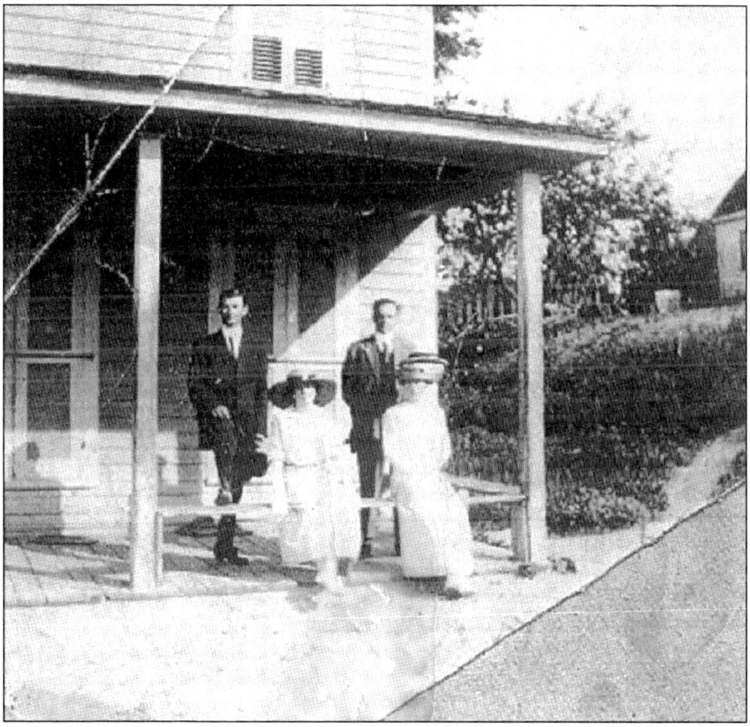

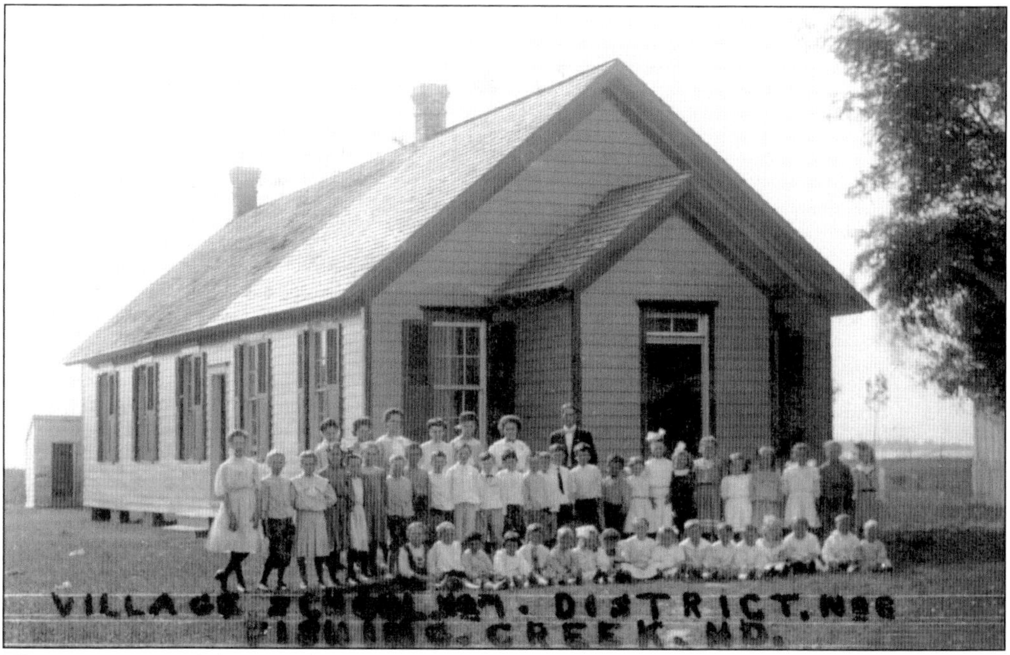

This 1911 postcard shows Fishing Creek School, "Village School No. 7, District No. 6, Fishing Creek, Maryland." It appears to have a new addition, making it a two-roomer. Debating usage of "under God" in the Pledge of Allegiance would seem most peculiar to these children of 1911, when school routinely opened with a Bible reading and the Lord's Prayer, along with the Pledge of Allegiance and a hymn or patriotic song.

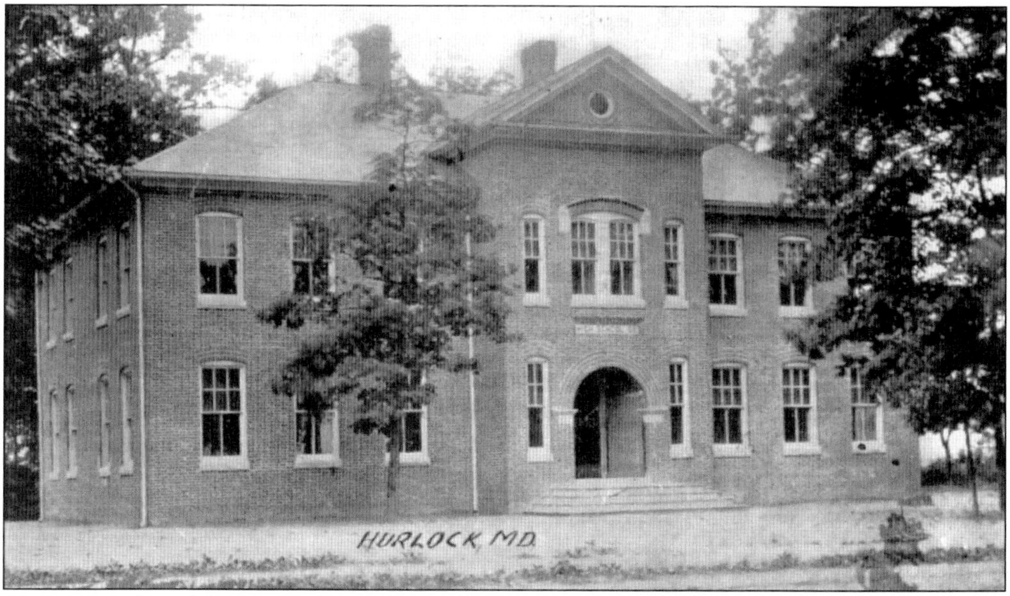

This postcard mailed in 1911 shows the second Hurlock High School, which replaced an earlier structure in 1908. Despite opposition as a "great waste of the county's money," the school soon filled with students as Hurlock continued to grow. African-American high school students rode by bus to Cambridge. North Dorchester High School opened in 1954, and eventually replaced East New Market and Vienna High Schools and the bussing of students to Cambridge.

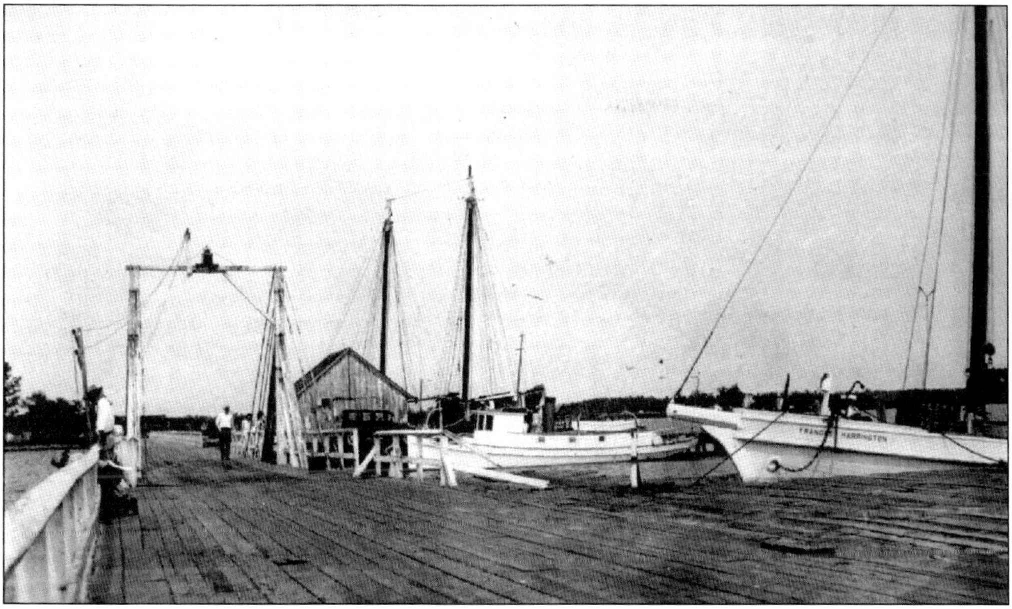

In 1854, a bridge replaced the ferry across Slaughter Creek. "Down below," other ferries crossed Fishing Creek to Hoopers Island, Blackwater River at Shorters Wharf, and the Transquaking at Bestpitch. A ferryman's salary was legislated, as was the fare he was to charge, though disagreements could arise in the hinterlands. In any case, a swing-span bridge expedited travel. The skipjack tied up here in 1931 is the *Frances Harrington*.

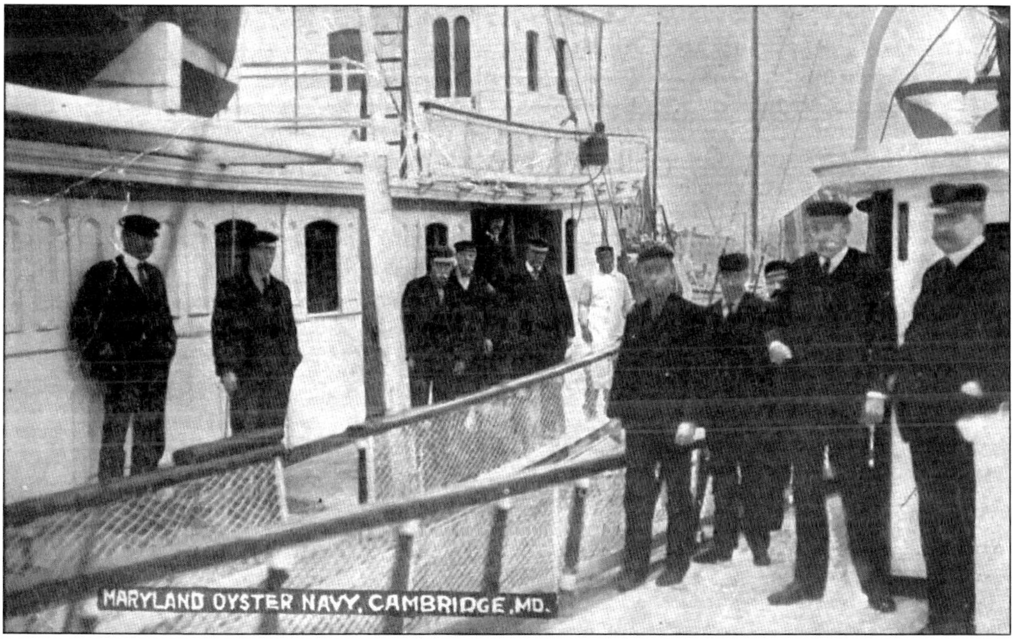

The Maryland Oyster Navy was organized in 1867 to combat out-of-state dredge boats that were destroying the state's rich oysterbeds. They also enforced regulations that restricted each oysterman to harvesting in his local county waters. Since Dorchester County lines were drawn largely along waterways with natural oysterbeds, the Oyster Navy's steamers *Governor Thomas* and *Governor McLane* were often seen in local waters.

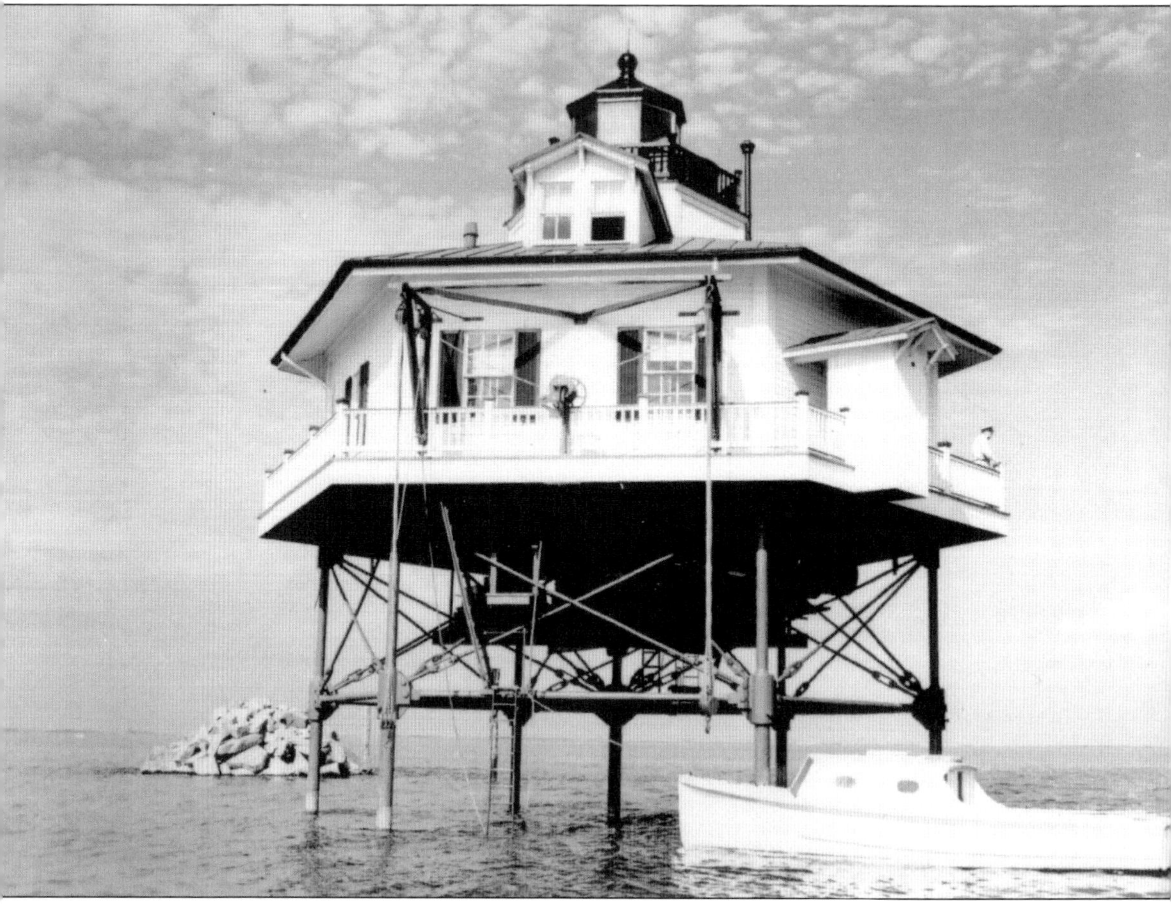

Screwpile lighthouses and the crews who manned them were once beloved fixtures of Dorchester County waters. A screwpile lighthouse was erected in Hooper Straits in 1867, replacing a lightship stationed there since 1827. This lighthouse was carried away after 10 years by an ice floe and found days later five miles south of the Straits. A second Hooper Strait Lighthouse was completed in 1879 and manned until 1954. After it was declared Coast Guard surplus, a tug-of-war developed between Historic Dorchester Inc. and the Talbot County Historical Society, who ultimately dismantled the lighthouse and barged it from its historic site 60 miles northward, where it now marks the Chesapeake Bay Maritime Museum in St. Michaels. Pictured here is Sharkfin Shoal Lighthouse, which in 1892 replaced a land-based lighthouse lost to erosion from Clay Island. Sharkfin Shoal Lighthouse stood at the confluence of Tangier Sound, Fishing Bay, and the Nanticoke River from 1892 until 1964. Before the Coast Guard burned it, its keepers were known to every waterman. They logged every weather change and passing vessel for seven decades.

Department of Commerce
Lighthouse Service

Office of Inspector, 5th L.H.Dist.
Baltimore, Md., June 7,1916.

DISTRICT CIR.LETTER NO. 63.
Instructions for Journal of
Light Station. Form 306.

You will paste this letter on the inside of the front cover of your present "Journal of Light Station" if there are no similar printed instructions therein.

You will see that the following instructions are <u>strictly</u> observed and any disobedience of the above instructions shall be reported by letter to the Lighthouse Inspector by any employee of the Service:

1. This Journal shall be a complete record of the important events at the stations having resident keepers, including weather, work in progress, officials visiting the station, visibility of adjacent lights and gas buoys, absences of light keepers, and any irregularity in working of equipment or appliances at the station, or noticed in that of other stations. Use as much space on a page as is necessary to record the important events for each day.

2. Keepers shall make the required entries in the Journal at the close of each day for that day. Postponements of entries will not be permitted. This record shall be kept in ink. No entry in this book shall be erased. Necessary changes may be made by drawing line through certain words and interlining others.

3. This Journal shall be presented for examination at each inspection of the station, and on such occasions will receive the signature of the Inspecting Officer, together with any comments or instructions relevant to his visit.

4. In addition to noting shore liberty or annual leave in the body of the Journal, a record of such absences shall be kept in the back part of the Journal to be examined when the station is inspected.

5. This book must be correctly kept, and when filled shall be preserved as a permanent record at the station.

KING

Lighthouse Inspector.

Early 1900s lighthouse instructions were signed simply "King." From the instructions, King appears uneasy, afraid that some keepers might relax while beyond observation. Meticulous records were required, verified periodically by inspectors. Journals were matter-of-fact, noting schooners in and out, packets on their rounds, floors cleaned, davits painted, occasional airplanes sighted, tenders delivering coal. Going ashore for mail or provisions, a keeper's absence was noted. Weather permitting, two family visits ashore were possible monthly. Prosaic entries were interrupted by sudden storms or frigid weather. Ice could strand keepers for days, weeks, or months, as family and shore communities watched anxiously each evening for the lamp to be lit. Frightful conditions followed as the rivers melted and vast ice floes boomed and cracked, free to move with the tide. Sharps Island Light in 1881 was tossed on its side and carried away, its keepers clinging to it for 16 hours before being rescued. South Dorchester felt bereft when Hoopers Straits lighthouse left its historic site and those who, as one said, "tended it, rang its bell, blew its fog horn, cleaned its globe of accumulated soot and preened its wick for another night of vigil."

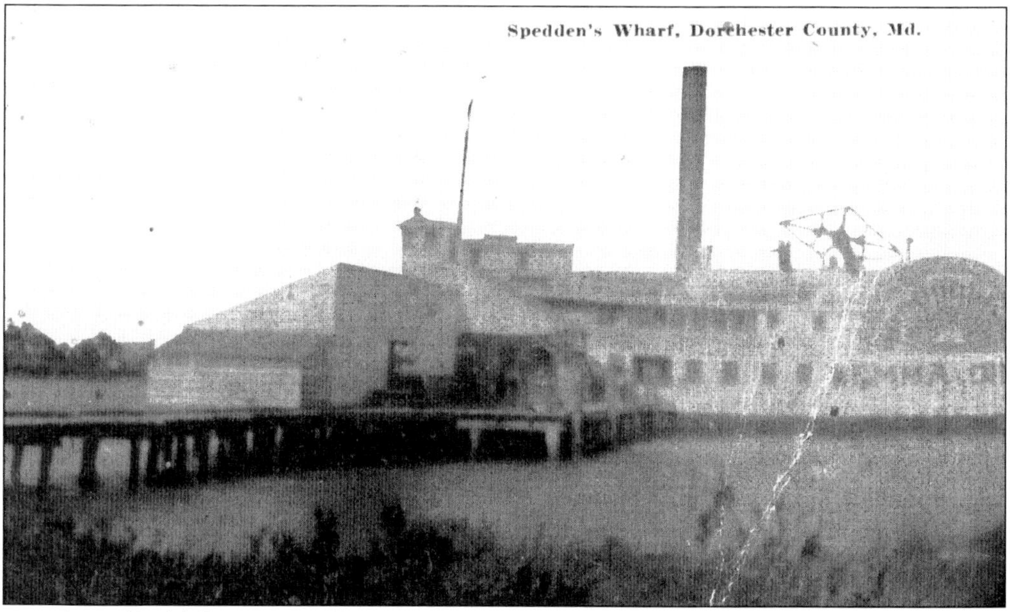

Travelers tell of following a well-worn road to a steamboat landing when the whistle sounded and finding chaos: coops of chicken and ducks piled about the gangway, bleating sheep crowded at the bow to make room for calves, stevedores twisting the tails and belaboring the horns of resistant steers. This early 1900s shot of the *Emma Giles* at Spedden Wharf caught a rather tranquil moment.

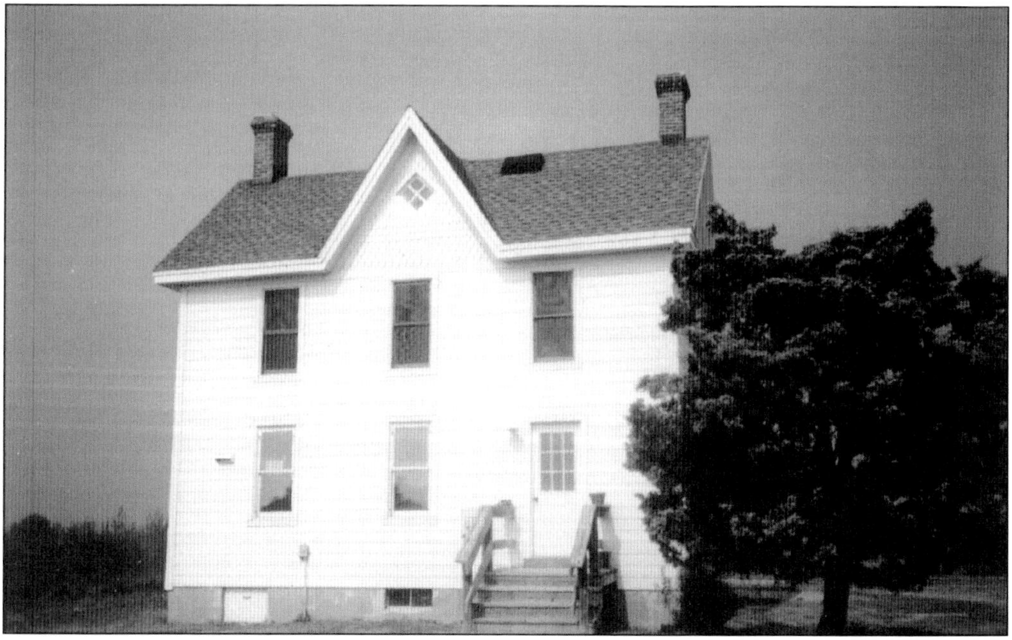

Hollands Island once supported a thriving community. Located south of Bishops Head, like much of Dorchester County, it was subject to erosion from wind and wave. Eventually, the residents reluctantly abandoned their home places and family graveyards to natural forces. Some houses were barged intact and others were dismantled board by board. A number of them were relocated to Cambridge. Others, like this house, are at Bishops Head.

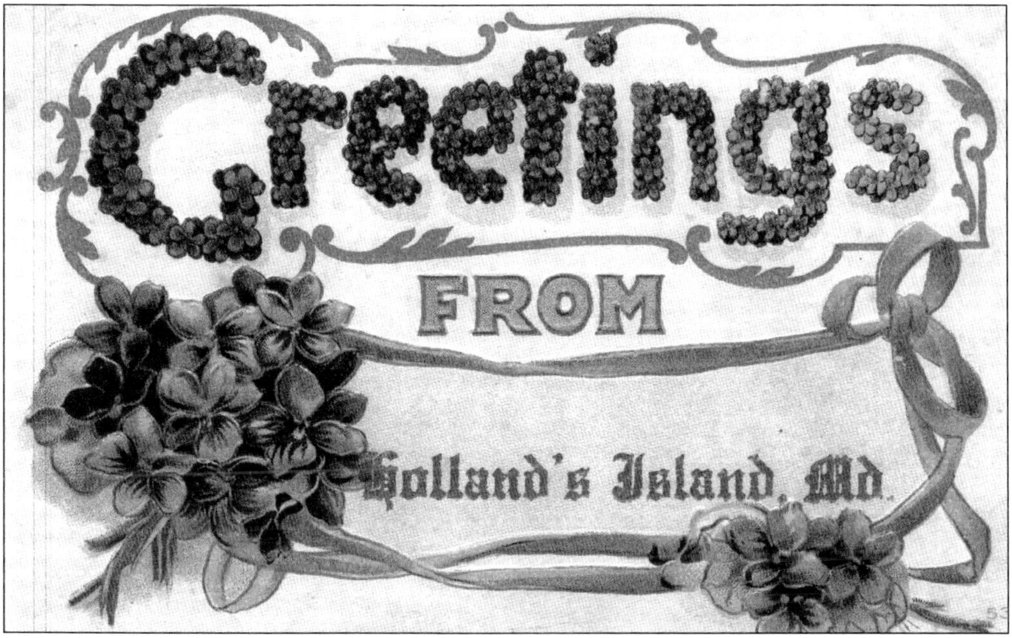

This postcard was sent from Hollands Island to Oriole in Somerset County, Maryland in 1909, from a Ms. Lanie to Mrs. Fonsie to let her know, "Randolph has just come for me. Will meet you later." Within 10 years, the last residents had left Hollands Island to eroding forces, loading their houses on barges and sailing off, it was said, "whichever way the wind was blowing."

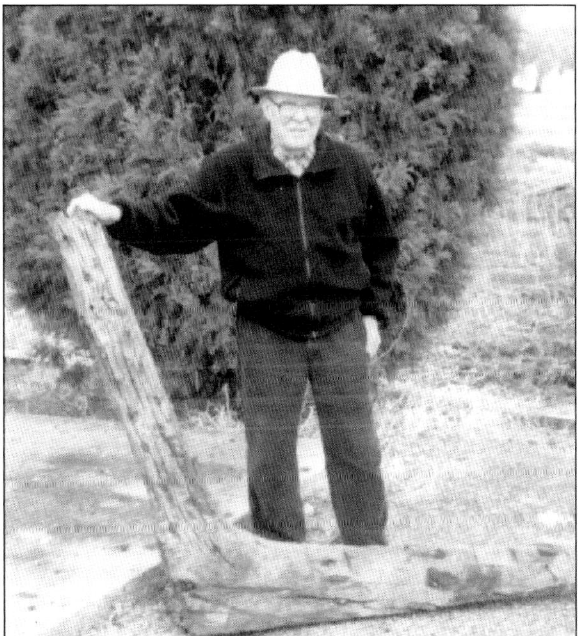

Capt. C. Calvert "Katz" Evans supports the stem of the schooner *Mamie and Lillie*, which was unearthed during an excavation at the former Coast Guard station on the Nanticoke River in Vienna. The schooner's captain, George Price of Hollands Island, sailed her up the Nanticoke, ran her aground, and went to work on the railroad. Captain Price was Mrs. Evans's grandfather. The *Mamie and Lillie* was a 44.6-foot schooner built in 1879.

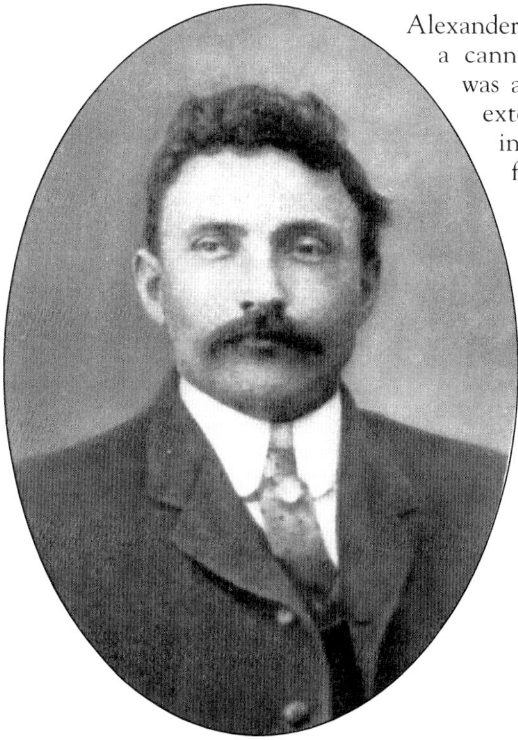

Alexander Goldsborough Robbins (1872–1921) was a canner in Robbins in southern Dorchester. He was also a trapper and fur dealer who conducted extensive research on humane steel traps for use in the muskrat trade. Of his children, five sons followed him into the canning business. Three sons, Henry, Louis, and M. Baker Robbins were associated in Robbins Brothers Canning Company in Dorchester County.

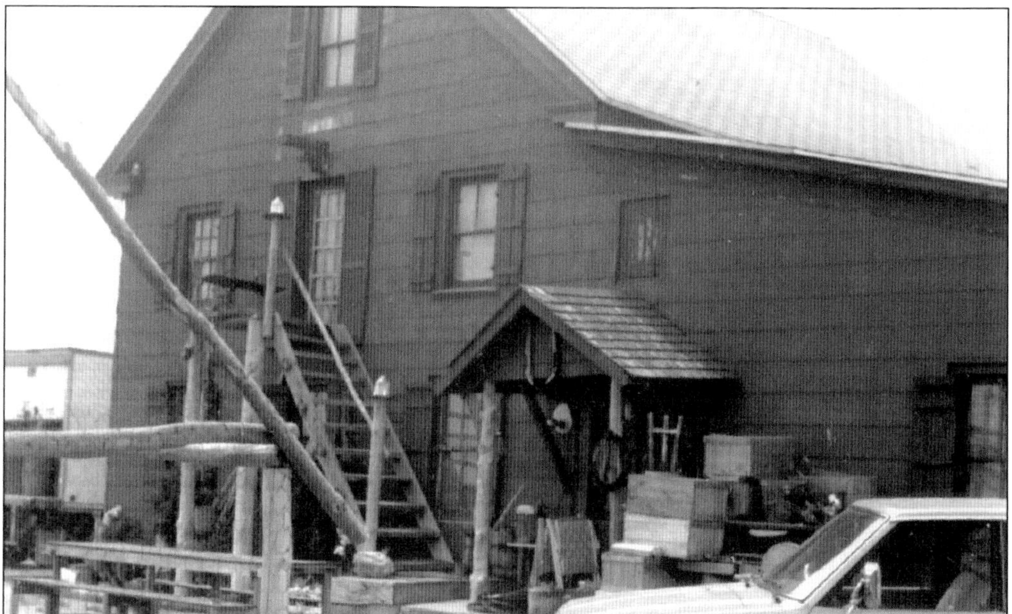

New Yorker Nathan Crocheron, after failing in the Gold Rush, came back east and struck it rich on Fishing Bay. There his complex eventually included barbering, a blacksmith shop, a crabhouse, a shedding operation, and a post office. His son Eugene and grandsons Clarence and Irving Crocheron carried on this conglomerate. Their store carried everything from glassware to marine supplies, groceries, and fresh meat, cut with Minnie Crocheron's big knife.

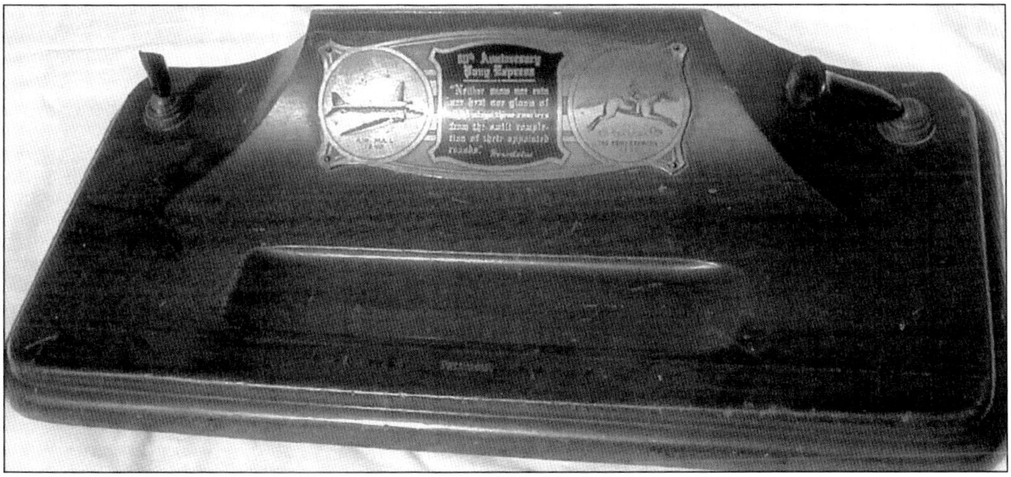

This desk set, presented to Minnie Short Crocheron, celebrated postal service with its historic motto: "Neither snow, nor rain, nor heat, nor gloom of night, stays these couriers from the swift completion of their appointed rounds." Minnie's father-in-law Eugene was the first postmaster when an office opened in his store in 1901. Minnie inherited the job on December 26 after her brother-in-law Clarence died on Christmas in 1934.

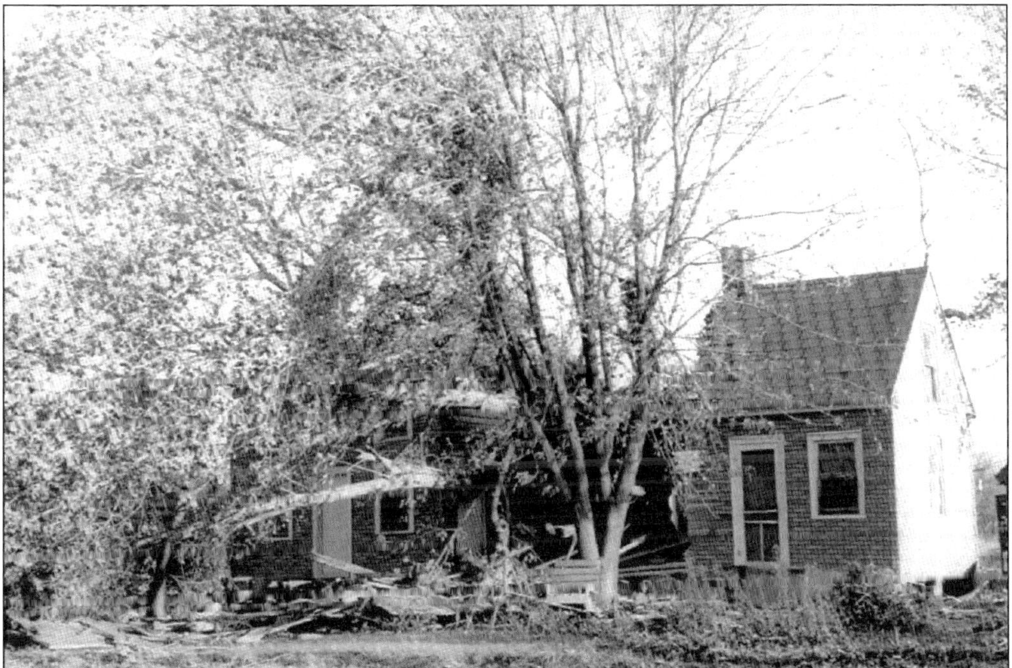

Hurricane Hazel, in October 1954, struck with winds over 100 miles per hour. Her fury drove tides six feet above normal. Boats were torn from moorings and landed days later inland as the storm surge subsided. Hoopers Island was cut off for days, as was Elliott Island, the county's second highest point. An elderly resident, Willie Ewell, lost her life when this tree blew onto her Elliott Island home.

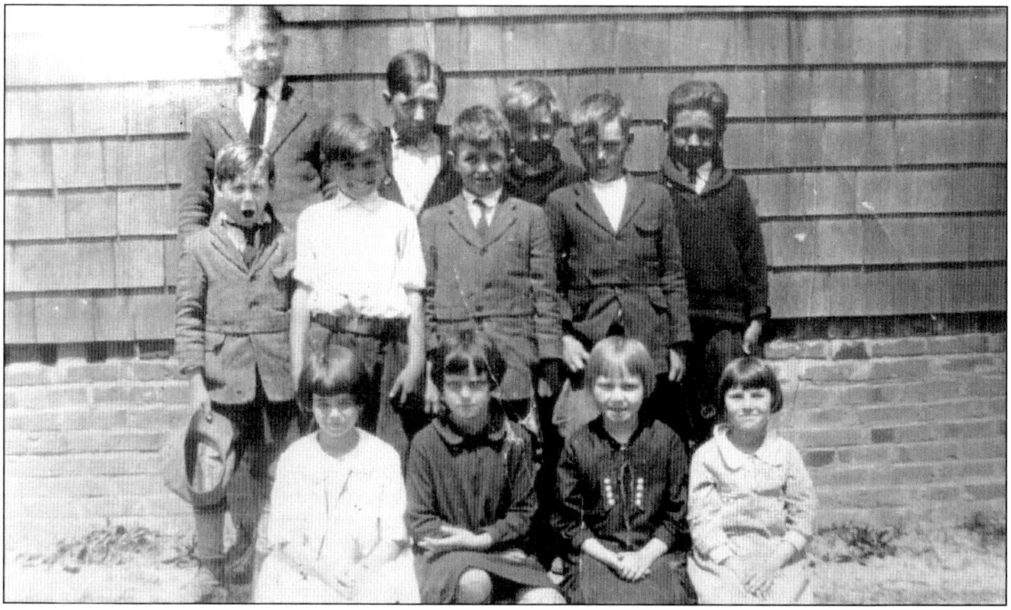

Helen Clifton taught the Rhodesdale School in 1926. Her students that year were, from left to right, (front row) Madeline Reid Koch, Isabel McWilliams Drugash, Margaret Short Turner, and Kathleen Collison Shanahan; (middle row) John Rhodes Jr., Robert McWilliams, Paul Collison, Harry Wainwright, and Everett Bestpitch; (back row) Emerson Reagan, George W. Payne, and Merrill Rhodes. The cedar-shingled school closed its doors in 1929.

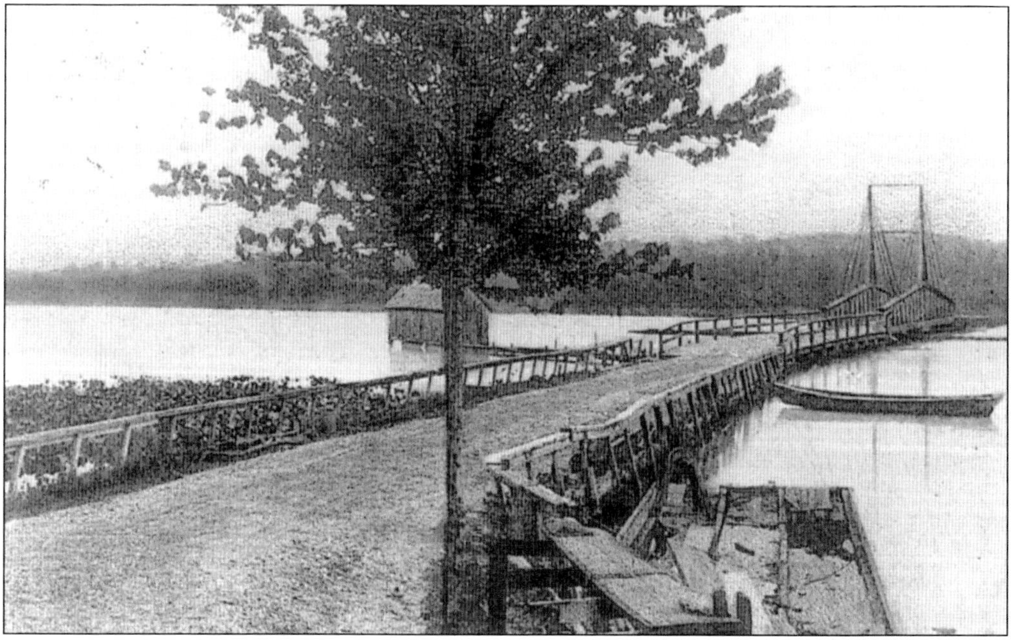

Today, a modern bridge has replaced the earlier Harrison Ferry bridges. Before this bridge was constructed (shown here in 1908), a ferry carried travelers in the Fork District over the Marshyhope Creek branch of the Nanticoke River. Crotchers Ferry crossed the Marshyhope farther downstream, where the town of Brookview is located, and another ferry was located at Vienna just below the mouth of the creek. Ferries were crucial to travel and strictly regulated.

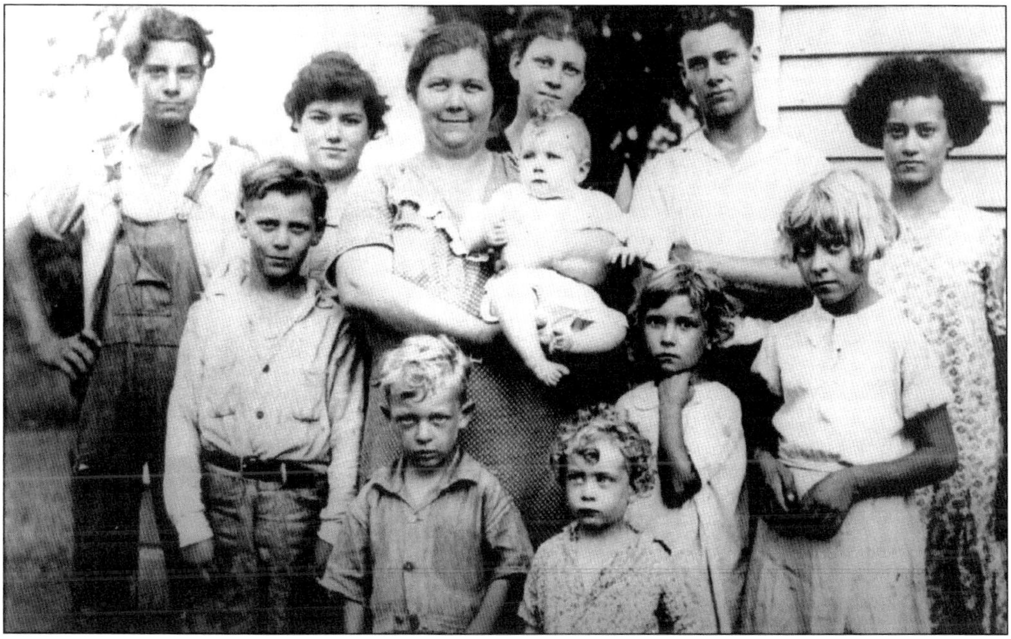

Mary Sellers Cheesman was obviously pleased when an itinerant photographer came along during the Depression. Her husband, James M. Cheesman Sr., was absent tilling their farm outside East New Market, but she had a chance to get a picture of her children. From left to right they are (front row) Albert and Betty; (middle row) William, Mrs. Cheesman holding Shirley, Hilda, and Audrey; (back row) Jimmy, Mary, Irene, Thomas, and Agnes. Baby Dot arrived somewhat later.

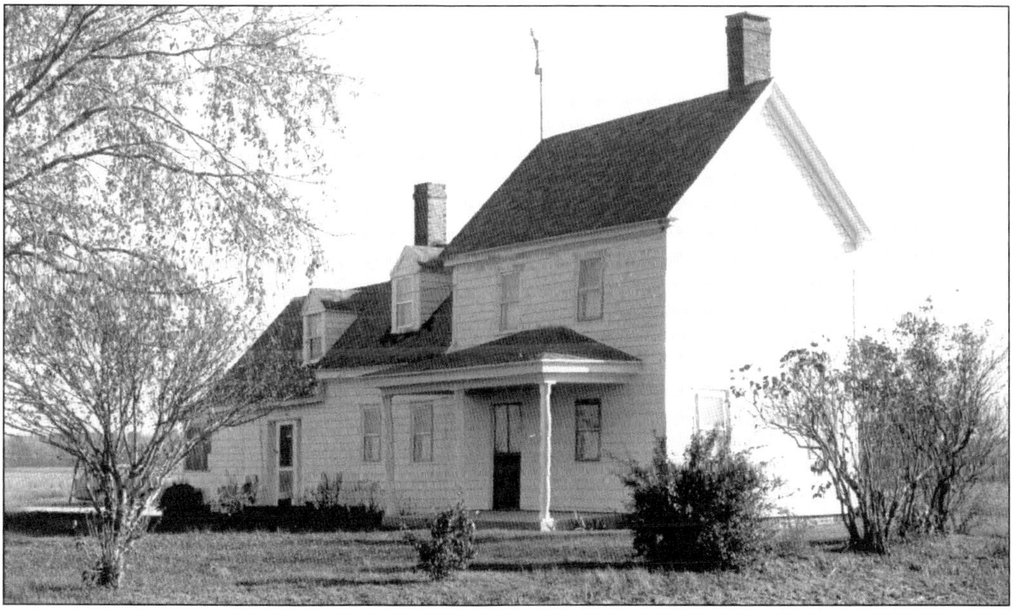

The Cheesman house outside of East New Market is a mid-1800s example of classic Eastern Shore telescope-style building—an original two-story section succeeded by two sections diminishing in scale. The land is still owned and tilled by members of the Cheesman family, who also operate the Home Pride Store in East New Market.

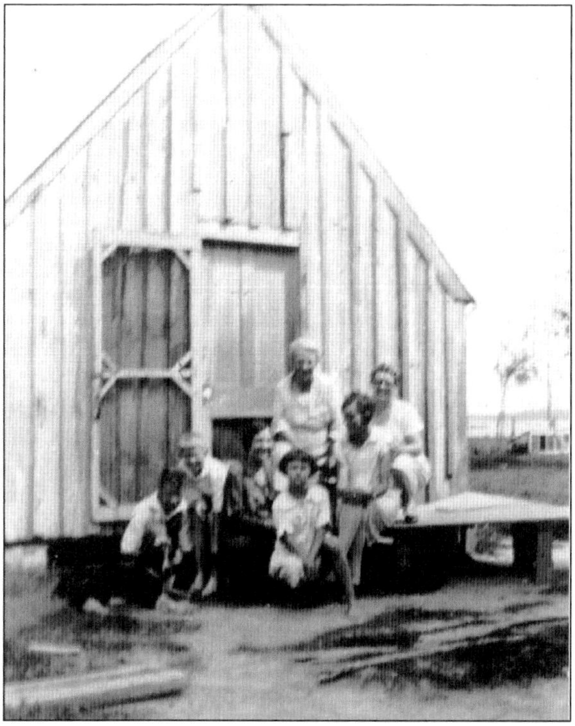

This summer kitchen and crew was photographed on Canning House Lane in Madison in 1929. A summer kitchen served seasonally to prevent excess heat from building up in the house, especially when the ladies of the house were laboring at a woodstove canning vegetables and fruits for later use. Besides keeping the residence cooler, they benefited the cooks by being small enough to admit a breeze from any quarter.

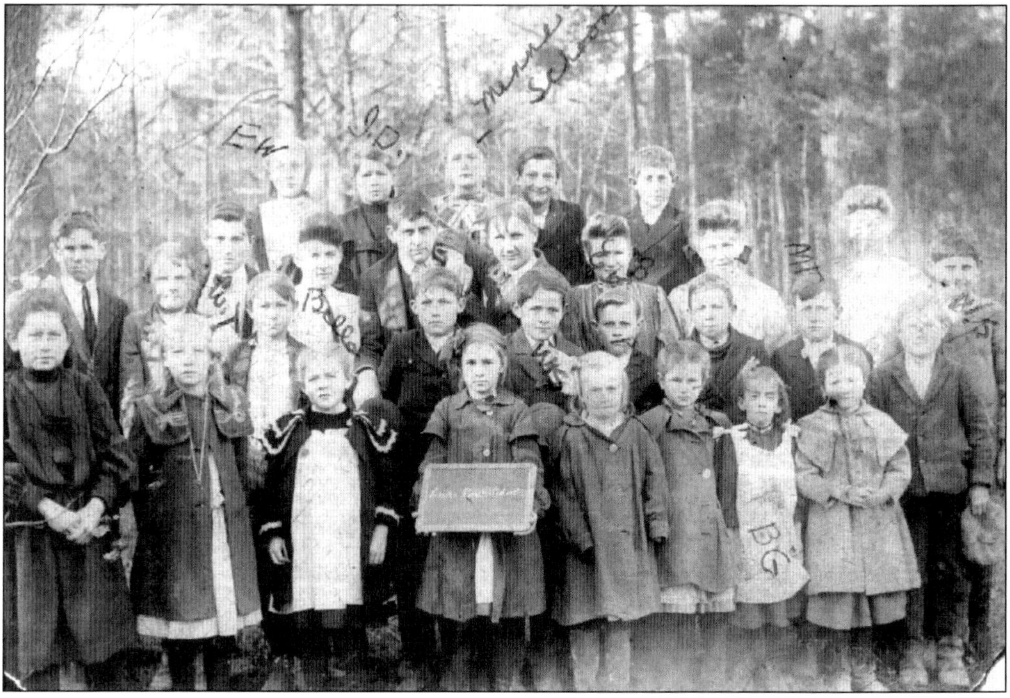

Things were relatively quiet on Cooks Point when this school picture was taken around the turn of the 20th century. Life would have changed drastically in the 1920s if the ferry proposal on the following page had materialized. Cooks Point might have developed into another resort like Tolchester or Betterton Beach.

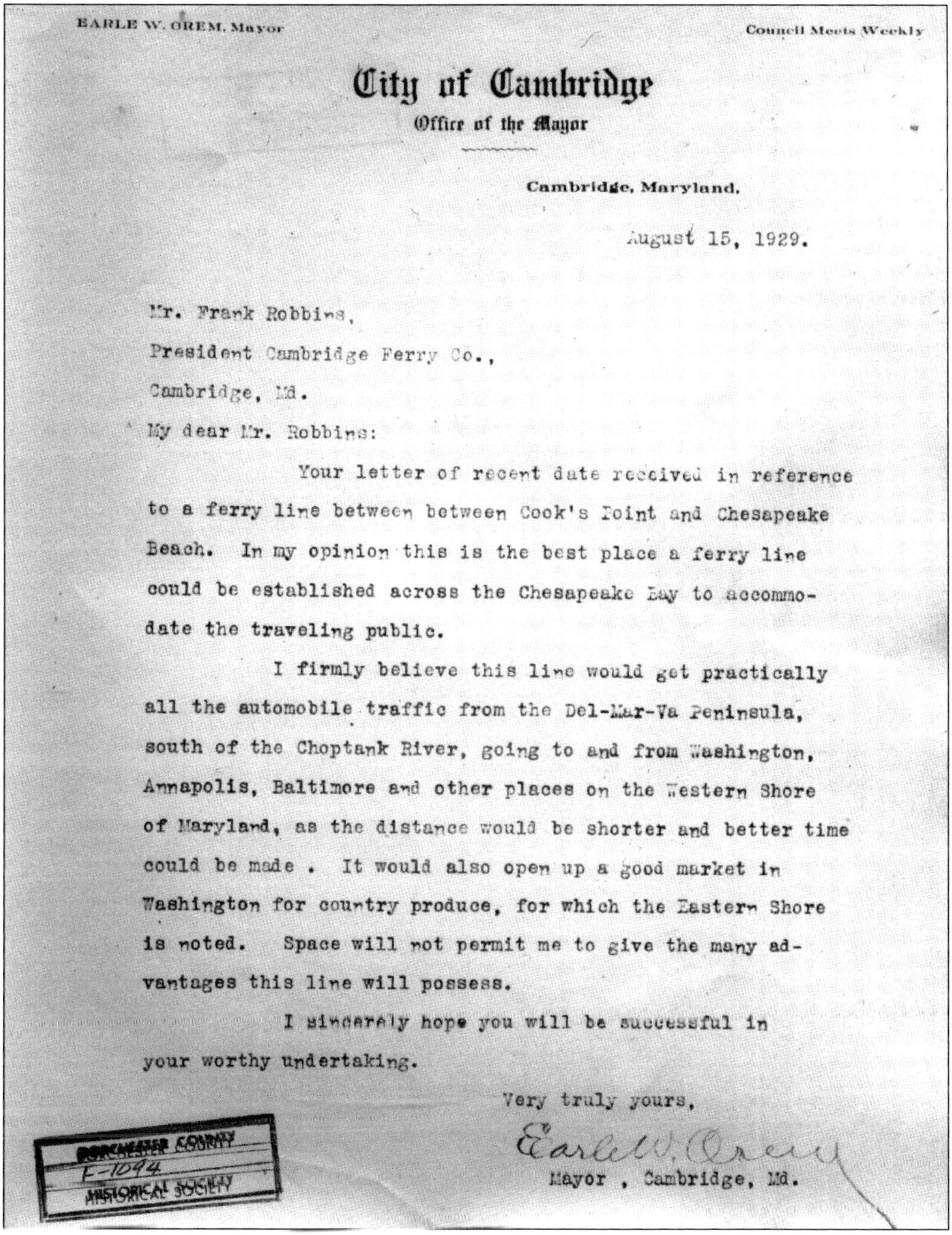

EARLE W. OREM, Mayor

Council Meets Weekly

City of Cambridge

Office of the Mayor

Cambridge, Maryland.

August 15, 1929.

Mr. Frank Robbins,

President Cambridge Ferry Co.,

Cambridge, Md.

My dear Mr. Robbins:

Your letter of recent date received in reference to a ferry line between between Cook's Point and Chesapeake Beach. In my opinion this is the best place a ferry line could be established across the Chesapeake Bay to accommodate the traveling public.

I firmly believe this line would get practically all the automobile traffic from the Del-Mar-Va Peninsula, south of the Choptank River, going to and from Washington, Annapolis, Baltimore and other places on the Western Shore of Maryland, as the distance would be shorter and better time could be made . It would also open up a good market in Washington for country produce, for which the Eastern Shore is noted. Space will not permit me to give the many advantages this line will possess.

I sincerely hope you will be successful in your worthy undertaking.

Very truly yours,

Earle W. Orem

Mayor , Cambridge, Md.

As the song says, "Everything old is new again." In 1920, Mayor Earle Orem of Cambridge was enthusiastic to endorse the concept put forward by the Cambridge Ferry Company and its president Frank Robbins. They proposed a ferry between Chesapeake Beach and Cooks Point. At that time, a train line carried excursionists from Washington, D.C. to Chesapeake Beach in Calvert County on the western shore of Maryland. Along with the anticipated automobile traffic, day-trippers would undoubtedly have flocked aboard a ferry for a look at Cooks Point and Dorchester County. More recently, the proposal in Dorchester County has been for a ferry terminal on Taylors Island.

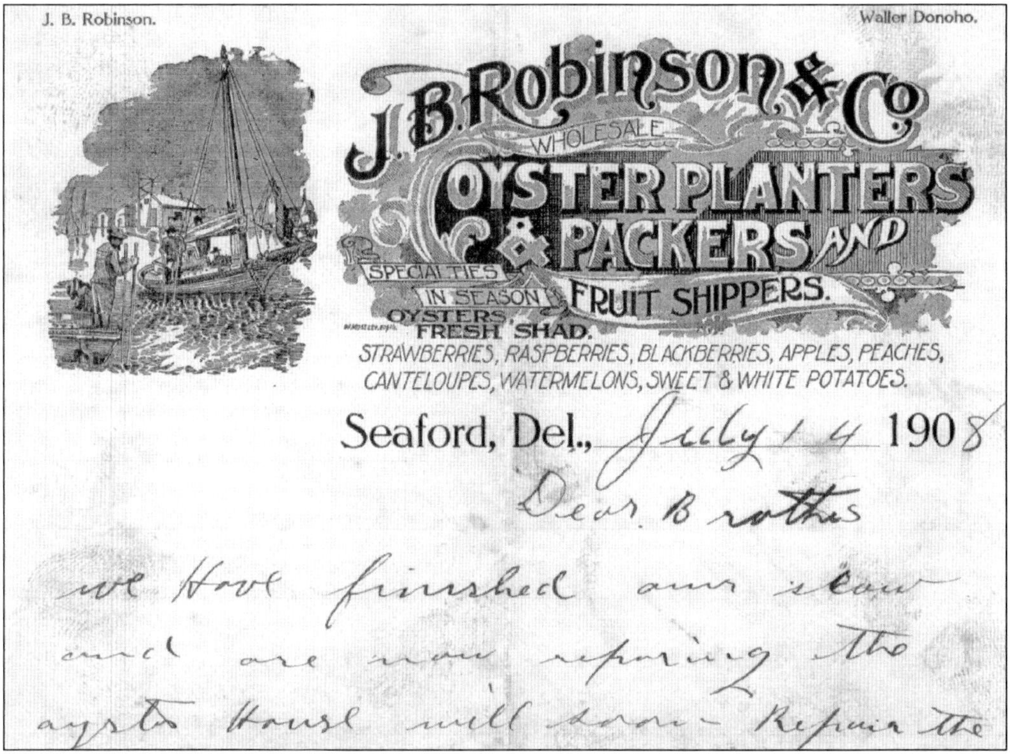
J. B. Robinson. Waller Donoho.

J. B. Robinson & Co.
WHOLESALE
OYSTER PLANTERS & PACKERS AND FRUIT SHIPPERS.
SPECIALTIES IN SEASON
OYSTERS FRESH SHAD.
STRAWBERRIES, RASPBERRIES, BLACKBERRIES, APPLES, PEACHES, CANTELOUPES, WATERMELONS, SWEET & WHITE POTATOES.

Seaford, Del., July 14 1908

Dear Brother

we Have finished our scow and are now repairing the oyster House will soon Repair the

Nanticoke River united Dorchester to Seaford, Delaware, where the railroad linked to northern markets in Philadelphia and beyond. Seafood and produce traveled upriver, along with seasonal workers for canneries, shucking houses, and other industries. One worker wrote home in 1908, "We have finished our scow and are now repairing the oyster house. Will soon repair the *Lizzie Bert*.," probably the schooner *Lizzie Burt* built in 1872, one of many sailing the Nanticoke.

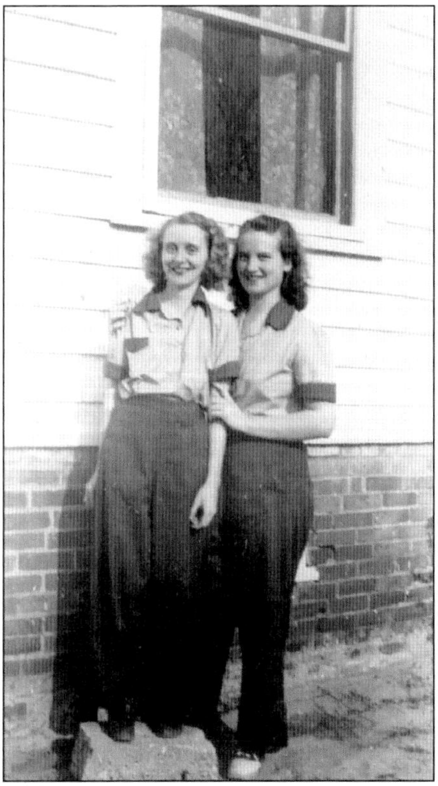

Migration of Dorchester County workers to Seaford accelerated in 1940, when DuPont opened the world's first nylon manufacturing plant. Sisters-in-law Anna Lankford Blocker (left) and Grace Wolff Blocker were among the Dorchester County women employed there during World War II. Women in slacks were uncommon in those days except for factory settings, where they were worn for modesty's sake.

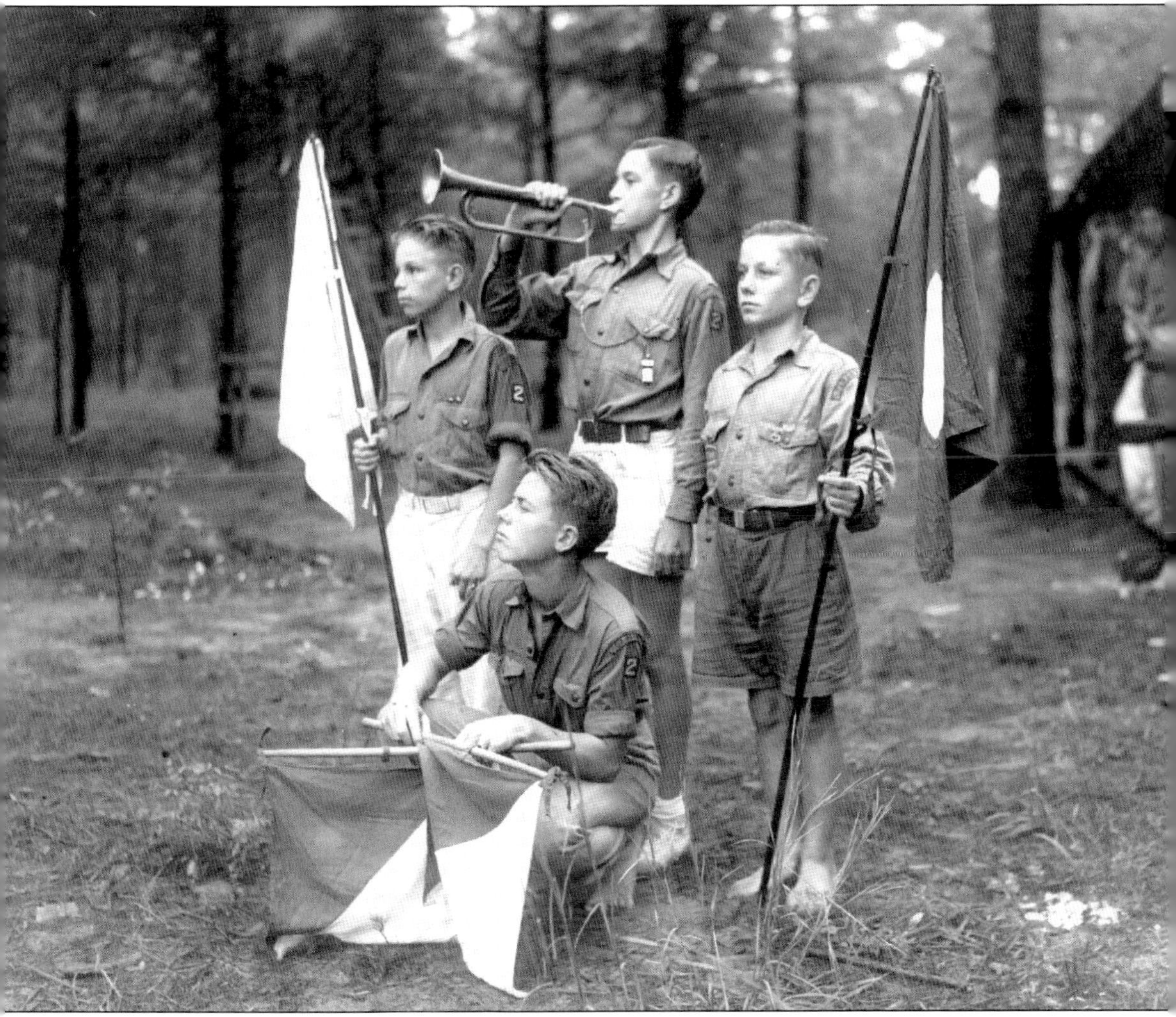

This photo of local Boy Scouts was taken in the 1930s by photographer George S. LeVarn. The scouting tradition in Dorchester County received a big boost with the purchase in 1964 of 1,265 acres on Marshyhope Creek for $165,000. In honor of the original inhabitants, the Delmarva Council of Boy Scouts named the camp Nanticoke Scout Reservation. The name was changed in 1987 to Richard A. Henson Scout Reservation in gratitude of a donation from the pioneering test pilot and founder of Henson Airlines. Before the land had a price tag, it was home to Nanticoke Indians. The junction of Marshyhope Creek and the Nanticoke River was an important intersection. As European settlers began arriving with claims of their own, a 10,000-acre Indian reservation was created by the general assembly, intended to solve disputes, but had little effect. The Nanticoke Indian Reservation stretched from Chicone Creek, just above Vienna, to above Brookview. Between the times of the Indian Reservation and the Boy Scouts, the community of Red Banks thrived on the site with a sawmill, houses, a wharf, and later, a moonshiner's still.

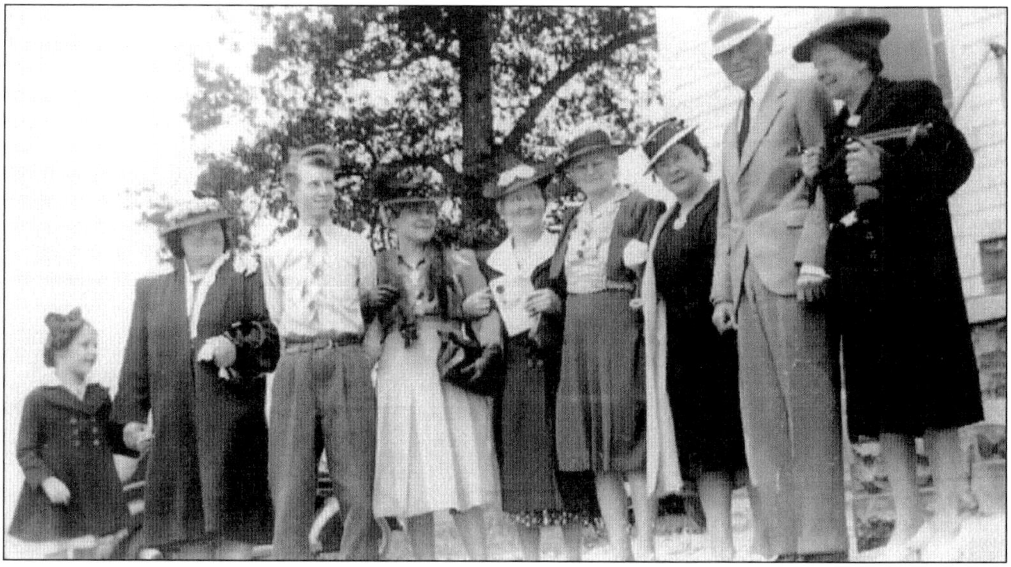

Brookview Methodist Church members, c. 1930s, were identified from left to right as Anna Laura Collison Messick, Hazel Collison Murphy, John Edwin Taylor, Hilda Wheatley, Edith Murphy Collins, Elsie Taylor, Zelda Milligan, John Rhodes Sr., and Ruby Rhodes Collison. John Taylor later entered the ministry and served several local churches. This building, dedicated in 1884 to replace a chapel that burned, was originally back from the road and later moved by members.

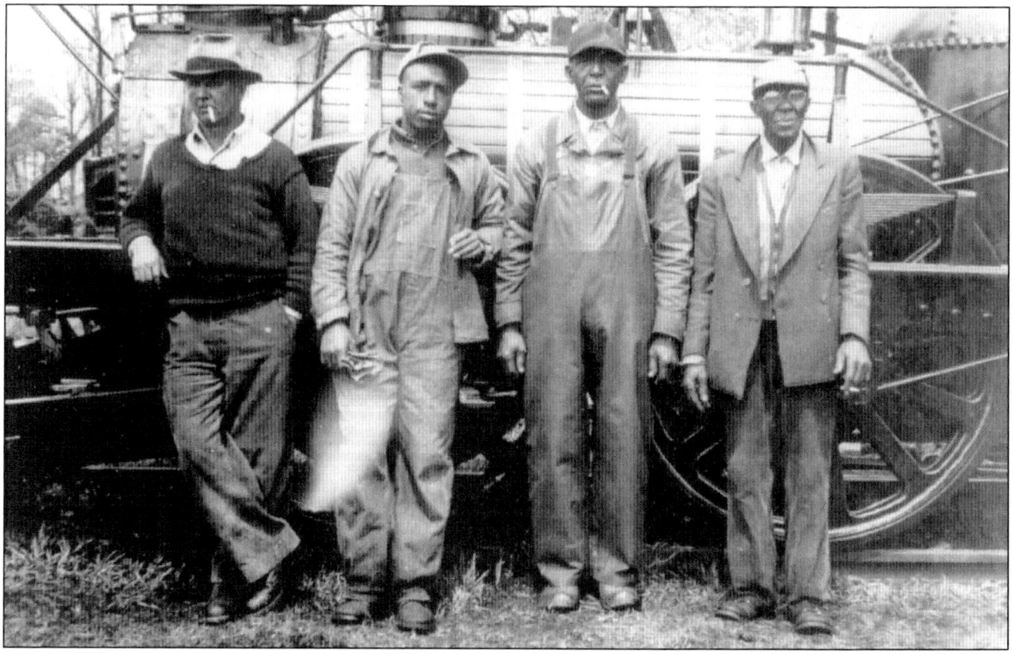

The trackmen standing in front of a wood-burning engine are, from left to right, foreman Adam Powell, Leonard Jackson, Fulton Jolley, and Walter Hudson. Pictured in the 1940s, the crew worked out of Hurlock, where this picture was taken. Riding a motor car with a trailer, they tended track from Preston to Vienna. Between them, they had nearly 200 years of service on the BC&A Railroad.

Before independence, those with 50 acres or 50 pounds of sterling could vote if they were male and white and, in Dorchester County, if they journeyed to Cambridge. In 1798, the county was divided into three election districts, and it has since been sub-divided into 18 districts. The last election district added, Elliott Island, saw the causeway-like road linking it to the rest of Dorchester paved during Austin Gray's second term as county commissioner.

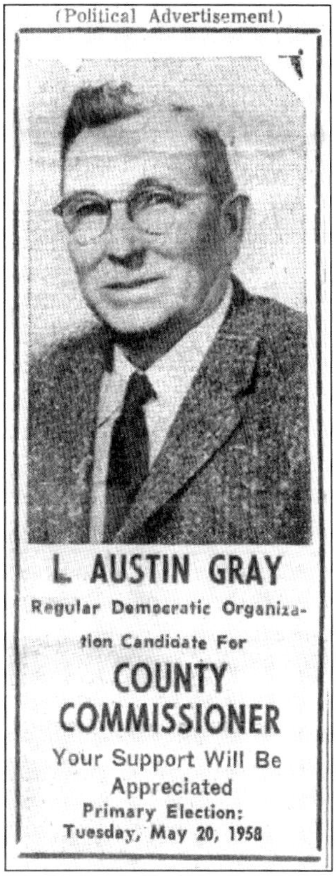

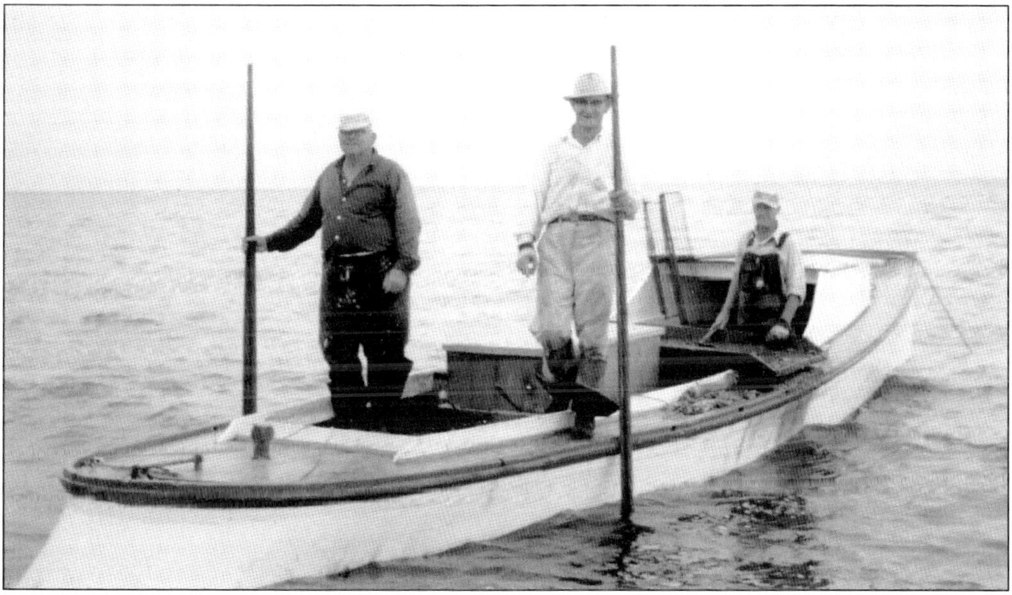

Hoopers Island dove- or drake-tails were round-sterned workboats with reverse-sloped transoms. Tricky to construct, island builders originated the design early in the 1900s, perhaps inspired by torpedo boat destroyers passing up and down the bay. Drake-tails made cramped workboats, but they were also the fastest of their day and certainly pleasing to the eye. Tonging Fishing Bay are Will Horseman (left) and Alonzo Gray while Capt. Randall Ewell culls.

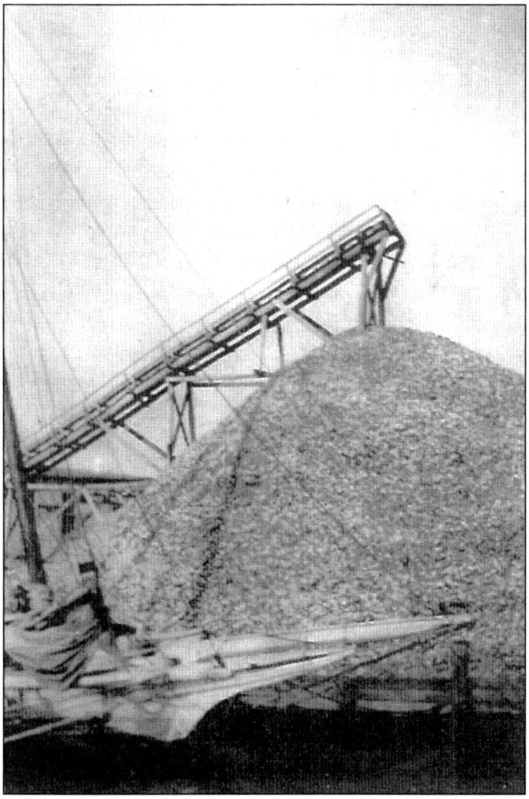

When pungy boats dredged county waters, shell conservation occurred automatically. Shucked shell supplied ballast aboard pungys sailing from shucking houses to oyster rocks. It was then returned to the bottom as the next catch supplied weight. Centerboards on skipjacks eliminated need for ballast. As skipjacks became more popular, rapidly accumulating shell piles were utilized for road building or ground as fertilizer until conservation measures were enacted to prevent depleting natural oysterbeds.

Capt. Charles Bromwell of Madison relaxes here with son Robert Bromwell aboard the Maryland Tidewater Fisheries patrol boat *Calvert*. The photo was taken in 1933 at the Taylors Island wharf by the bridge. In Captain Bromwell's time, the Tidewater Fisheries were more inclined to recruit from local communities than their successor, Maryland Natural Resource Police, is today.

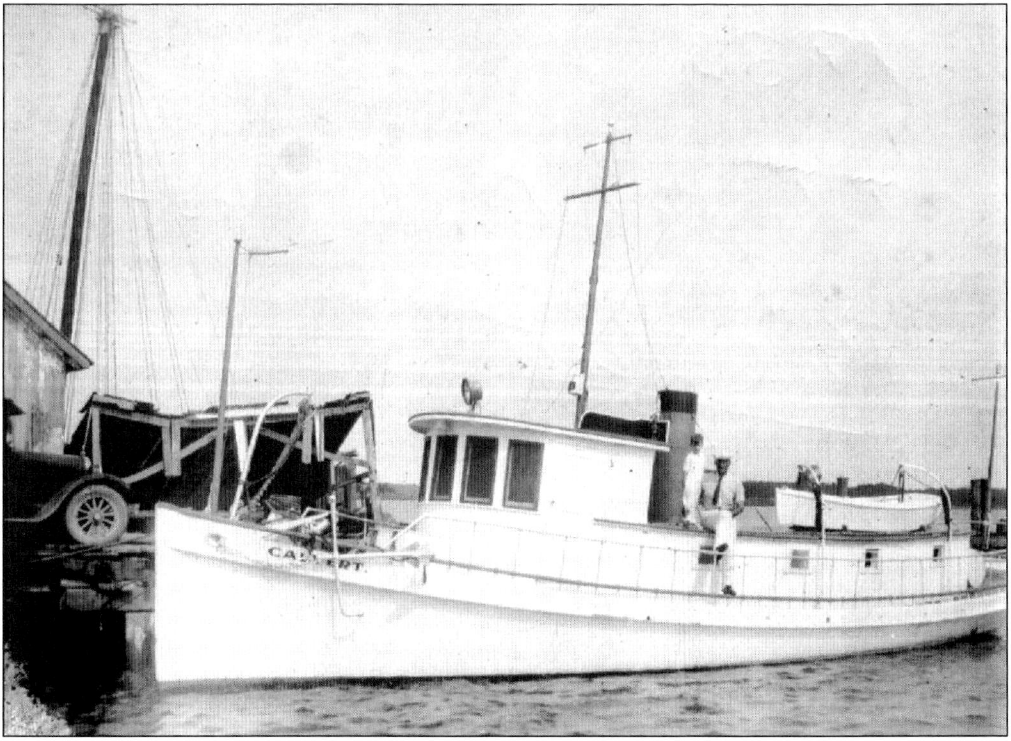

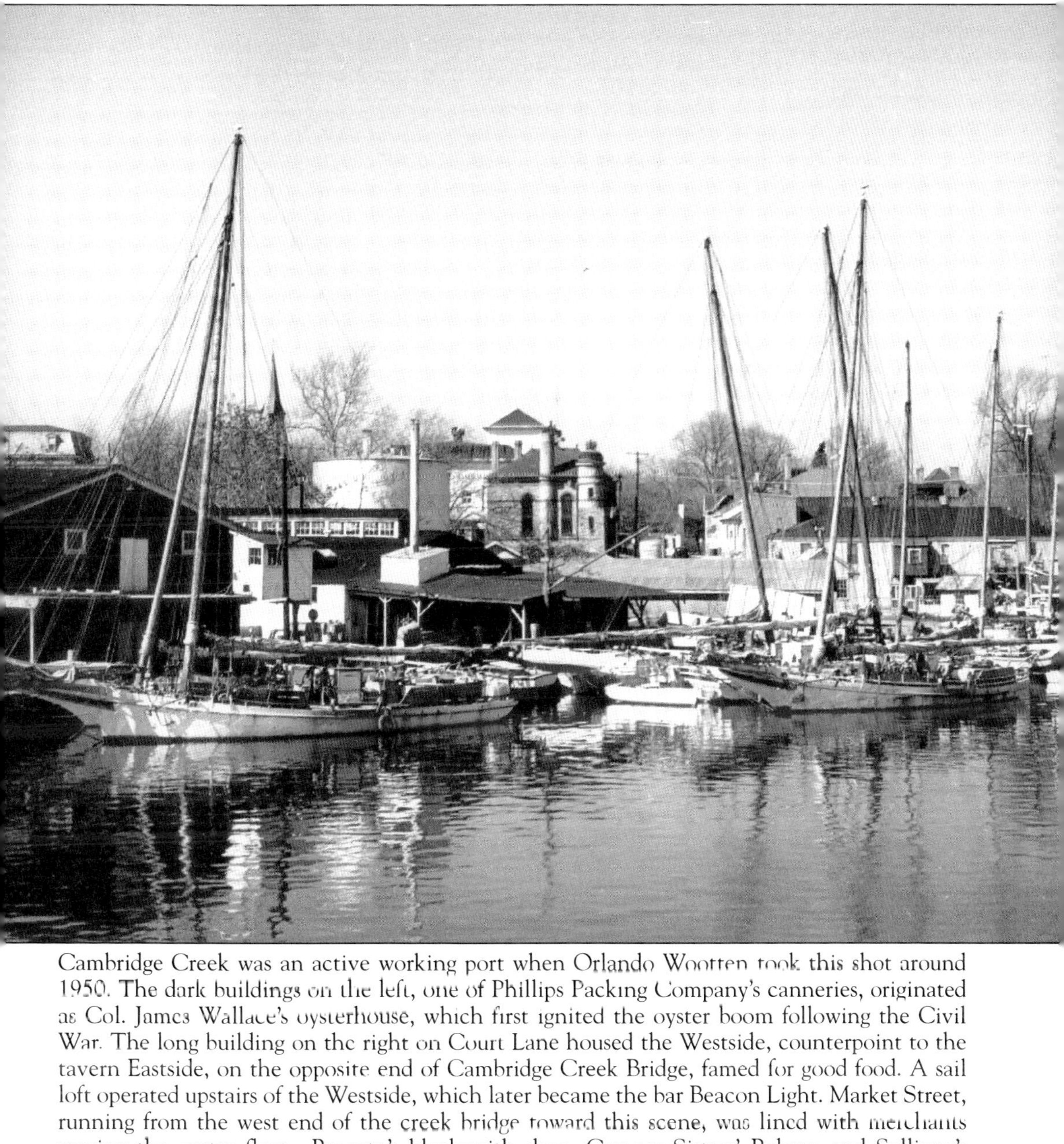

Cambridge Creek was an active working port when Orlando Wootten took this shot around 1950. The dark buildings on the left, one of Phillips Packing Company's canneries, originated as Col. James Wallace's oysterhouse, which first ignited the oyster boom following the Civil War. The long building on the right on Court Lane housed the Westside, counterpoint to the tavern Eastside, on the opposite end of Cambridge Creek Bridge, famed for good food. A sail loft operated upstairs of the Westside, which later became the bar Beacon Light. Market Street, running from the west end of the creek bridge toward this scene, was lined with merchants serving the oyster fleet—Brocato's blacksmith shop, Camper Sisters' Bakery, and Sullivan's Chandlery. The skipjack in the left foreground is the *Wilma Lee*, built by Bronza Parks of Wingate and now listed on the National Register of Historic Places. Also listed on the National Register is the old jail dominating the scene, now literally history, as are all the buildings mentioned. Only the *Wilma Lee* survives.

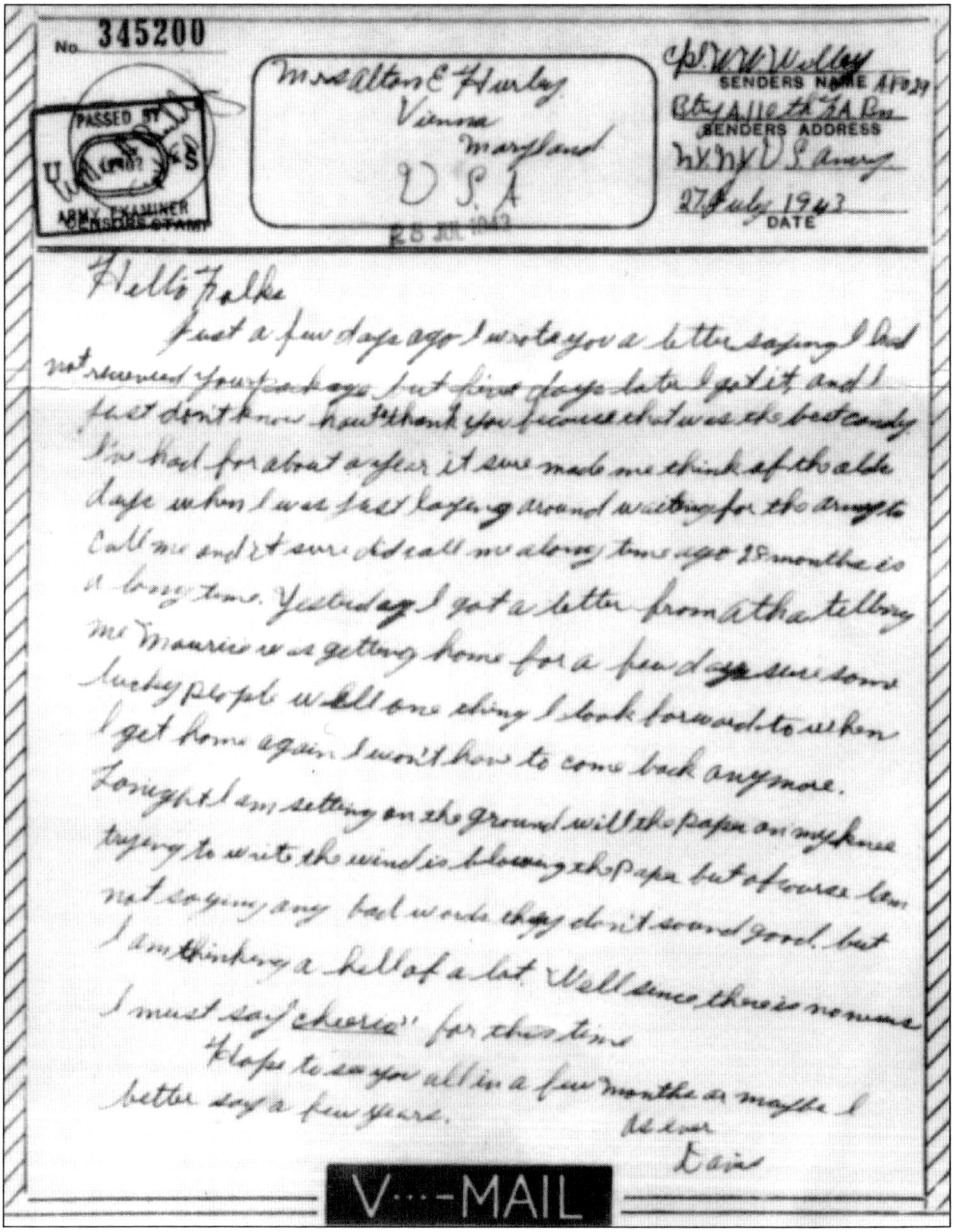

No. 345200

Mrs Alton E Hurley
Vienna
Maryland
USA

SENDERS NAME
SENDERS ADDRESS
27 July 1943
DATE

PASSED BY
ARMY EXAMINER

Hello Folks

Just a few days ago I wrote you a letter saying I had not received your package but five days later I got it and I just don't know how to thank you because that was the best candy I've had for about a year it sure made me think of the olde days when I was just laying around waiting for the army to call me and it sure did call me a long time ago 18 months is a long time. Yesterday I got a letter from Retha telling me Maurice was getting home for a few days sure some lucky people. Well one thing I look forward to when I get home again I won't have to come back anymore. Tonight I am setting on the ground with the paper on my knee trying to write the wind is blowing the paper but of course I am not saying any bad words they don't sound good but I am thinking a hell of a lot. Well since there is no more I must say "cheerio" for this time

Hope to see you all in a few months or maybe I better say a few years.

As ever
Dain

V···-MAIL

During World War II, military V(ictory) Mail filtered through censors who scanned each special stationary page to black out any information that might fall into the wrong hands. It was stamped with a number and the censor's approval and signature, photocopied, greatly reduced in size, and forwarded postage-free. This GI censored himself this windy day, sitting on the ground with the paper against his knee, sending thanks home for a package of candy. As he said, "I am not saying any bad words, they don't sound good, but I am thinking a hell of a lot." One suspects he was in Great Britain as part of the build-up of troops for the D-Day Invasion launched less than a year later. He managed to slip by the censor his signing of "cheerio," underlined. The other message that seems to come off the page is homesickness for the "USA," the last line of the address requiring no magnifying glass.

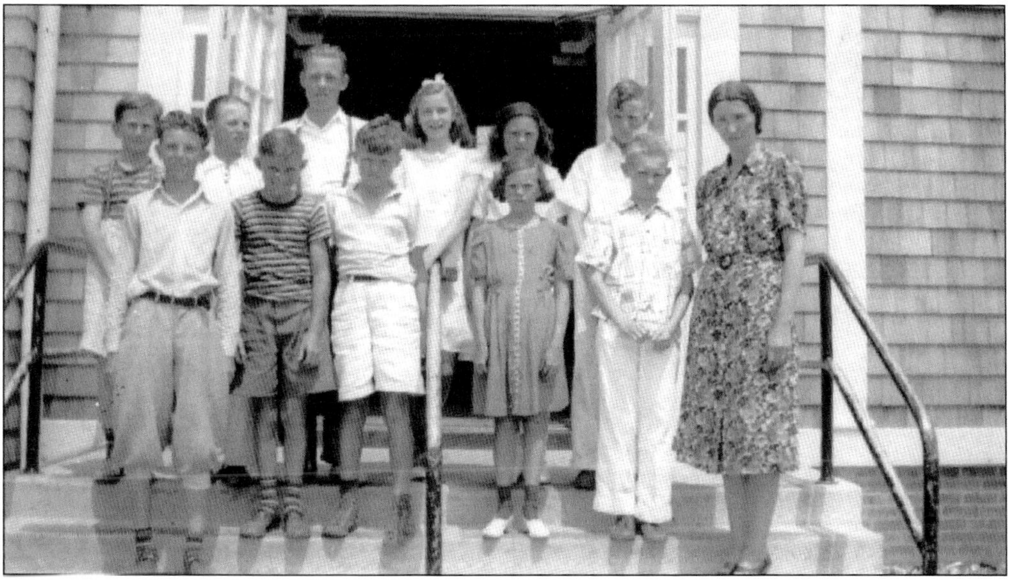

Hoopers Island, one of Dorchester's oldest settlements, was separated over years from the mainland by erosion. There are now three islands, only the upper two inhabited. In the 1940s, teacher Louise Linthicum Bromwell and pupils posed on the steps of Hoopers Island High School, since consolidated into Cambridge-South Dorchester. Younger children are now bussed to Golden Hill. In 1983, Joanne Ashton purchased this school and renovated it into Old Salty's Restaurant.

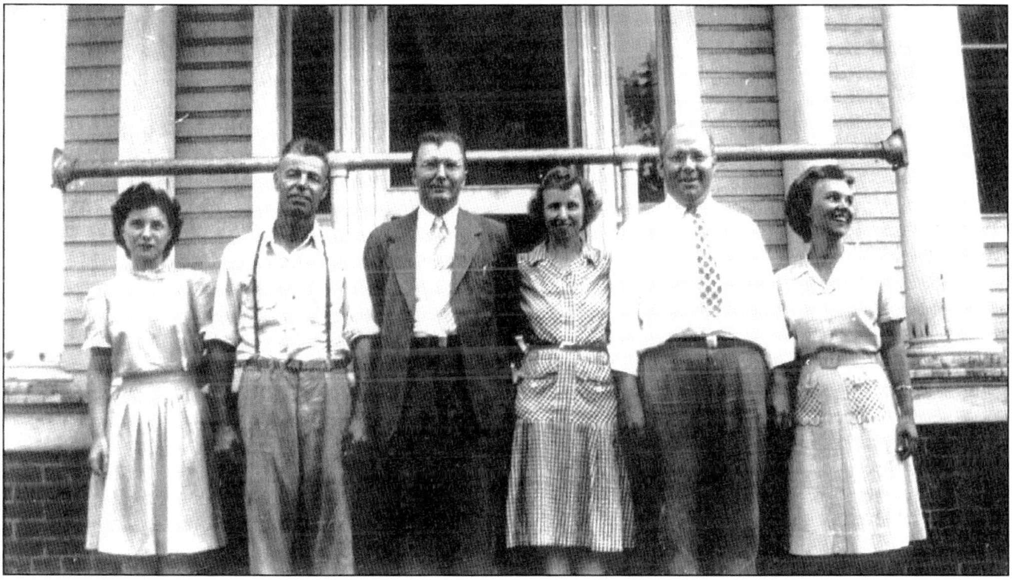

Pictured at his office on Court Lane is the superintendent of schools, W.T. Boston, and his entire staff. From left to right are Theda Warren Brerewood Stubbs, Wilbur Slacum, Superintendent Boston, Mary W. LeCompte, Hubert Kinnamon, and Gwynette Carruthers. Somehow, before consolidation and desegregation, they administered a system that included one or two primary schools in every community and high schools in every town.

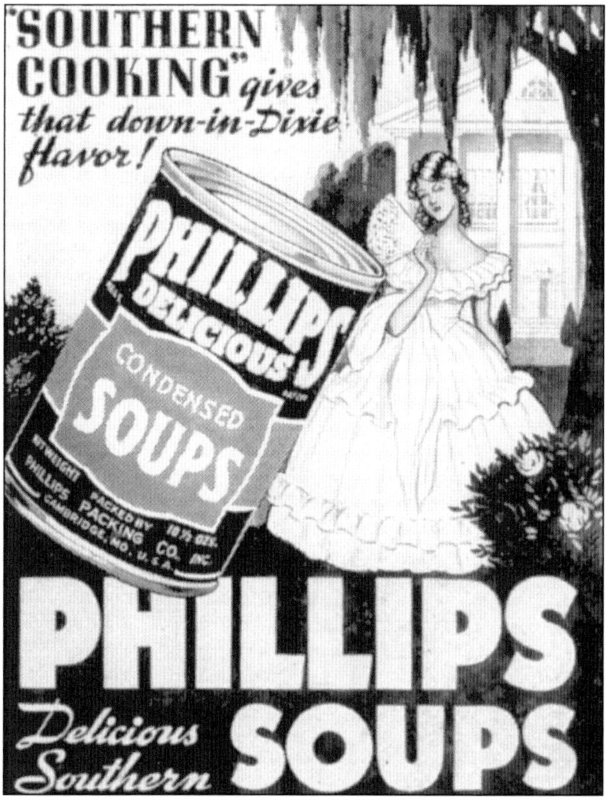

Albanus and Levi Phillips and W. Grason Winterbottom joined forces in 1902 to form the Phillips Packing Company, which became the county's largest employer. Their ad from 1938 may be excused for overstating a bit the time-honored southern tradition of condensed soup. The ad's publication coincided with the popularity of the best-selling novel of all time, *Gone With the Wind*.

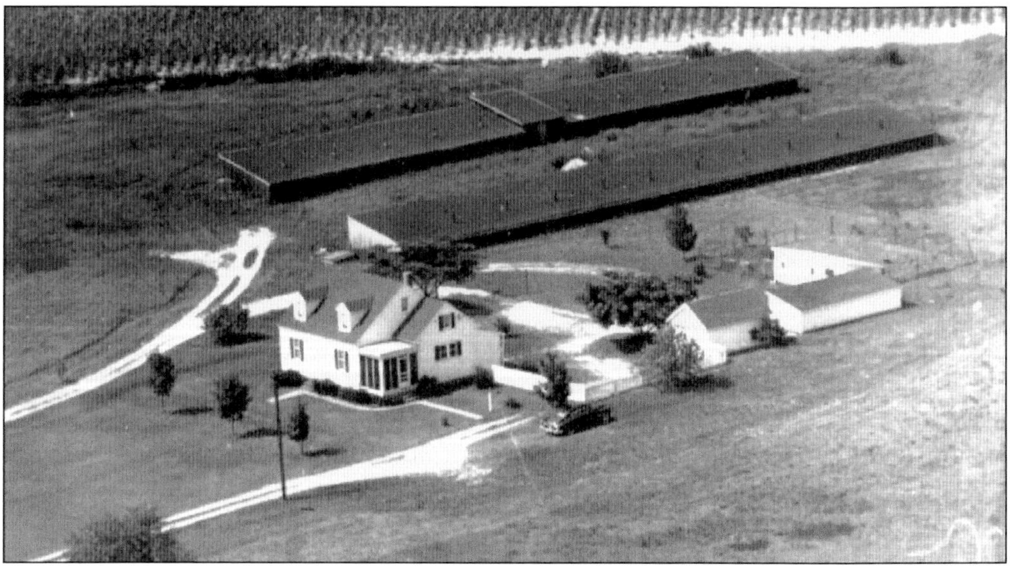

Poultry raising evolved from a few chickens pecking around every farmyard into one of Delmarva's most important industries. Chicken became a major source of protein due to the shortage of available pork and beef during World War II; therefore, since the 1930s, commercial chicken raising has become an important industry. A modern poultry farm may have several hundred thousand laying hens. The renowned Perdue family expanded from Wicomico into Dorchester County with several facilities.

An abundance of wildlife sustained settlers and provided a living for many of their descendants. Migrating Canada geese trumpeting the change of season drew waterfowlers in their wake, filling hotels with sportsmen and prompting migrating magnates to acquire waterfront estates. Visiting deer hunters generally encamped in more modest shelters. Native sons such as Bruce "Tucker" McCready were equally at home on land or water and hadn't far to travel for sport.

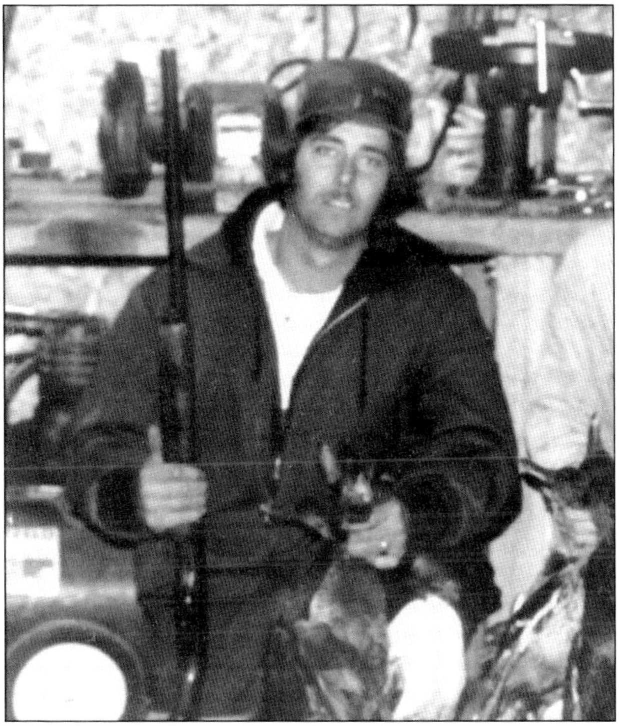

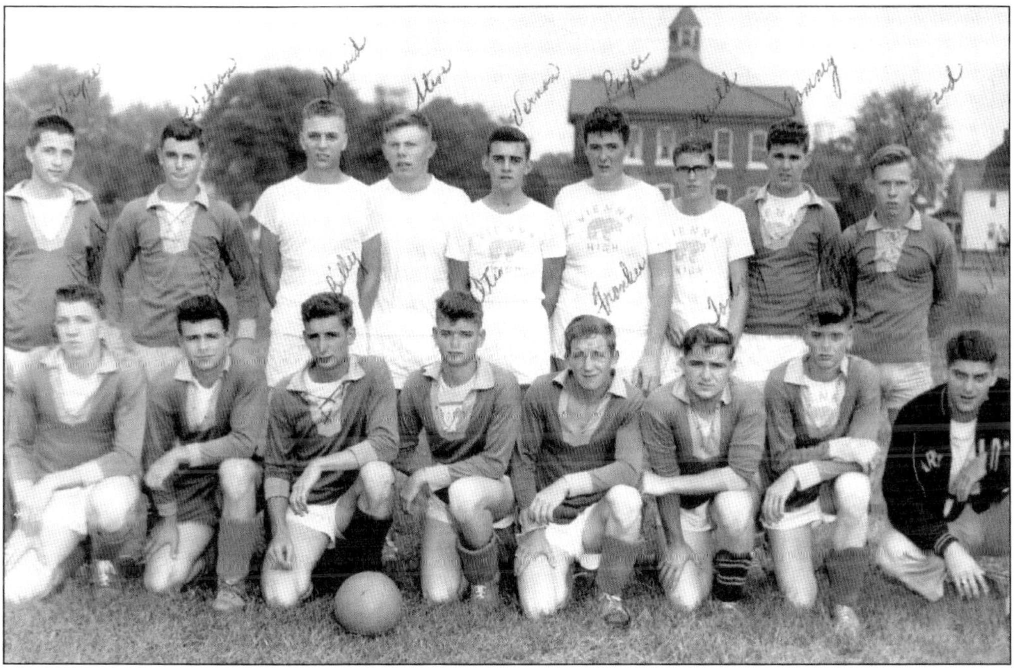

The last soccer team fielded by Vienna High School in the 1952–1953 season are listed as, from left to right, (front row) David Trader, Billy Willey, Billy Dennis, Otis Bramble, Frankie Marine, Tommy Lewis, Fred Bramble, and Coach Hopkins; (back row)Wayne Gray, Wilson Gray, David Bennett, Steve Gray, Vernon Phillips, Royce Brinsfield, Gerald Foxwell, Tommy Ralph, and Howard Harding.

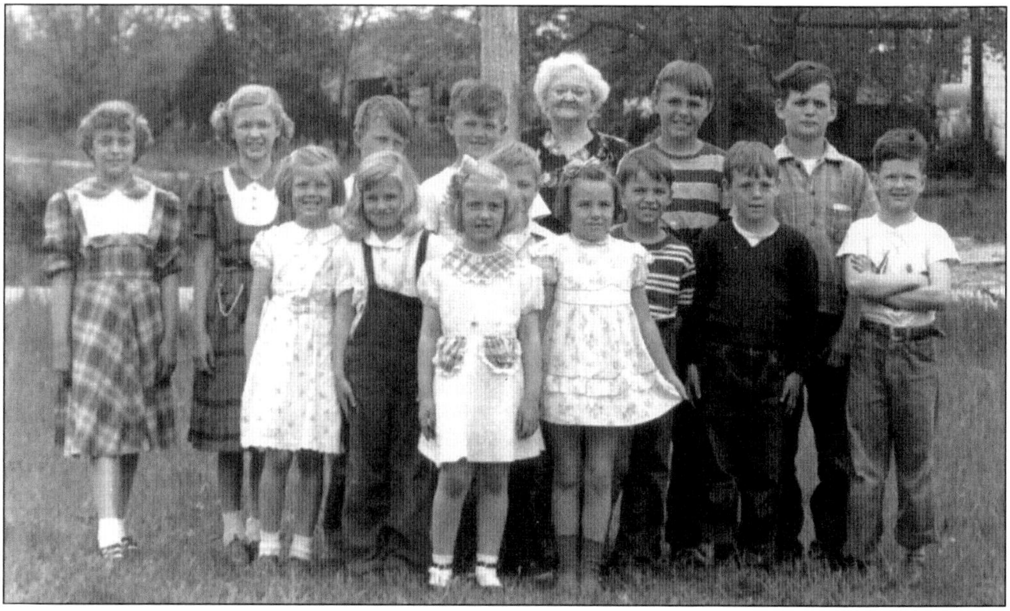

Community primary schools were being closed and consolidated when this photo was taken on May 15, 1950 of the last classes of the one-room Woolford School. The last students were, from left to right, (front row) Sylvia Brannock and Gayle Bramble; (middle row) Shirley Linthicum, Evelyn Shenton, Wayne Asplen, Tommy Klopp, Graham Bramble, and George Asplen; (back row) Joyce Bramble, Deanna Asplen, Bobby Shenton, Billy Shenton, Ruth Jones (teacher), Dennis Bramble, and Terry Bramble.

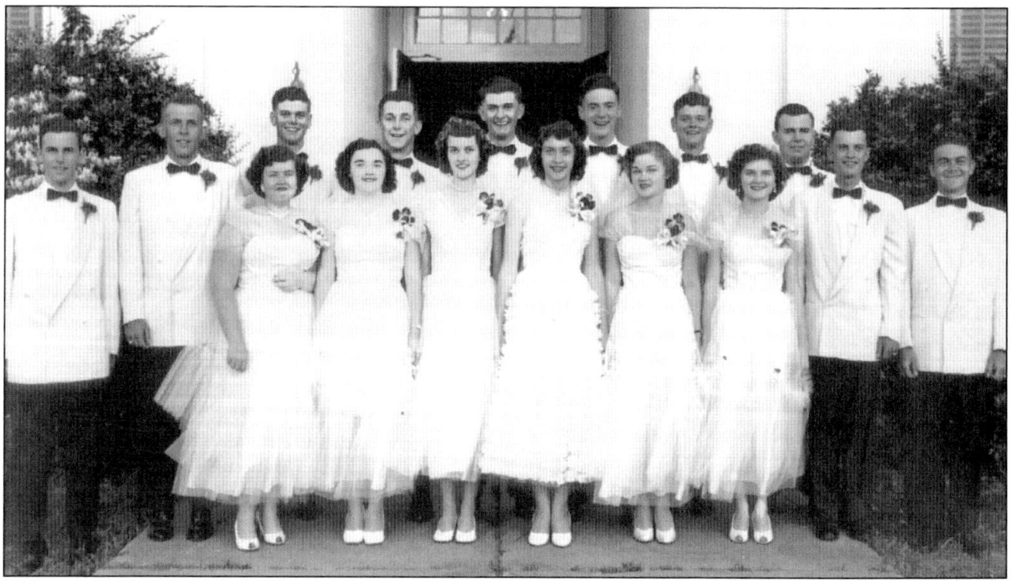

Knowing their school was closing for good, the seniors of Vienna High School spent six months persuading principal Orem Robinson and their parents to let them bow out formally. In their 1954 finery are, from left to right, (front row) Ruth Hurley, Shirley Dayton, Bernice Coates, Fay Forester, Rita Olson, and Shirley Hughes; (back row) Wilson Gray, Howard Harding, Freddie Bramble, Phil Baumgartner, Vernon Sellers, Royce Brinsfield, Otis Bramble, Calvert Evans, Roy Coates, and Edward Willey.

Three

Wheels of Time

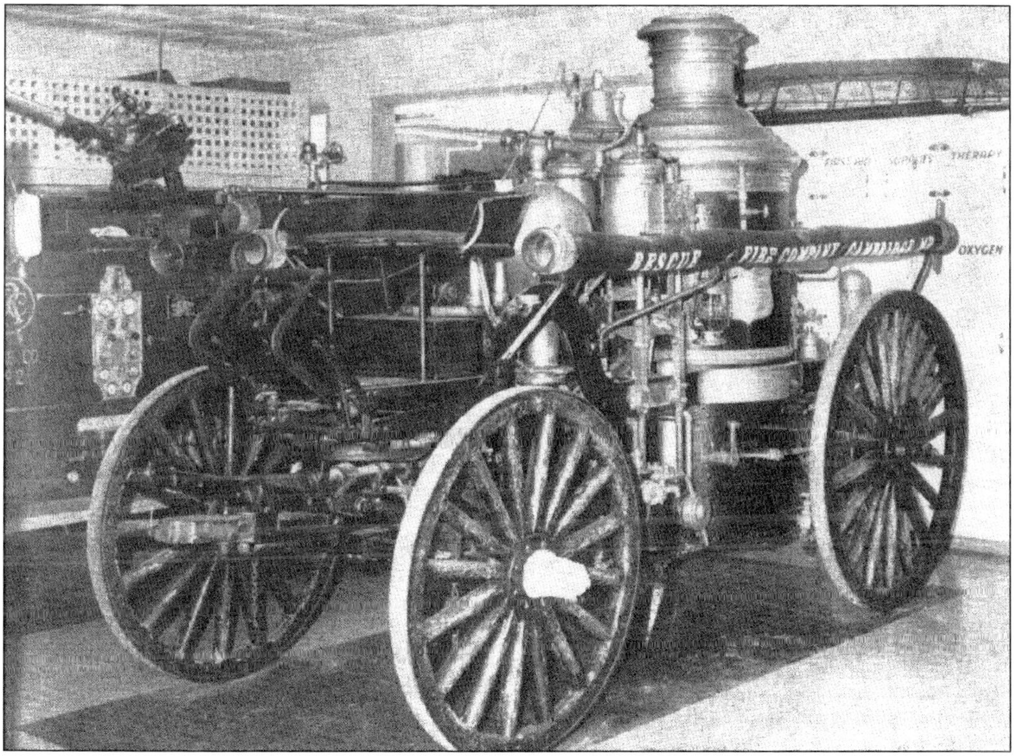

This 1910 American LaFrance steam pumper has been refurbished by Cambridge's Rescue Fire Company, which, in 1882, succeeded the United Fire Company, organized in 1843. United was headquartered in Cambridge's original jail building on Locust Street. The Municipal Building on Gay Street houses Rescue Fire and its steamer, which last saw fire duty in 1928 when Green Valley Mill's boiler exploded. Between runs, it served as a cooker at company oyster scalds.

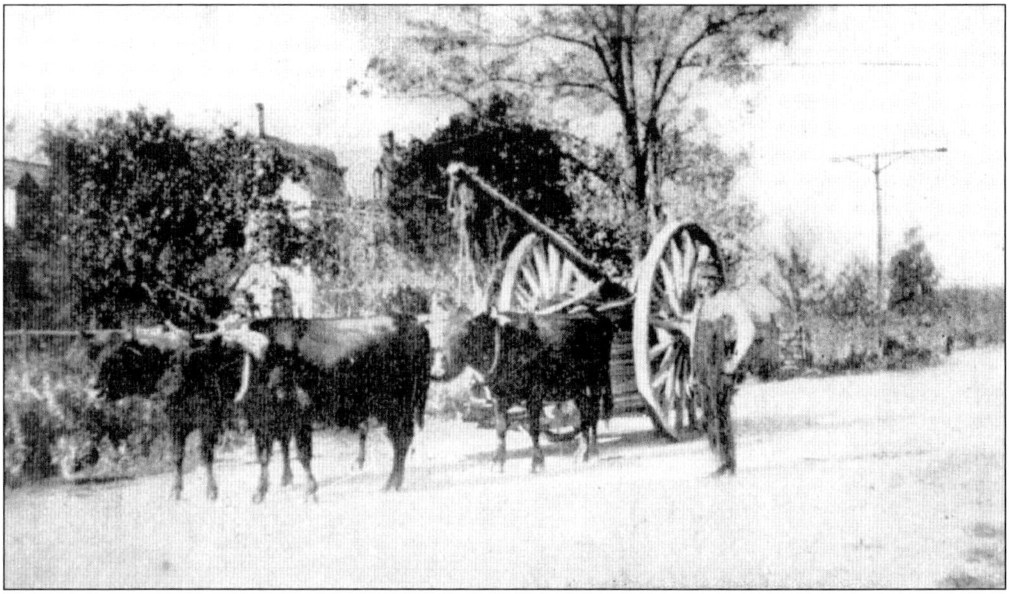

Dorchester timber carts were objects of curiosity to visitors. Their wheels were up to eight feet tall and logs were suspended over the axles nearly to the ground. Oxen were suited for heavy loads that had to be hauled over mired paths. As timber was cut near waterways, canals were hand dug in different locations into forests to facilitate removing much sought-after virgin oak and pine.

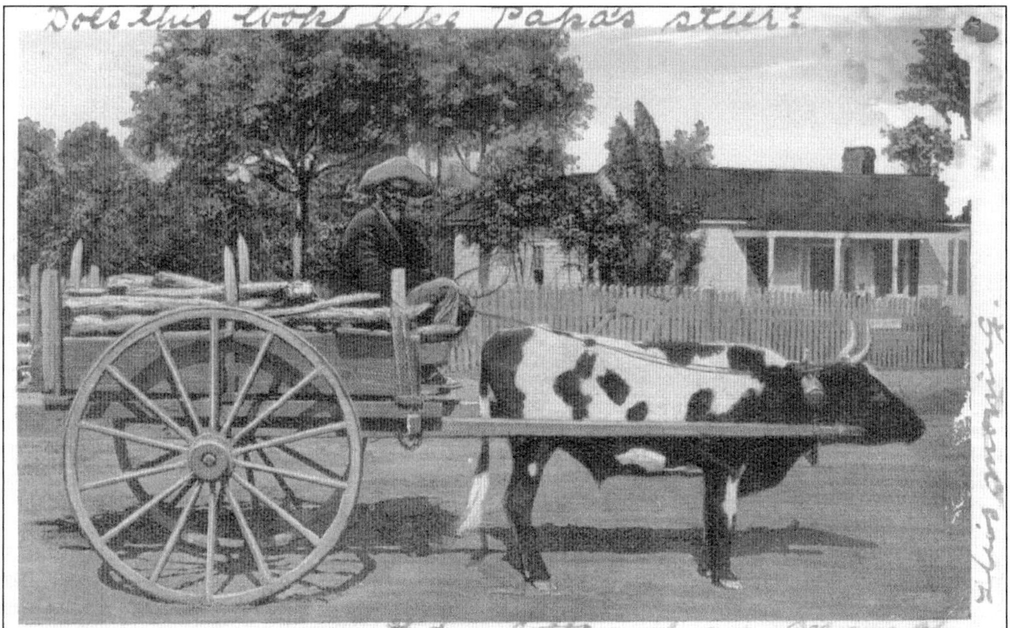

Oxen were indispensable in logging and, if not rapid, economical on smaller jobs like the one depicted here. Their split hooves were ideal on muddy log roads where cut timber needed hauling to a waterway for shipment. Oxen temperament was better suited for such tough going than that of a draught horse. "Does this look like Papa's steer?" the sender asks on this early 1900s postcard sent between sisters.

In 1908, Sears, Roebuck and Company carried the American Beauty line of buggies, along with enough models, styles, options, and accessories to make a modern-day used-car salesman's head spin—road wagons, road carts, spring wagons, business wagons, farm wagons, runabouts, top buggies, phaetons, cabriolets, and surreys with and without fringed tops.

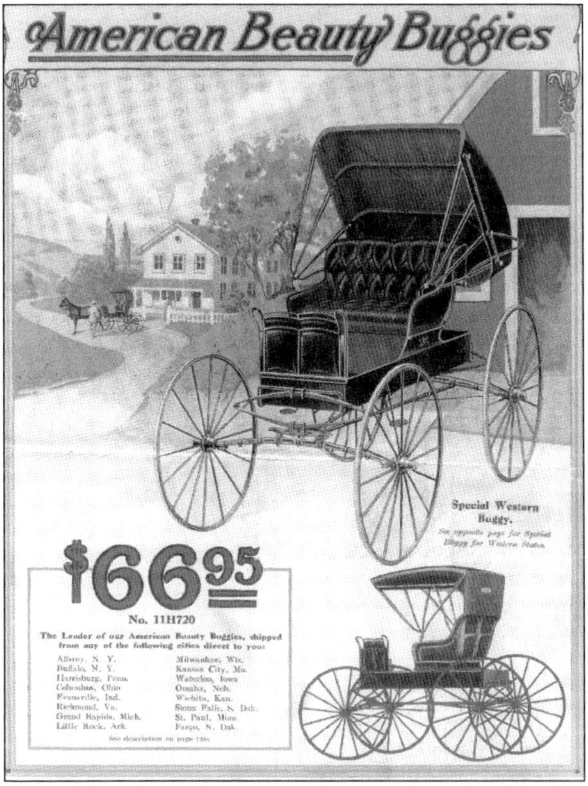

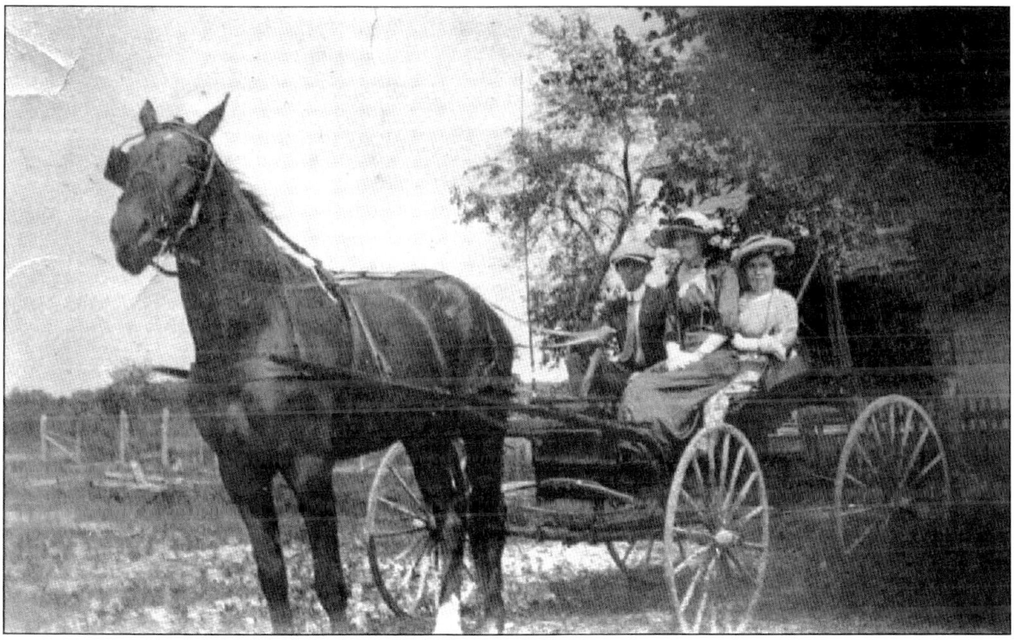

In this 1920s photo, Leon and Hattie Marine Lankford and Roxy Wheatley (right) are en route to Sunday service at the historic Wheatley Church in North Dorchester's Fork District. On the Sabbath, horse Ruth was not at the plow and performed lighter duties for the Lankfords. During winters, she carried the family over the snow in a wicker sleigh.

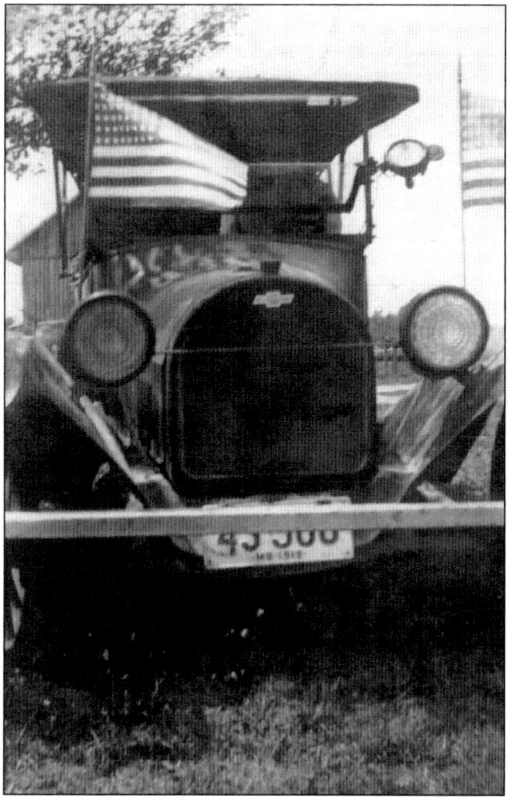

Drivers of cars such as this patriotic Chevrolet would fall in behind parades when every automobile still had curiosity value. After a Fourth of July parade, Francis duPont and party from Horn Point enjoyed viewing fireworks over the Choptank from the bridge of the Cambridge Yacht Club. DuPont endowed a fund to perpetuate the Cambridge display, but every corner of Dorchester County has its own celebrations, as well.

This 1930s photo shows Carl V. and Mabel Wainwright Marine outside the *c.* 1870 home of relatives Charles G. and Cora Marine. Operating the adjoining 80-acre farm, Carl raised chickens and grew truck crops. Mabel was employed at Douglas Canning House in Galestown, where she set a record for wrapping labels on quart cans. This Eldorado home, now called Twin Gables, was reconstructed in the 1970s by the present owner, Donald Hackett.

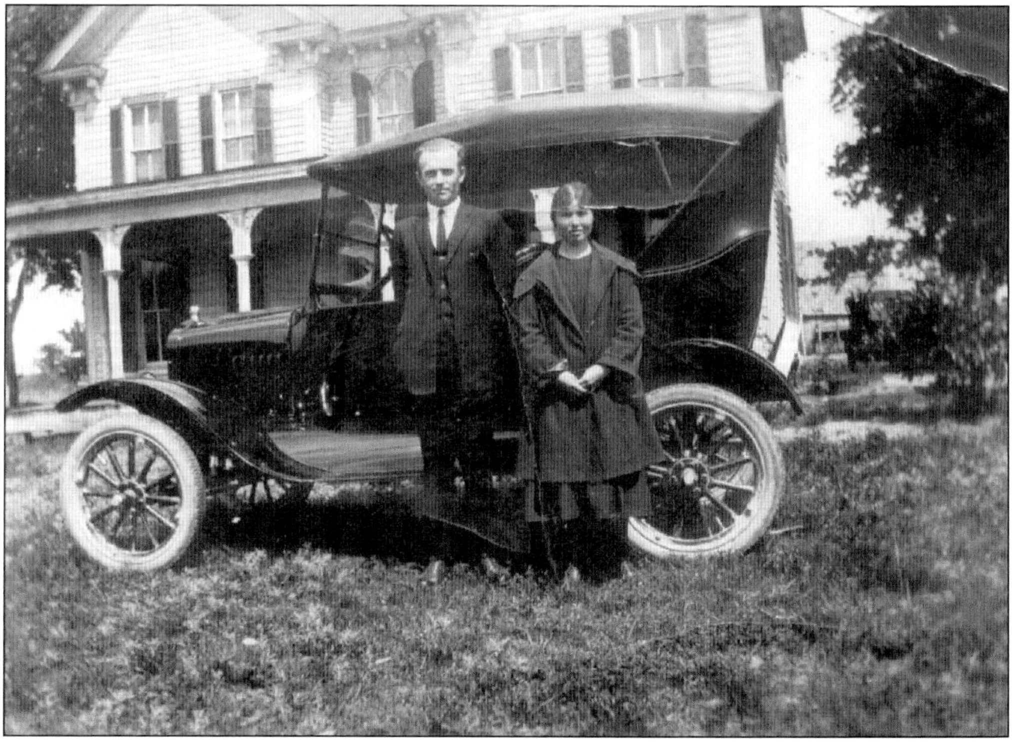

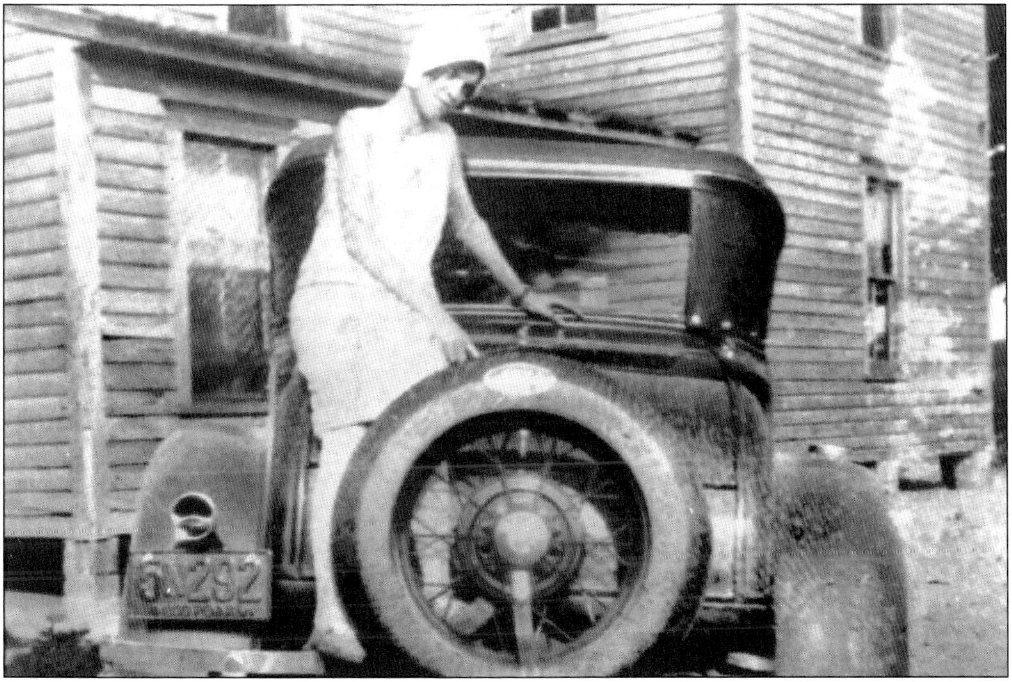

Evelyn Wheatley poses here in 1934 by the rumble seat of a Ford at her parents' Galestown home. The foldout, open-air rumble seat behind the roofed front seat was a delightful feature yet to be rediscovered by a retro car manufacturer. Evelyn, two years later, wed Harold Milligan of Hurlock and raised four girls and two boys on their 135-acre dairy farm on Milligantown Road near Williamsburg.

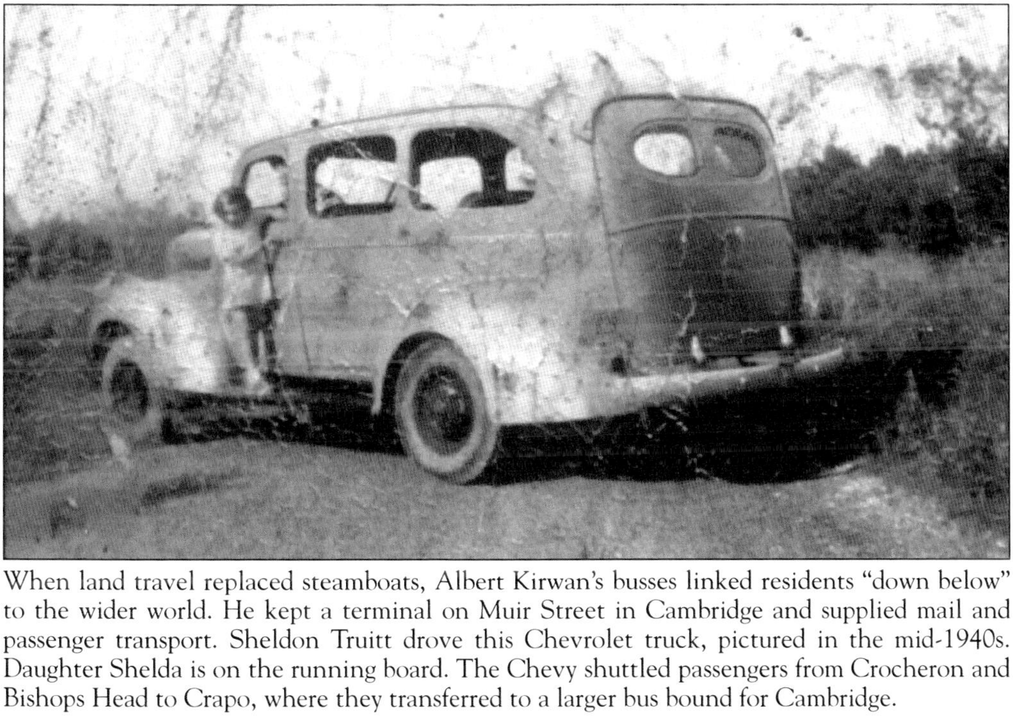

When land travel replaced steamboats, Albert Kirwan's busses linked residents "down below" to the wider world. He kept a terminal on Muir Street in Cambridge and supplied mail and passenger transport. Sheldon Truitt drove this Chevrolet truck, pictured in the mid-1940s. Daughter Shelda is on the running board. The Chevy shuttled passengers from Crocheron and Bishops Head to Crapo, where they transferred to a larger bus bound for Cambridge.

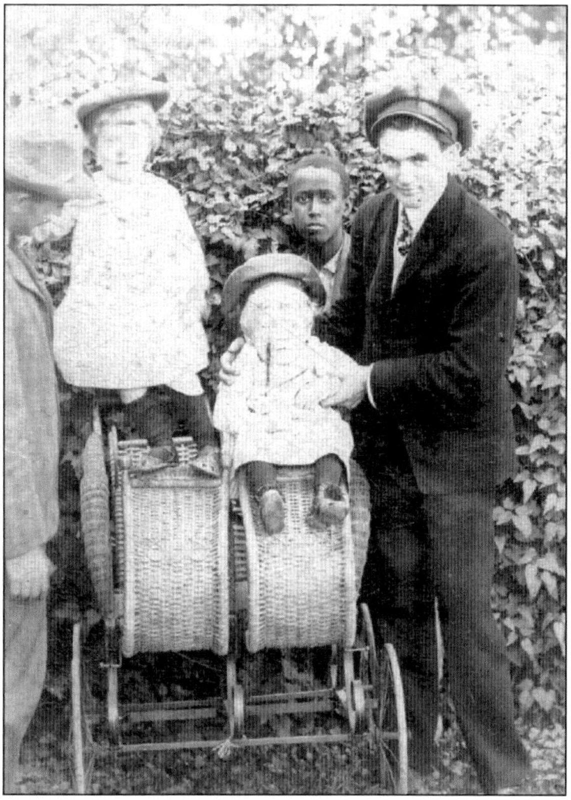

William Richard and Harry Franklin Bratten were adorable in their twin stroller. They almost didn't make it home from a visit to the Woodlands, where the admiring farm hands in the photograph enjoyed entertaining the children. Their Aunt Nell and Uncle Will Percy had invited the boys to visit a while at their farm on what later became Route 50. Their mother was obliging until Aunt Nell asked about adoption, when the mother fetched them home.

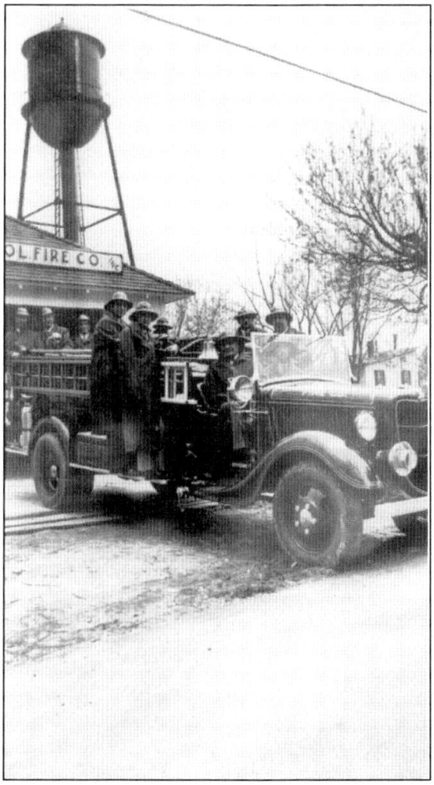

The Vienna Volunteer Fire Company celebrated dedication of their firehouse on Race Street in 1936 with a large parade, speeches, and an oyster and chicken supper. Festivities wound up at night with a free dance.

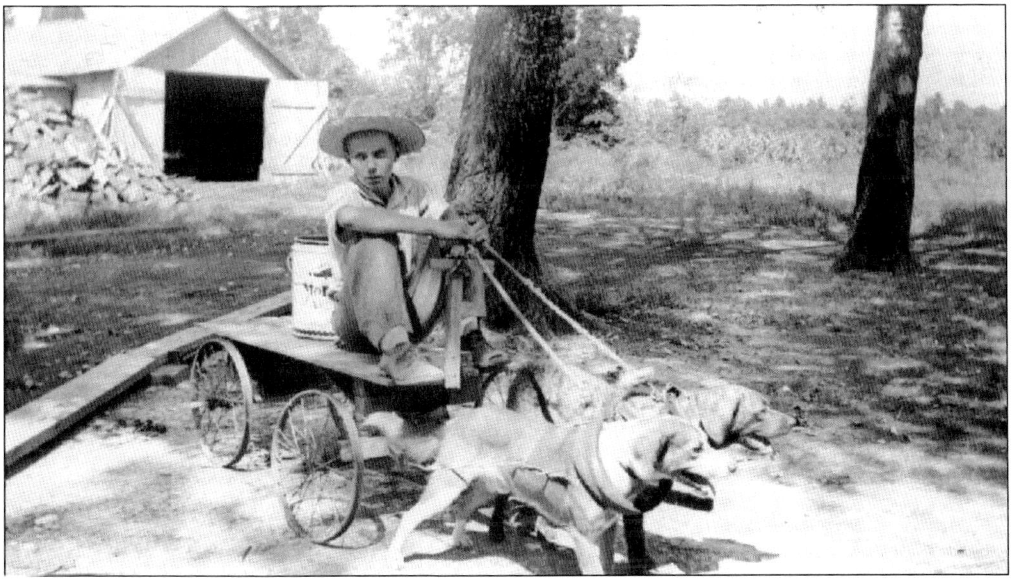

A boy needn't carry a bucket if he has a brace of retrievers in fitted harnesses. Robert L. Bromwell of Madison was a youngster in the 1930s, but many grown men benefited from owning a good dog and cart. Fulton Fisher of Hurleys Neck had fond memories of his father heading for work with Dash, the family German Shepherd, hauling five gallons of gasoline down the path for Mr. Fisher's workboat.

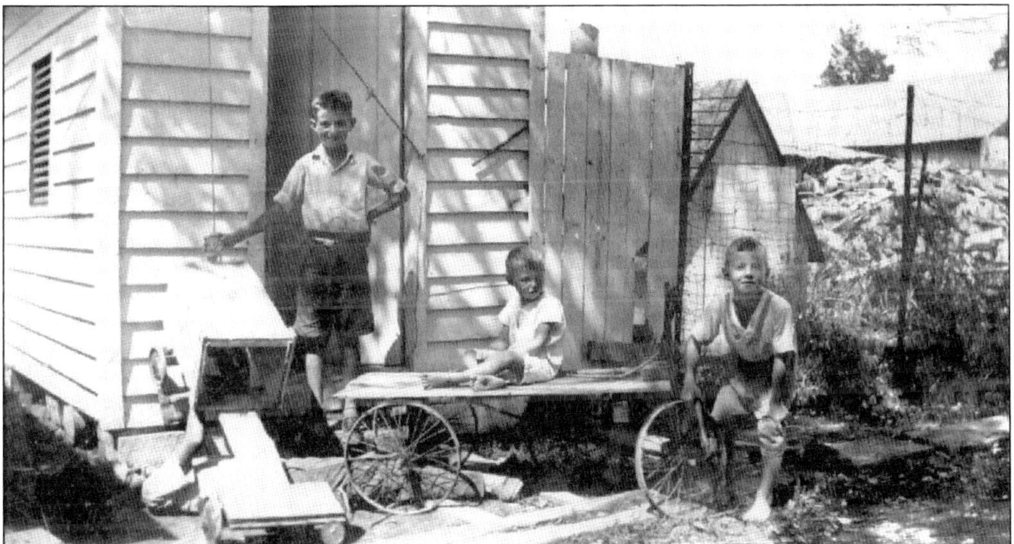

Before the expression "men and their toys," these lads in the summer of 1939 were known as "The B-Boys." These Madison boys are Johnnie Brannock (under soapbox racer), Robert Bromwell (in door), Wimpy Barrack (on wagon), and Howard Barrack.

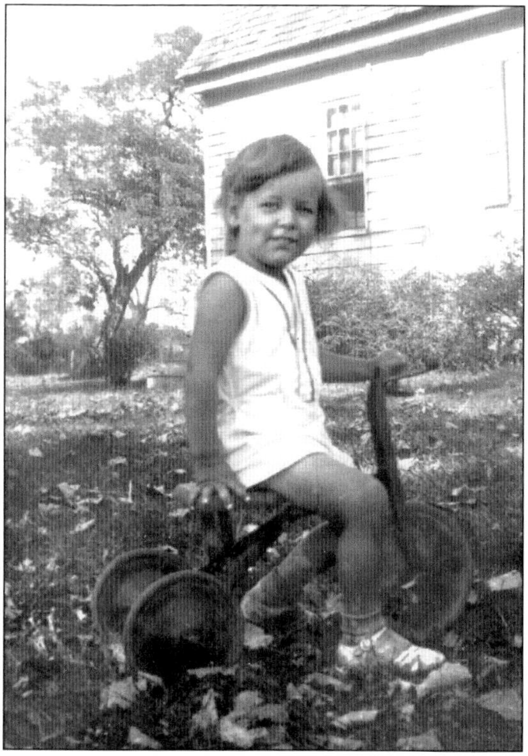

James H. McCready didn't realize in the 1930s that he was biking around one of the county's most historic properties, Jarvis Hill. When the Loyola Federal Savings Bank was built on Academy Street in Cambridge, it was modeled after Jarvis Hill, which is seen here in the background. It has since burned.

Skipper, in the 1940s, was messenger between the Handley family and their daughter, Nell Handley Fooks, whose husband was disabled after being gassed in World War I. The Handley's farmed in the Jacktown area and a three-fourths-of-a-mile lane separated their two houses. Skipper saved them many trips, shuttling the mail delivered to the house nearest the road, and otherwise relaying items the two households wanted to exchange.

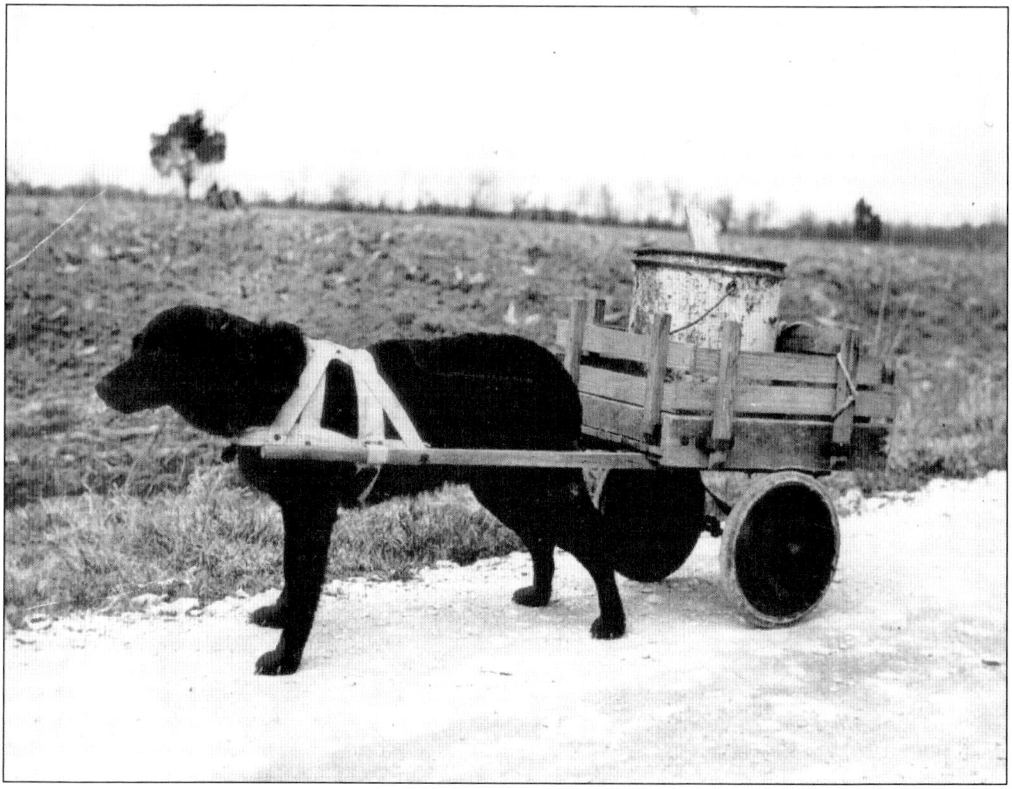

Four

ALL IN A DAY'S WORK

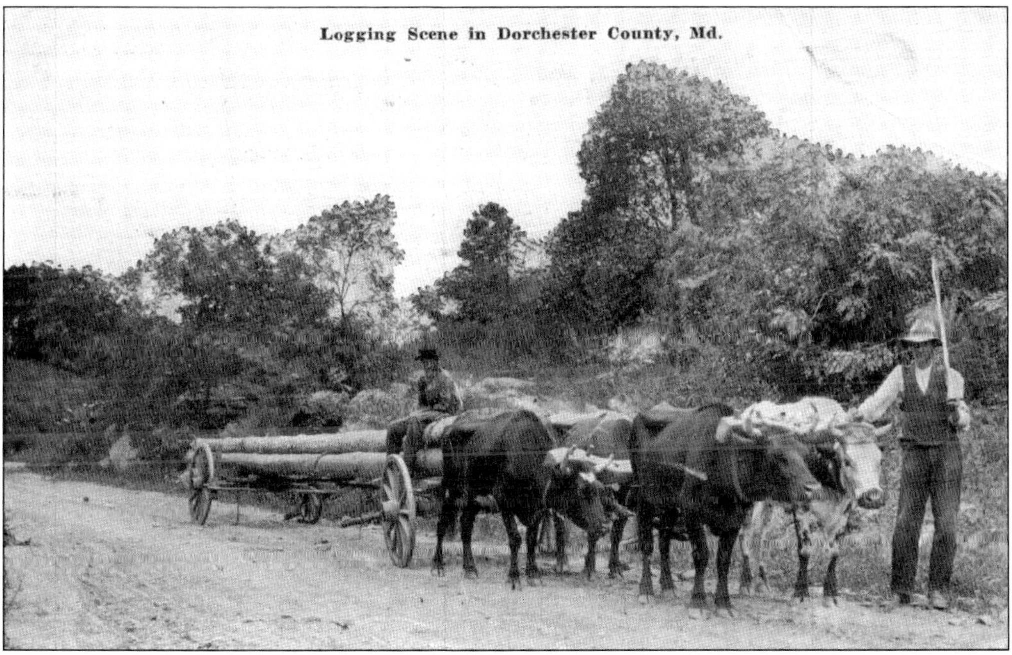

Virgin forests of pine and oak provided a livelihood for many newly arrived settlers of Dorchester County. Back in England, where forests outside of the gentry's private preserves were largely denuded, shipbuilders in particular were hampered by a lack of suitable masts and structural timbers. This 1912 postcard from Secretary shows that logging methods changed little in the first 300 years of settlement.

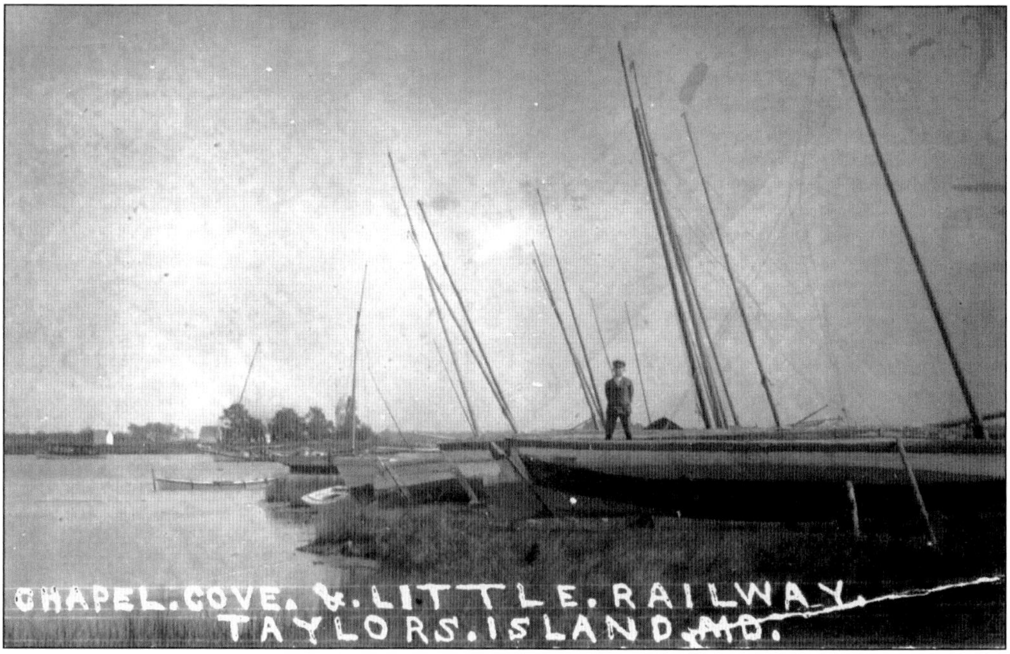

Hoopers and Taylors Islands, the first of Dorchester County to be settled by Europeans, saw several patents for land issued around 1660. Laced with creeks and coves for excellent harboring and thick with virgin forests, they were ideal for shipbuilding. This postcard mailed January 11, 1910 from Taylors Island shows the importance of the marine railway in hauling out the extensive oyster fleet to prepare for the annual harvest.

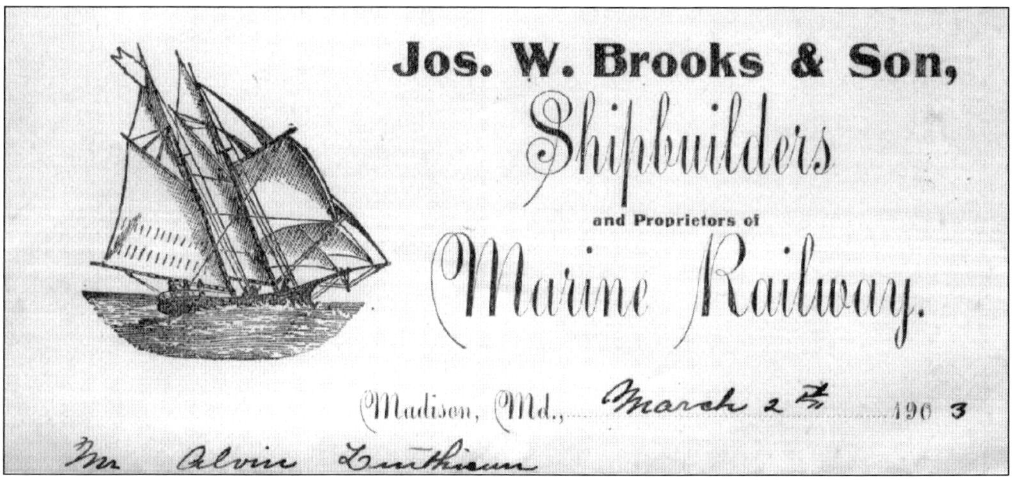
Jos. W. Brooks & Son,
Shipbuilders
and Proprietors of
Marine Railway.
Madison, Md., March 2nd 1903
Mr Alvin Linthicum

Joseph W. Brooks of Madison launched many ships into the coasting trade, which freighted produce between the Chesapeake Bay and the West Indies. In the 1870s, when Madison was still called Tobacco Stick, Brooks was advertising his steam saw mill and shipyard. In addition to his marine railway maintaining ships of the coasting trade and local oyster fleet, he later oversaw the local steamboat wharf and built a hotel at Madison.

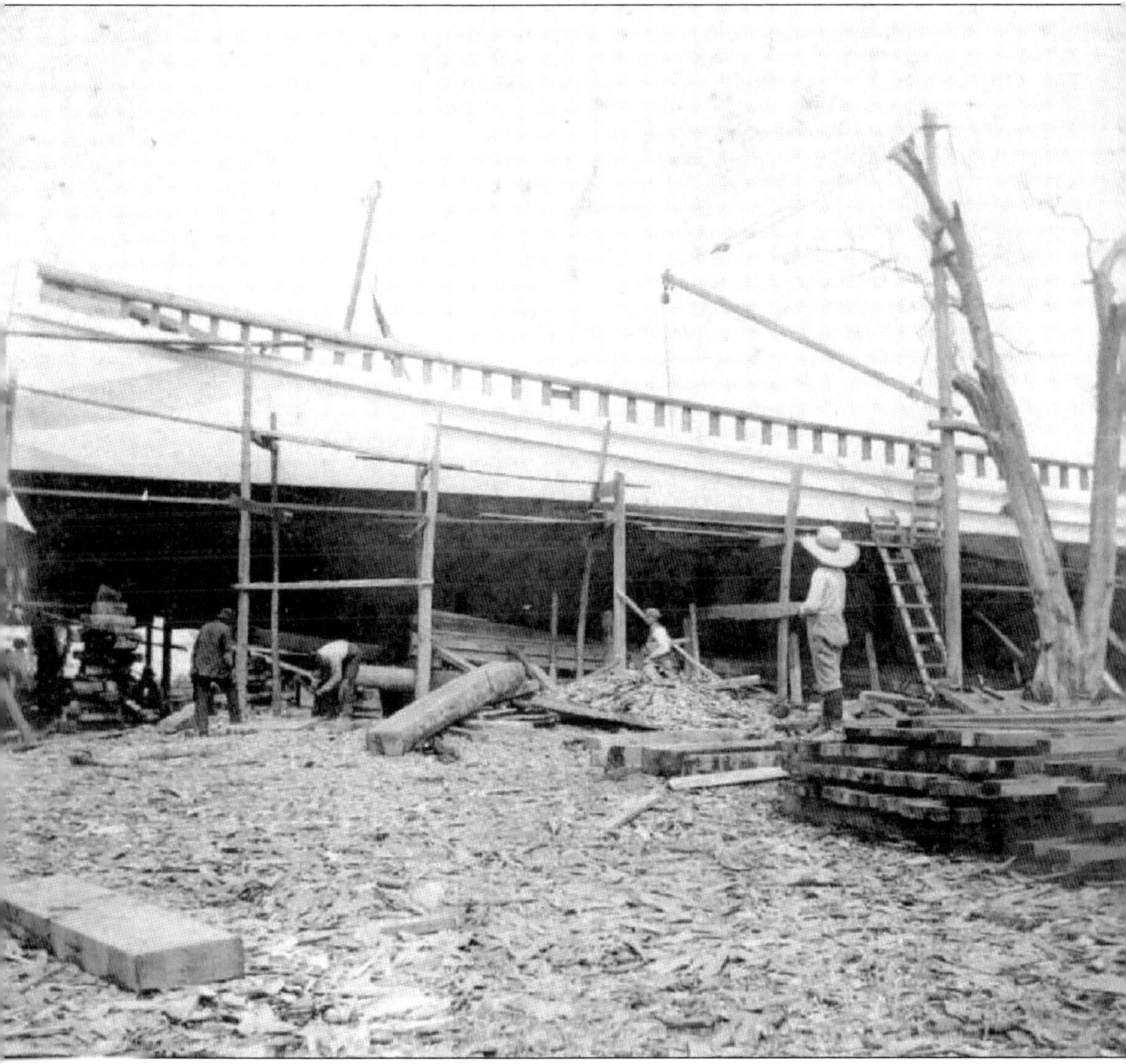

This lad in the straw hat was pictured May 15, 1898 watching from a safe distance the activity in Joseph W. Brooks's boatyard. According to M.V. Brewington's definitive *Chesapeake Bay Log Canoes and Bugeyes*, Joseph W. Brooks (1832–1915) of Madison designed and launched more vessels than nearly any one man in the world. Geoffrey Footner cites him in his groundbreaking *Tidewater Triumph* for having built the last pilot schooner, a pungy boat, in 1885. Pilot schooners are also called Baltimore Clippers. In 1884, he built the *Amanda F. Lewis*, the last surviving clipper type vessel in freight service on Chesapeake Bay. She was converted to power in 1940. Originally built for the oystering Lewis family of Lewis Wharf on the Nanticoke River, in later days *Amanda F. Lewis* sailed out of Virginia under Capt. Gus Rice. Captain Gus was asked once how paint was mixed to achieve the distinctive colors of green and pink used on pungys. He shot back that the colors were not green and pink, "They're pungy bronze and flesh."

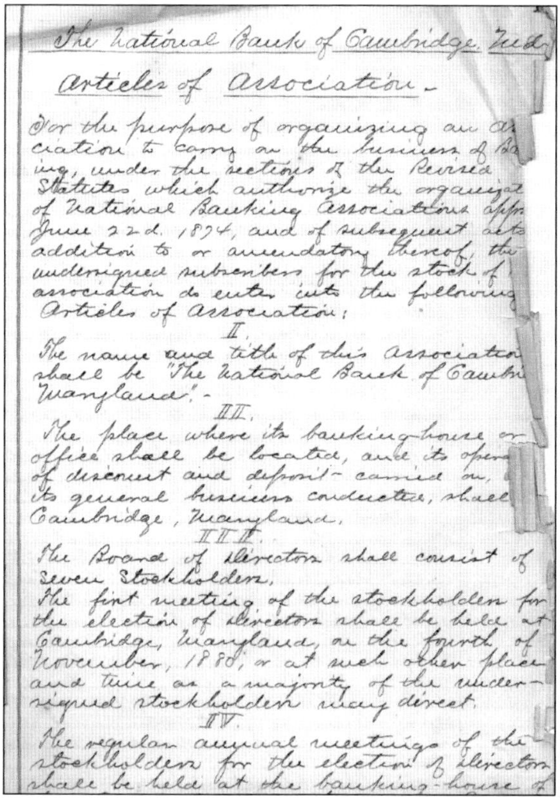
The National Bank of Cambridge, Md.
Articles of Association -
For the purpose of organizing an as-
ciation to carry on the business of Ba
ing, under the sections of the Revised
Statutes which authorize the organizat
of National Banking Associations app
June 22d. 1874, and of subsequent acts
addition to or amendatory thereof, the
undersigned subscribers for the stock of
association do enter into the following
Articles of Association:
I.
The name and title of this associatio
shall be "The National Bank of Cambri
Maryland". -
II.
The place where its banking-house or
office shall be located, and its oper
of discount and deposit carried on,
its general business conducted, shall
Cambridge, Maryland.
III.
The Board of Directors shall consist of
seven Stockholders.
The first meeting of the stockholders for
the election of directors shall be held at
Cambridge, Maryland, on the fourth of
November, 1880, or at such other place
and time as a majority of the under-
signed stockholders may direct.
IV.
The regular annual meetings of the
stockholders for the election of directors
shall be held at the banking-house of

These articles of association marked the creation of Dorchester County's first banking establishment and crowned the efforts of many of her leading citizens. The first president was William H. Barton Jr., a graduate of the United States Naval Academy and veteran of the Civil War. Depositors at the bank sailed unscathed through the Great Depression, being paid dollar for dollar on their money.

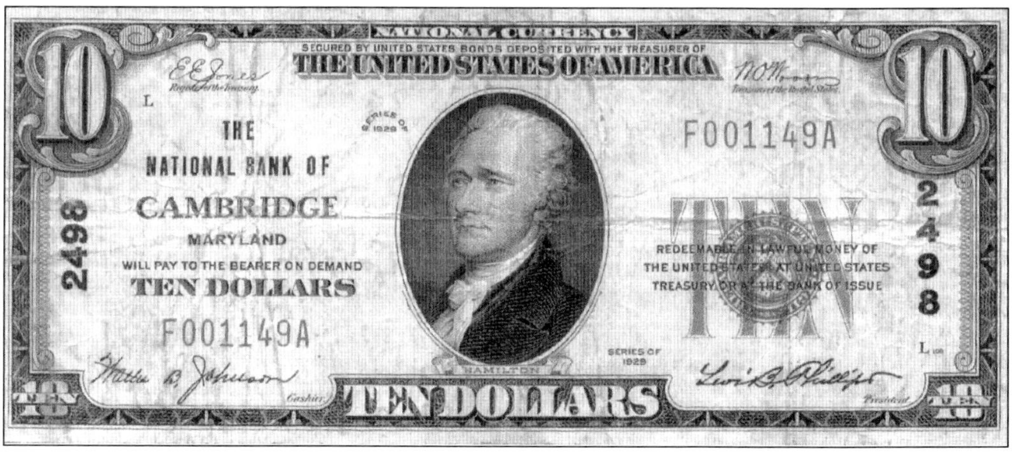

By 1880, when the National Bank of Cambridge was chartered, paper money had replaced tobacco as the medium of exchange, making commerce considerably more convenient. The government furnished chartered banks with large notepapers of different denominations, along with printing plates. When this $10 bill was printed, paper money had assumed its current size, but they still included the bank's name. Appropriately, Cambridge currency also carried the signature of Levi Phillips, bank president for 32 years.

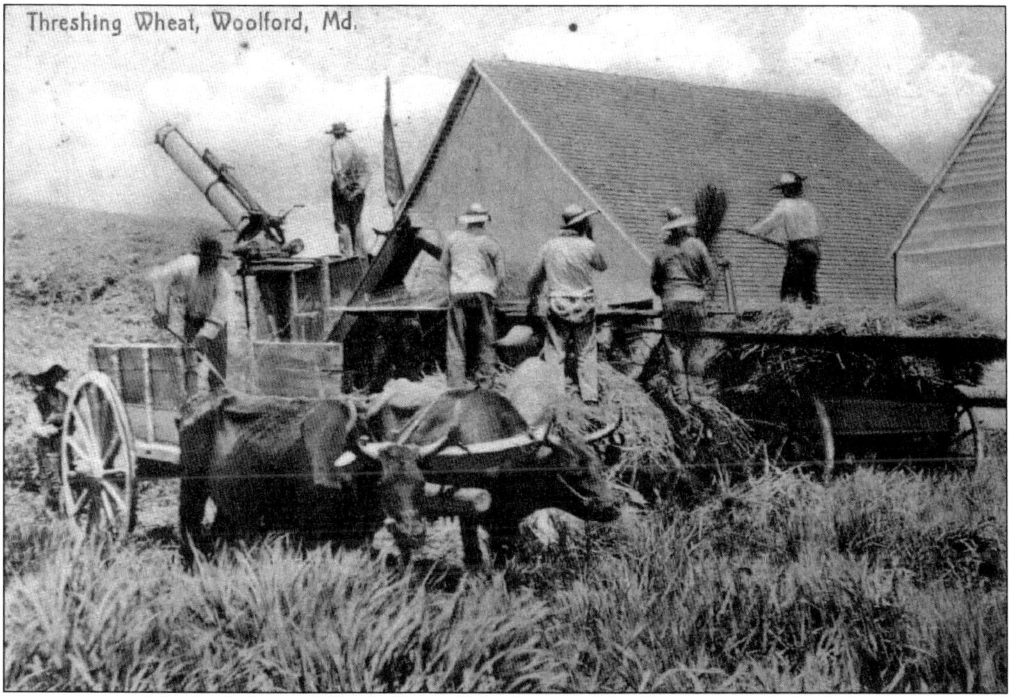

As tobacco crops waned, wheat became the primary cash crop on the Delmarva Peninsula, which was called the Breadbasket of the Revolution for the important role it played in supplying Gen. George Washington's Continental Army with provisions. This 1900s postcard from Woolford depicting wheat thrashing could have originated nearly anywhere in Dorchester County. A Church Creek firm, Buker and Jester, in 1912 listed their specialties as wheat thrashing, house moving, and wood sawing.

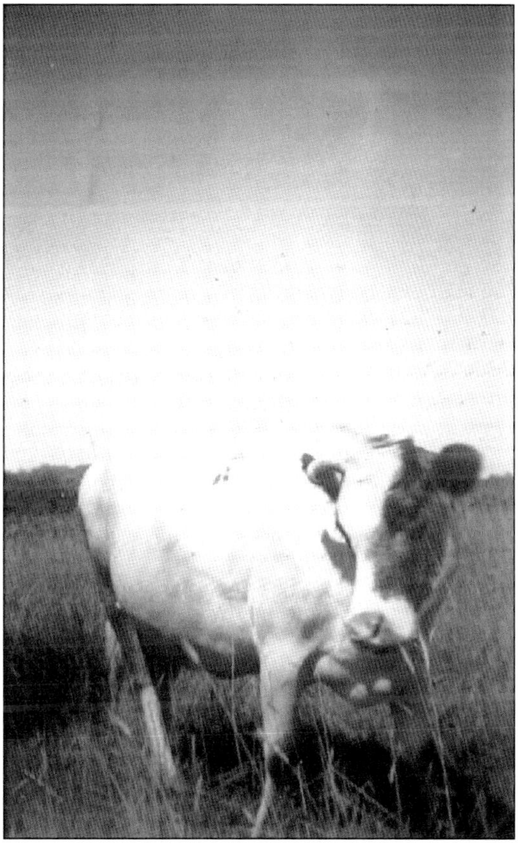

Cows were once so ubiquitous they strayed streets in town, grazing unfenced in neighborhood gardens as happily as in rural pastures. Harbison's milk-cooling station in Hurlock operated collecting routes throughout the upper county where a dairyman could place milk at his gate early in the morning for collection. The cow is now an endangered species throughout the county, its benevolent demeanor a sentimental motif in country decor.

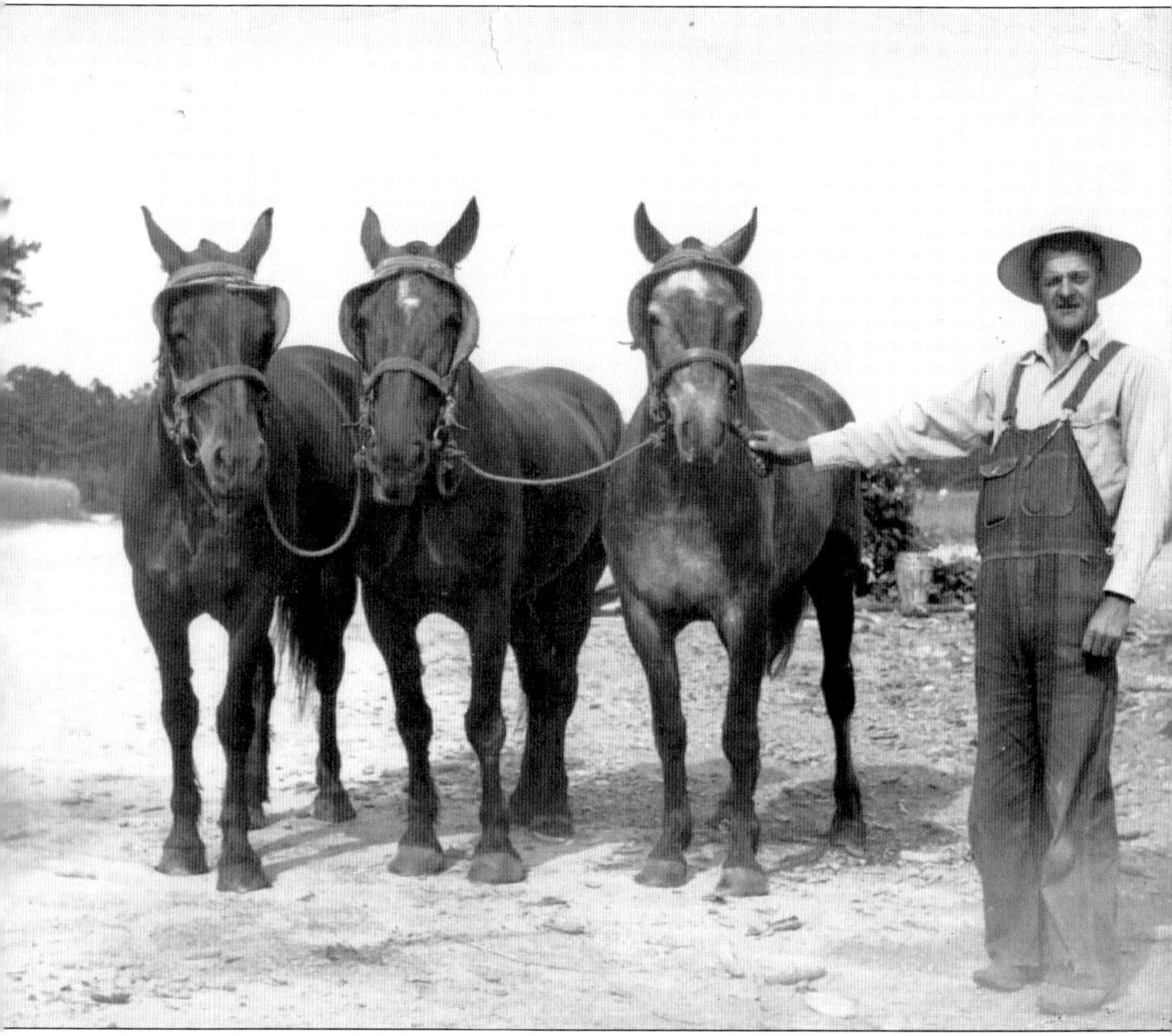

Before the internal combustion engine usurped their jobs, mules saved many farmers from backbreaking labor. When tractors took over tilling the fields, some farmers faithfully maintained their mules despite jibes from more practical neighbors, who thought idle beasts an unnecessary expense. Here, a proud Tom Howard pauses during the 1940s long enough to be photographed with his mules. He tilled an 88-acre farm on Adams Road near Reliance purchased from Oliver Holmes Collins. He married Aline Collins on December 24, 1935, worked as a farmer, and enjoyed the sport of rabbit hunting. Tom Howard also served his community as what was sometimes called a "water witch." He had the gift of dousing for water using the forked branch of a fruit tree. As a water witch walked around and held the forked ends in his hands, the main stem of the branch would dip when over an underground stream, thus saving the landowner much futile digging.

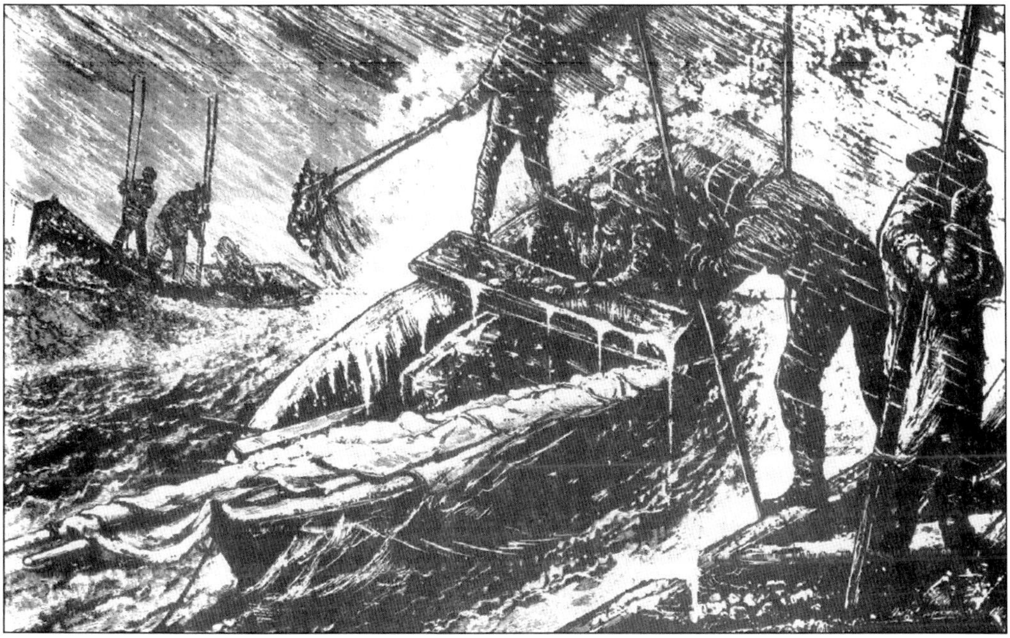

This February 1879 depiction from *Frank Leslie's Illustrated Newspaper* of half-frozen, storm-tossed watermen tonging for oysters may be an exaggeration of what they endure in the winter season, but it only slightly overstates the discomforts. Balancing on icy washboards of today's workboats as they rock over frigid water is not for the faint of heart.

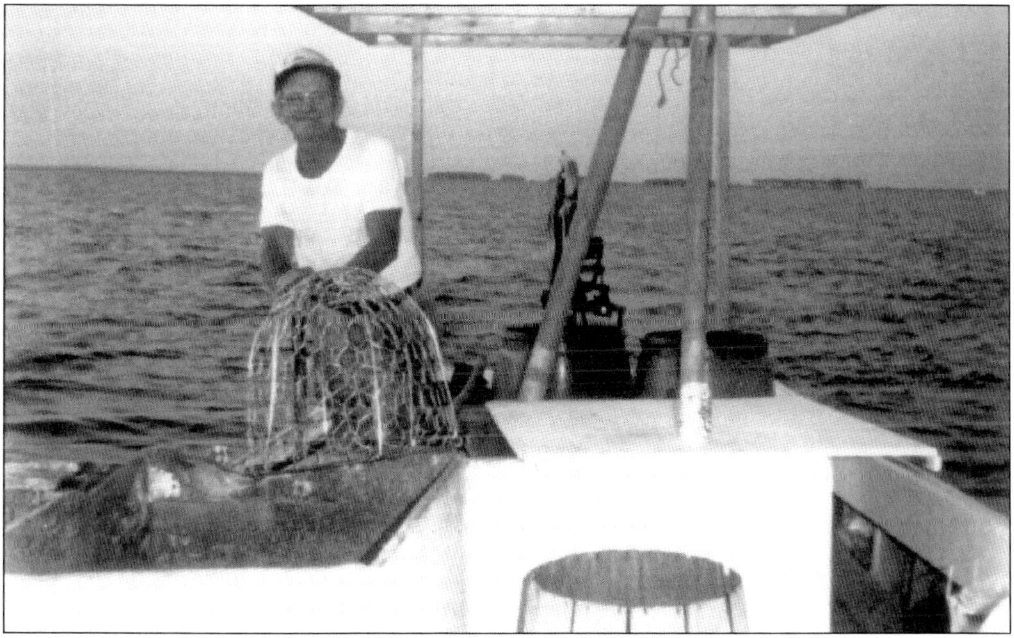

Trotlining is the only crabbing method allowed in interior waters. A trotliner runs a line perhaps a half-mile long, baited every five feet or so. After laying lines, the crabber runs slowly along, dipping crabs clinging to the bait as it lifts over a "roller chock" fastened to the side of the boat. Shriver Mills trotlines from *Miss Magdalene*, a 50-year-old workboat that Paul Jones of Crocheron built for him.

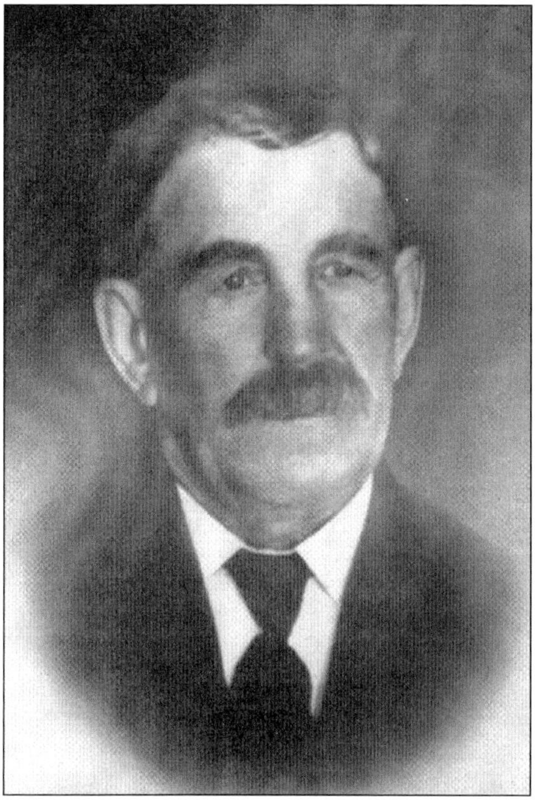

Albert Webb was born of an old Eastern Shore family with ties to such lines as McNamara, Lake, and Hicks. He founded and, until his retirement in 1918, operated a cannery at Vienna producing under the Bob White label. Sailing vessels and motorized buyboats of every description arrived laden with tomatoes. A railroad spur ran to Vienna and steamboat routes passed up and down the Nanticoke River facilitating shipment of cases leaving the plant.

After growing up in the business, Clay McAllister Webb joined his father in 1913 as a partner in producing the Bob White line. Besides the cannery employing 250 full-time people, Clay Webb operated farms where over 1,000 acres were cultivated and that held over 1,000 additional acres in timber.

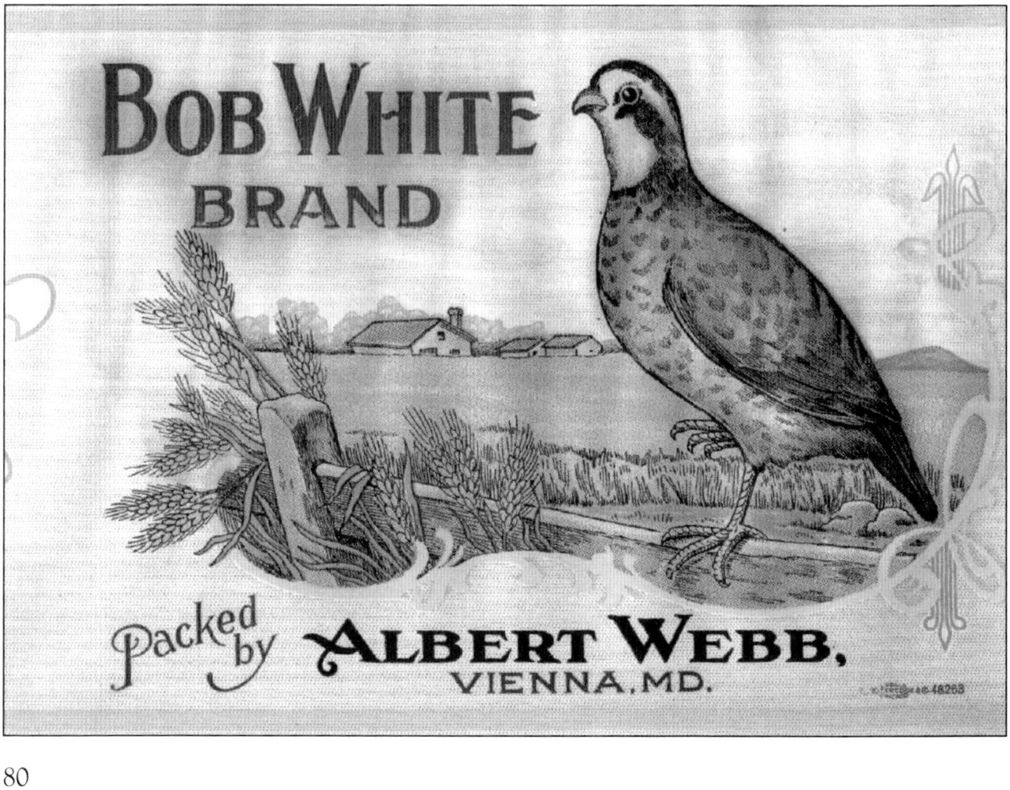

Leonard Simmons (left) stands in the door of his Madison Bay cannery with his son, Sewell Simmons. Another branch of the Simmons family operated a cannery in Andrews for decades, opened by Robert L. Simmons by 1915. An employee's receipt from 1942 shows that Triffinia Truitt earned $335.75 at Andrews skinning tomatoes for Roy L. Simmons' cannery and had $8.20 taxes withheld.

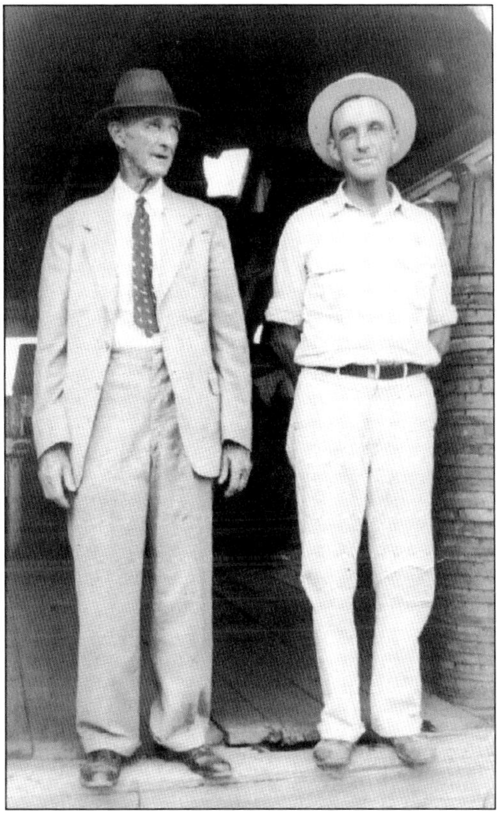

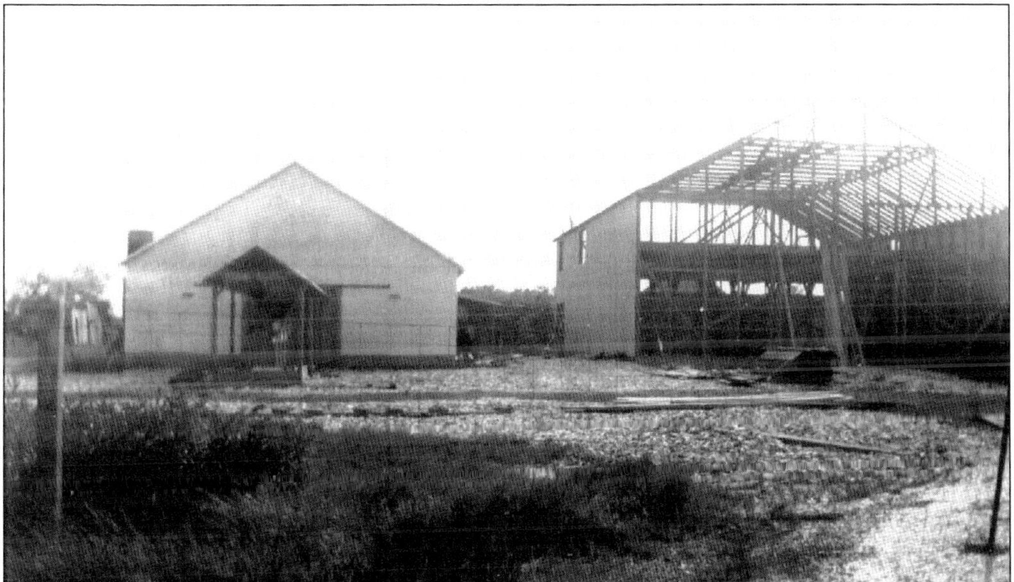

The cannery at Madison Bay, a restaurant in recent years, had to be rebuilt in the mid-1930s after a fire. After a couple of false starts, canning took root in Madison when Calvin Jones opened for business in 1919 and operated until the fire. Leonard A. Simmons took over afterwards and he and his sons operated the cannery for decades.

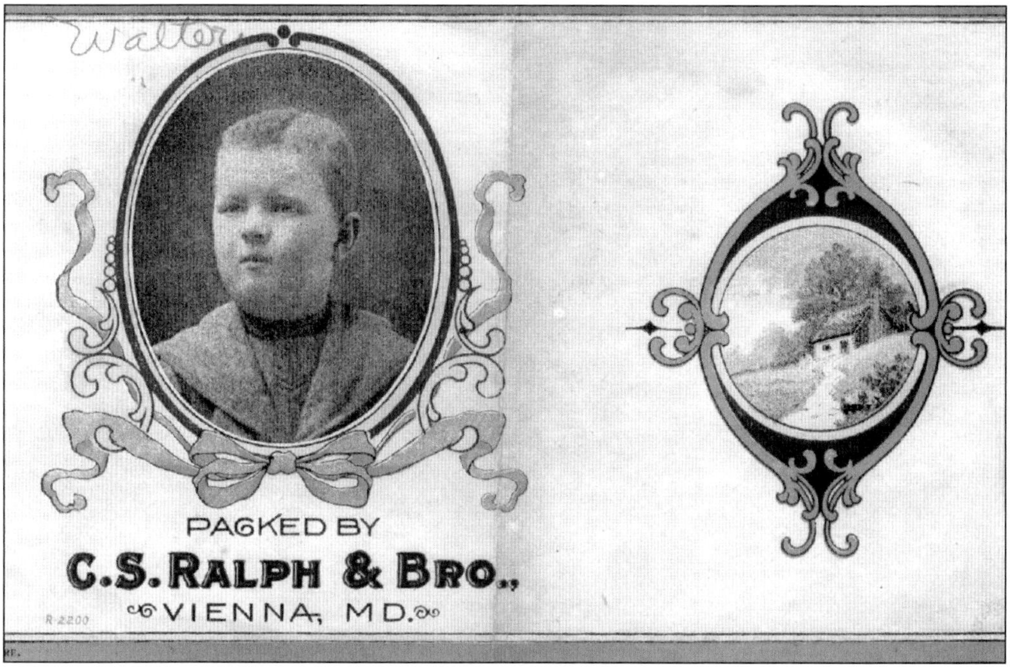

C.S. Ralph and Brothers cannery operated from 1908 to 1922 at Ralph's Crossing outside Vienna. Son Walter Ralph was born in 1899 and served as the model for the company logo. This label belonged to Walter's widow, Doris Ralph. Other canneries in the vicinity operated at Reids Grove and Rhodesdale.

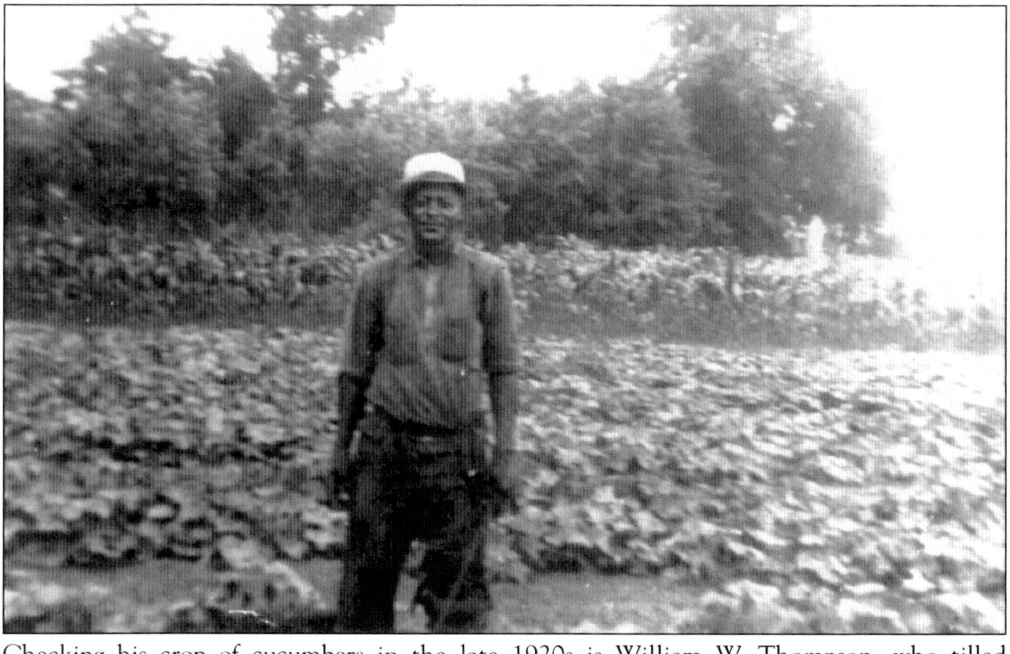

Checking his crop of cucumbers in the late 1920s is William W. Thompson, who tilled Thompsontown farms for decades with a horse-drawn plow. Tomatoes, cucumbers, and peppers were truck crops hauled by horse and wagon or truck to Rhodesdale Canning Company, later called Rhodesdale Pickle Company, owned by Frances Green of New York in the 1930s.

Dorchester climate and soil suit melons of many varieties. Otis Corkran (right) of Rhodesdale, "The Cantaloupe King," acquired and operated 1,200 acres of tillable land and received state recognition for his farming accomplishments. Organic chemist and author P.J. Wingate of Wingate claimed in *Bandages of Soft Illusion* that Elliott Island grew the best watermelons and attributed this to trace soil elements such as potassium, fluorine, selenium, and bromine.

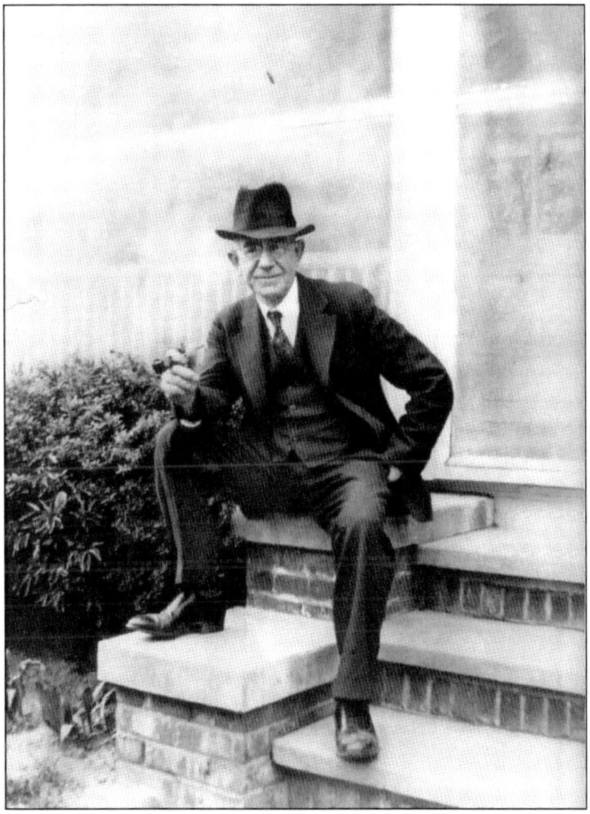

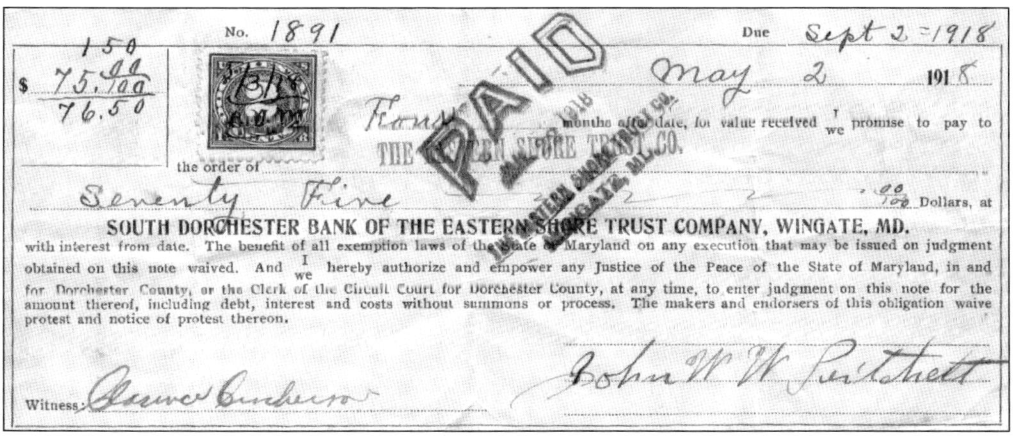

150

No. 1891 Due Sept 2 - 1918

$ 75.00/100

76.50

May 2 1918

Four months after date, for value received I/we promise to pay to the order of THE EASTERN SHORE TRUST CO.

Seventy Five 00/100 Dollars, at

SOUTH DORCHESTER BANK OF THE EASTERN SHORE TRUST COMPANY, WINGATE, MD.

with interest from date. The benefit of all exemption laws of the State of Maryland on any execution that may be issued on judgment obtained on this note waived. And I/we hereby authorize and empower any Justice of the Peace of the State of Maryland, in and for Dorchester County, or the Clerk of the Circuit Court for Dorchester County, at any time, to enter judgment on this note for the amount thereof, including debt, interest and costs without summons or process. The makers and endorsers of this obligation waive protest and notice of protest thereon.

Witness: Clarence Crocheron

John W W Pritchett

PAID

South Dorchester Bank of the Eastern Shore Trust Company in Wingate served the needs of people "down below." Clarence Crocheron's witnessing of this 1918 document might indicate that his general store served as an unofficial branch office. Many small banks of this type were wiped out in the Great Depression, while general stores carried their customers through the hard times, putting down necessities "on the book."

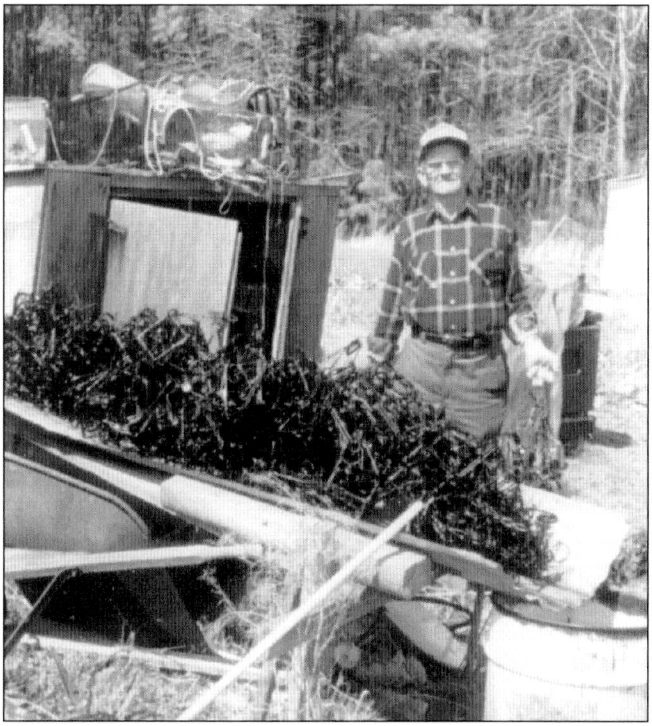

Shriver Mills of Golden Hill is shown oiling his traps, preparing to put them away for another season, when they will be washed in gasoline and put to work again. Conibear traps kill instantly and are used to keep muskrat populations in check by the most humane means possible. Shriver began trapping at age 11. The four Mills brothers, John, Shriver, Arthur, and Thomas, trapped as partners, setting 500 to 600 dozen traps each season, harvesting perhaps 1,500 muskrats.

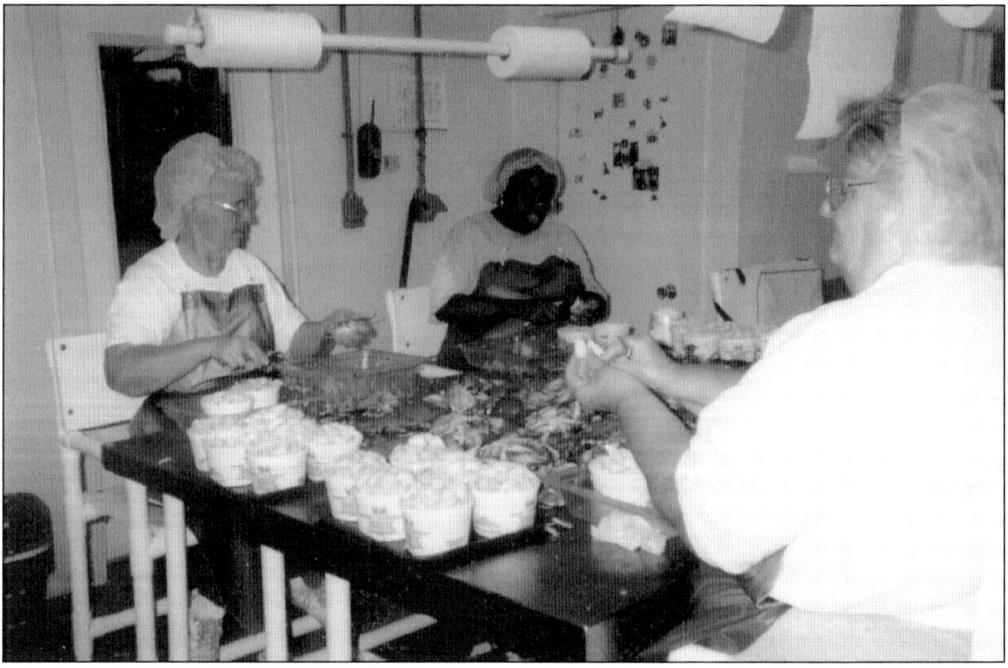

Crabhouses developed around waterfront communities early in the 1900s and provided income for local ladies. Some able-bodied women already shucked oysters, but those of any age or strength could pick crabs, as well. Here, from left to right, Janice Robinson Paul, Juanita Wheatley, and Magdalene Mills practice the fine art. In Maggie Mills's career, she has seen the price paid to a picker increase from 8¢ per pound to $2.40.

Five

Faces of Dorchester

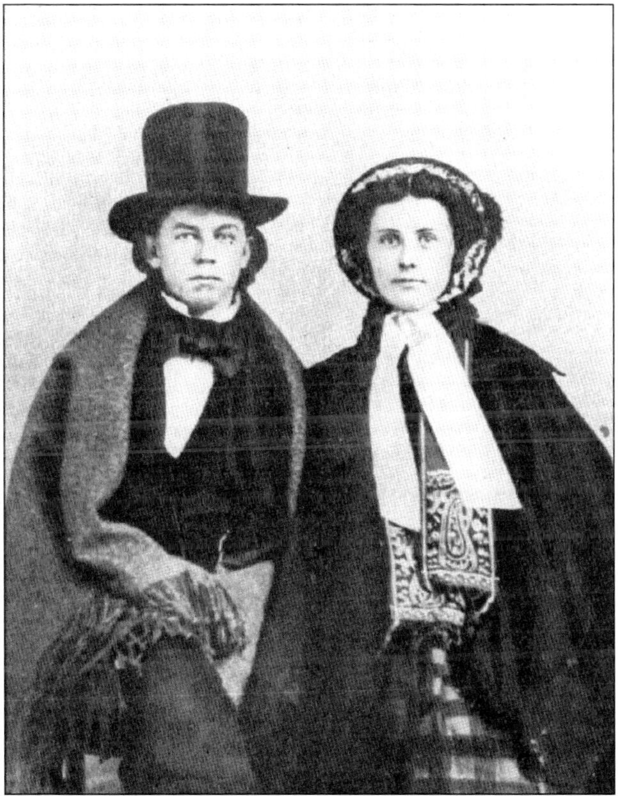

Future-bishop John F. Hurst's journal for 1855 records, "Now, my good old Journal, I will introduce to you a name with which you may become quite familiar—Miss LaMonte. Good Journal, take care of her, she will be doubly dear to you when you and she get better acquainted. She is my betrothed. I love her; she is beautiful, and has a heart." He is pictured with Catherine shortly after they wed.

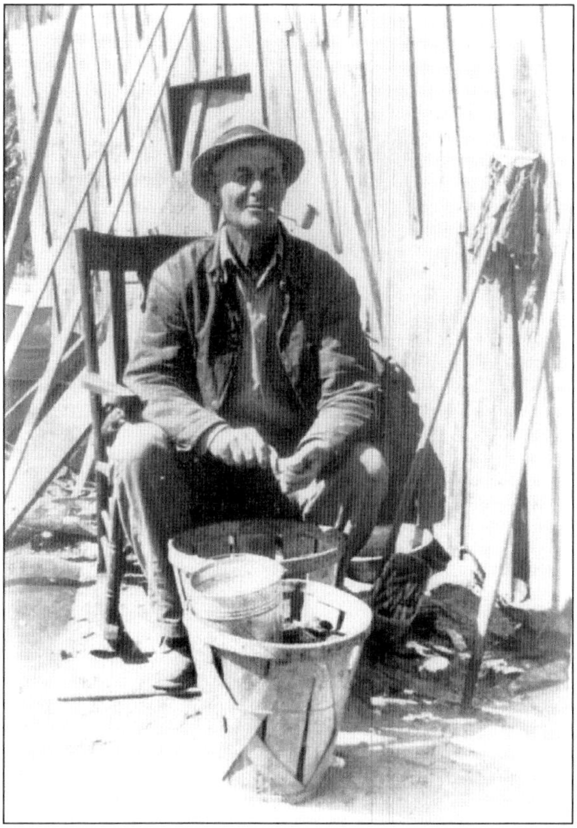

George W. Thomas (1876–1954) was the son of John "War Eagle" Thomas. George is pictured here shucking out a mess of oysters at his home on Elliott Island. His family relocated from an isolated island on Nanticoke River onto Elliott Island, where they taught even the experienced locals a trick or two about working creeks and marshes. George courted by boat and wed Angeline Stewart of Bivalve, Wicomico County.

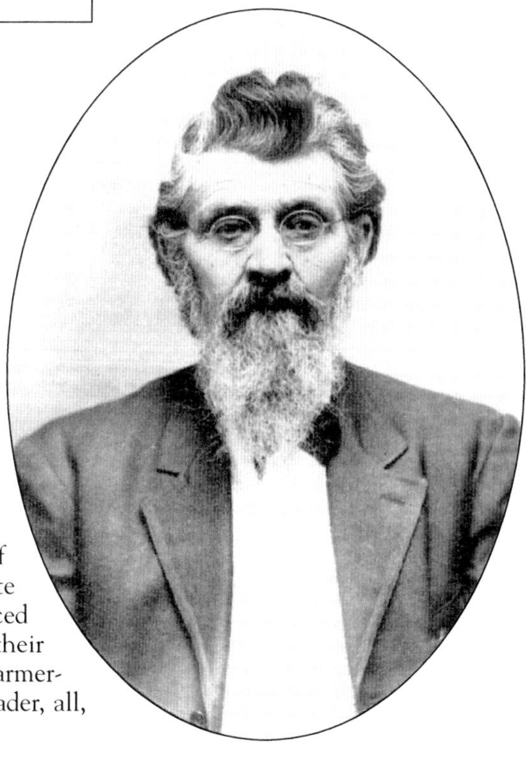

Capt. Levin Frank Hurley was a typical son of Hurleys Neck, a heavily forested area on the Nanticoke River. Only a couple of ramshackle roadside buildings indicate the site of this once-thriving community, but it produced a breed of men and women noteworthy for their self-sufficiency and longevity. They were farmer-fisherman, woodsman-boatbuilder, trapper-trader, all, or some of these in endless combination.

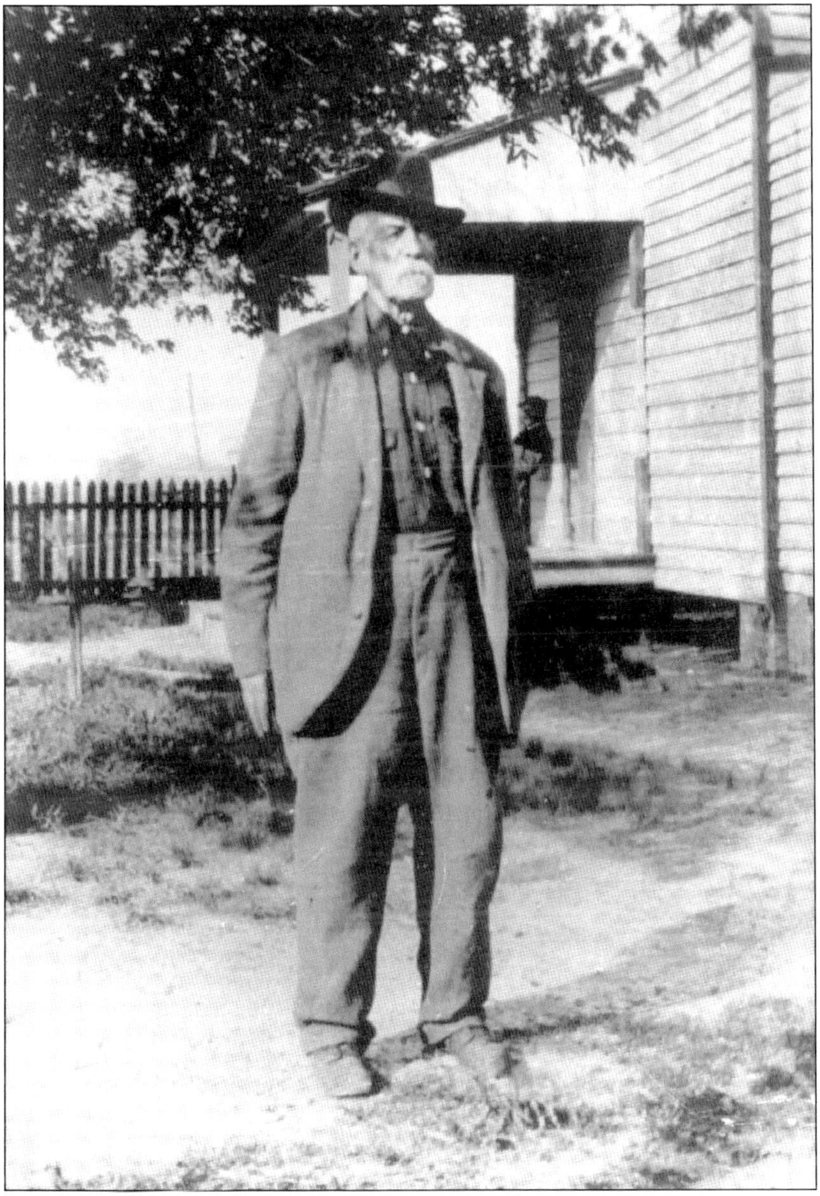

Robert H. "Bob" Richardson was born in 1865 on Greens Island, a patch of high land below Hurleys Neck on the Nanticoke River shore, surrounded by a sea of marsh that isolated the Richardsons from their landward neighbors. Thus, Richardsons were uniquely fitted for life on land, water, and everything in between. After leaving Greens Island, Mr. Bob farmed the Wainwright Farm in Hurley's Neck for 25 years. He was much respected in the vicinity, "a gentleman of the highest caliber," it was said at his passing. Many in the Richardson family were prominent in the area. George Richardson of Greens Island was a noted dealer in diamondback terrapin early in the 1900s, when they were popular with epicures and worth a dollar an inch. A neighbor recalled, "George Ricks lived up to Greens Island and he got big money for those salt water terrapins—turkles—six or seven dollars apiece. He kept them in a pen. When he called, 'Yo-yo-yo,' they knew he was getting ready to feed them and they'd come a-running."

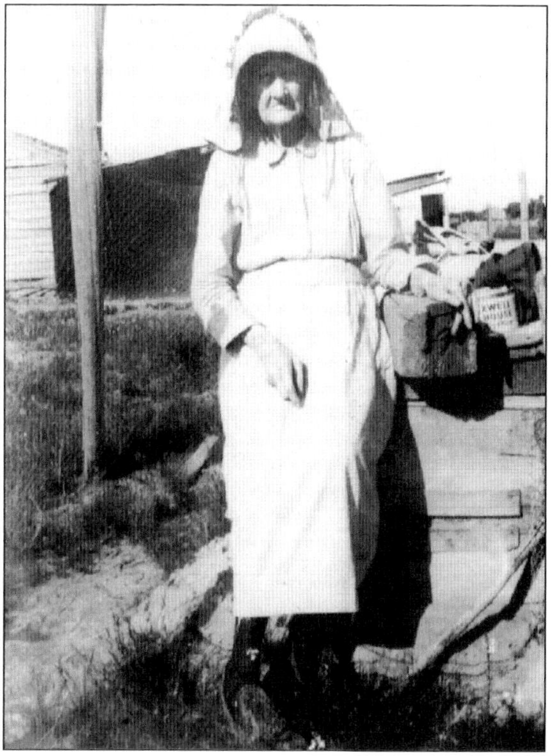

A lady at leisure could protect her complexion from the sun by carrying a parasol. On a farm, two free hands were usually needed and slat bonnets provided the solution. Anyone at all handy with a needle could whip up a bonnet out of scraps of material and a bit of cardboard, trimming it out with a bow in the back or a bit of rick-rack. To protect their hands from becoming aged-looking while doing field work, ladies wore "half-hands," gloves cut from scraps and sewn together to cover the back of the hand down to the first knuckle, leaving fingers free to pick crops. Margaret Fisher Marine is pictured above on the 40-acre farm on the Eldorado-Sharptown Road, where she and George Earl Marine raised five girls and two boys. Mamie Horseman McAllister of Elliott Island, right, was photographed around 1960. Ladies of the lower county like Miss Mamie favored scraps of old sail for making half-hands. Her husband, Samuel "Captain Jim" McAllister, was an island boatbuilder.

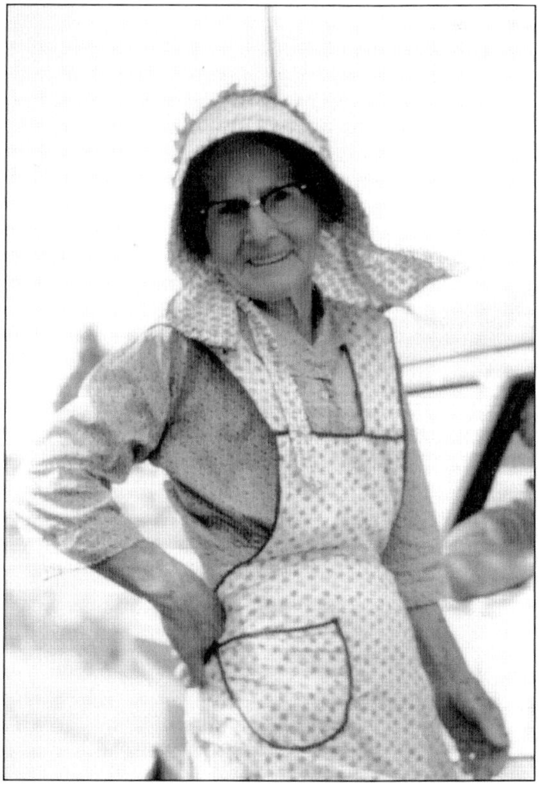

Mary Meekins Elliott was the daughter of Ann Meekins, who was born into slavery. She gave birth to Mary around 1876. Ann Meekins worked in the house of a doctor. Mary Elliott raised her family at the end of Blackwater Road near Barnes Landing. Before she died in 1968 at age 92, she recounted stories of slave days told by her mother.

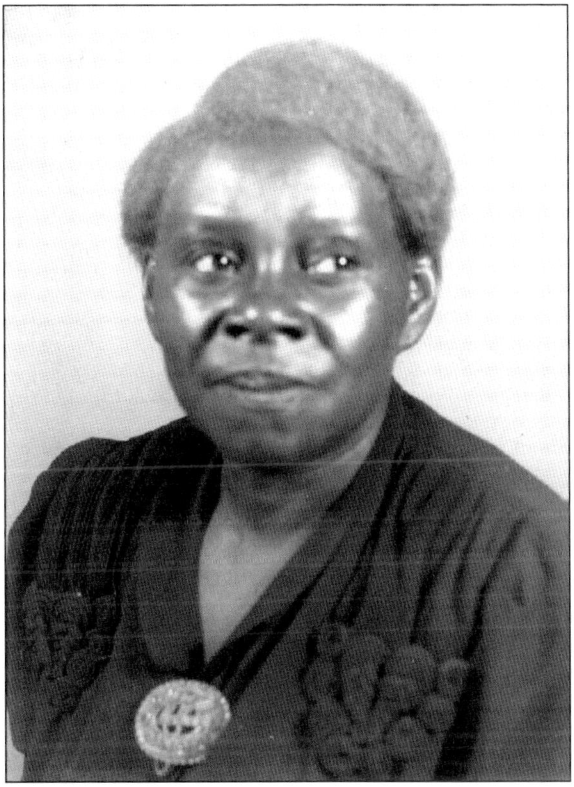

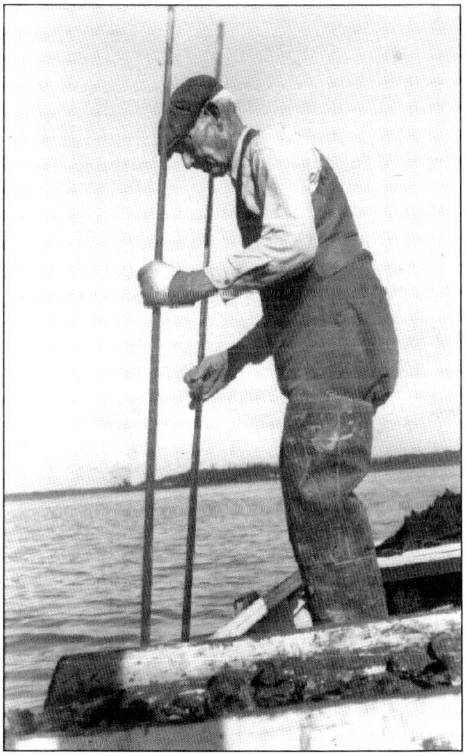

Capt. Charles Bromwell Sr. is pictured in the 1930s tonging oysters off Little Choptank at Brooks Creek. Men like Captain Charles find it unremarkable that they are able to "feel" the bottom through shafts anywhere from 14 to 36 feet long and separate live oysters from empty shells. Judging from the number of oysters on the culling board and the growing pile on his right, Captain Charles knew his business.

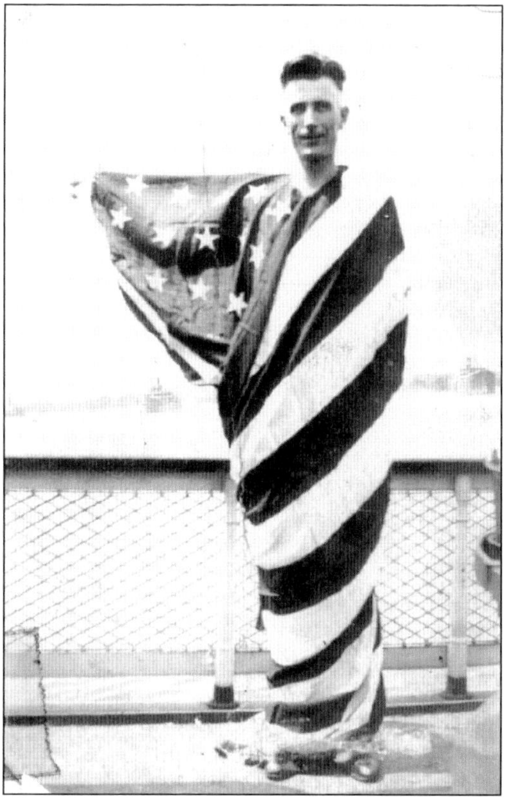

Wrapped up in patriotism is Capt. Edward Bromwell of Madison, who went on to captain a tugboat out of Baltimore. This photo was taken several decades before flag-wearing became discredited in the 1960s. As the 21st century begins, red, white and blue attire has again come into style.

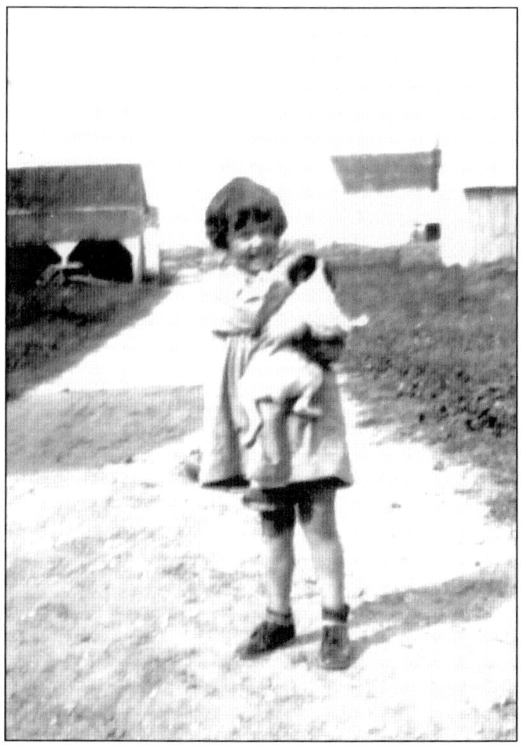

Frances Hurley entered the world on a February night in Steeles Neck, a blizzard separating her mother from the town doctor. Frances wasn't one to let a wiggly puppy get the best of her. Like a legion of other Dorchester ladies, Frances once sewed for a shirt factory, but she's better remembered for her many years as Nanticoke Inn's skillful cook.

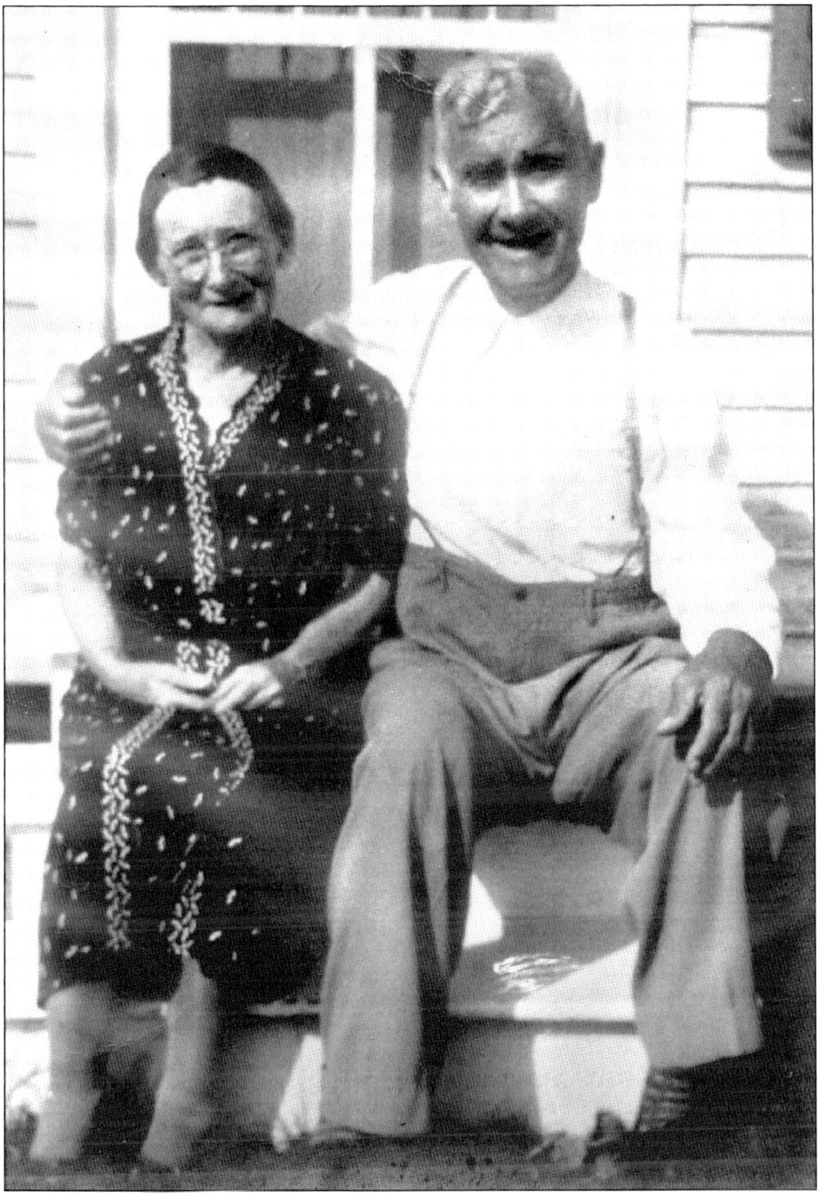

Melvin and Shilley Jones are pictured around 1950 at their home in Wingate across from the church. Typical of their time and place, they lived simple, devout lives centered on home and church. Keeping the Sabbath meant Sunday's chicken and dumplings were cooked Saturday. In the summertime, they were cooked on a kerosene stove in the summer kitchen beside the house and kept for the next day in an icebox. Mel loved the old hymns. When church windows were open, his deep bass voice resounded through the community. Also typical of the time, despite spending his working life on the water with Maryland's Tidewater Fisheries, he never learned to swim. A neighbor once came up on Mel neck-deep in the Honga River after being knocked overboard by his boom. "Mr. Mel," he asked, "why didn't you walk ashore?" "If I'd stepped in a hole, I'd drowned, so I waited for some'n to come along." Mr. Mel knew the tides and his neighbors equally well. Nor was Mrs. Jones a stranger to the water, born Shilley Amanda Bloodsworth in 1875 on Bloodsworth Island.

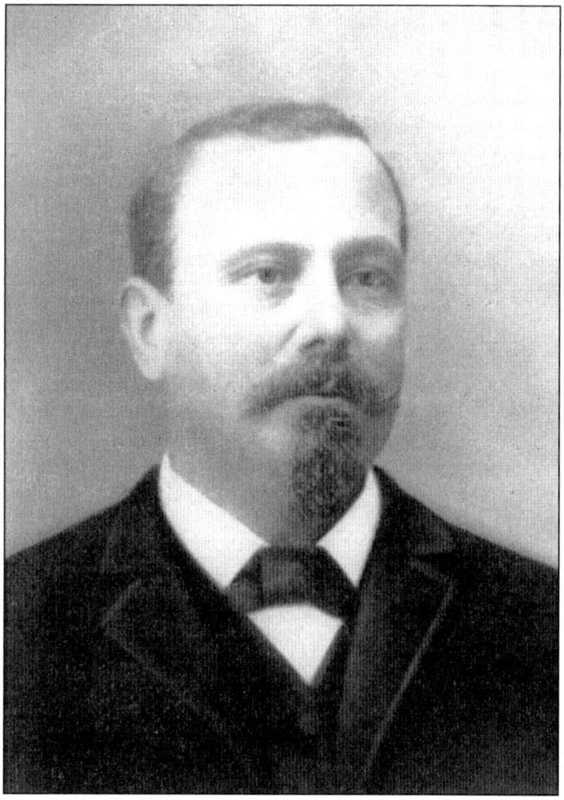

Meyer Nathan came to Dorchester County around 1870 peddling items door-to-door and farm-to-farm from a pack on his back. Gradually he acquired a mule, then a wagon, and finally a High Street store and residence. His first store and home burned in the 1892 fire that devastated both sides of the High Street block above the courthouse. He rebuilt and left the business to his son Milton upon his death in 1911. In 1919, Nathan's was advertising, "Furniture of All Kinds, Carpets, Mattings, Oil Cloth, Window Shades, Chinaware—133 High Street, Cambridge." Milton Nathan eventually operated 18 stores. Milton, his wife Estelle, and his sister Bertha Nathan created and endowed the Nathan Foundation, a charitable entity administered for many years by attorney Edward H. Nabb. The Nathan Foundation operates for the exclusive benefit of Dorchester Countians, who were fortunate indeed that Meyer Nathan adopted Cambridge as his home.

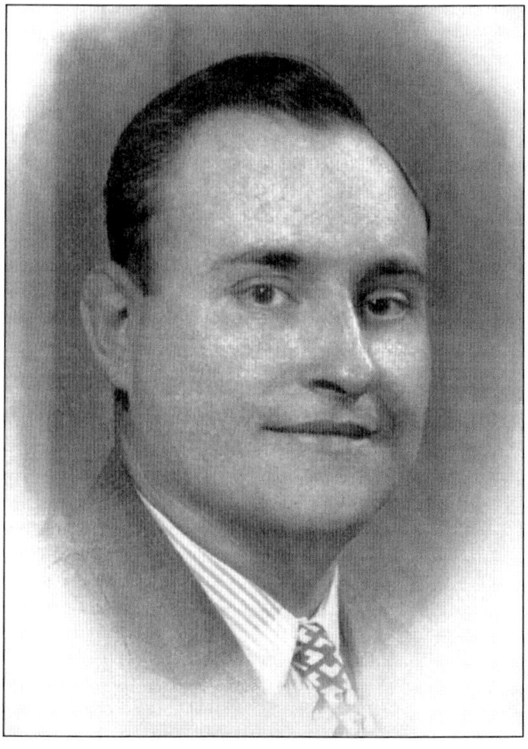

Mark Baker Robbins of Robbins and two brothers followed their father into business. They operated canneries at Andrews and Vienna, from which 250,000 cases a year of Robbins Brand tomatoes were shipped all over the United States east of the Rockies. In the fur trade, Robbins Brothers accumulated 10,000 acres of marshlands and employed 40 trappers. As a county commissioner, Baker Robbins championed road development.

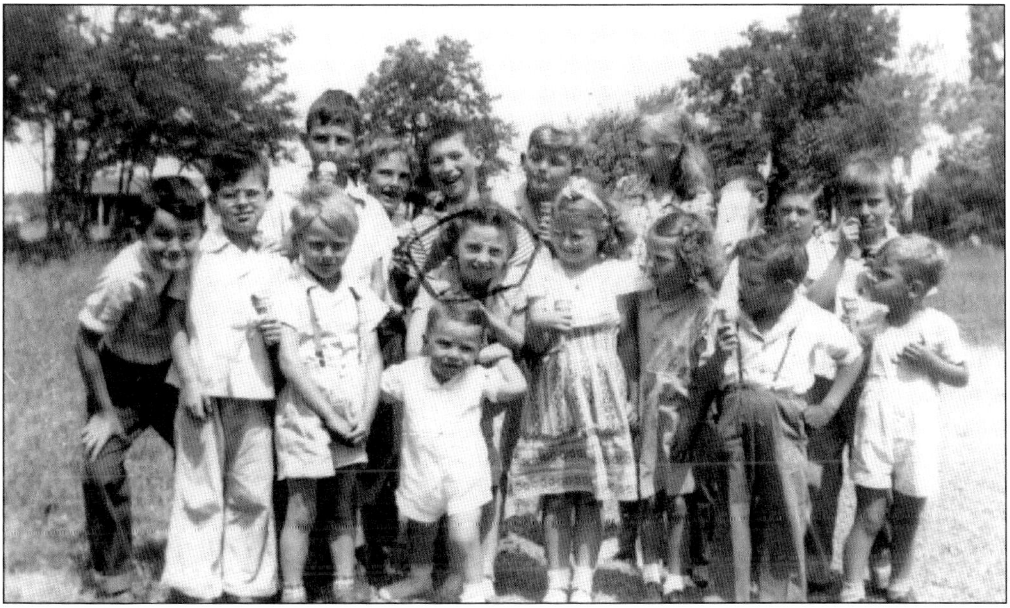

Hills Point School in the Neck District enjoyed very involved and cooperative parents. Before being consolidated, along with all the other community schools in the county, Hills Point School students included, among others, LaRue Warfield, Donald Hubbard, Sara Louise Marshall, Dennis Marshall, Barbara Lee Hill, Dorsey Hubbard, Nelson Marshall, Billy Marshall, Glenn Hubbard, Kenneth Warfield, and Tommy Condon.

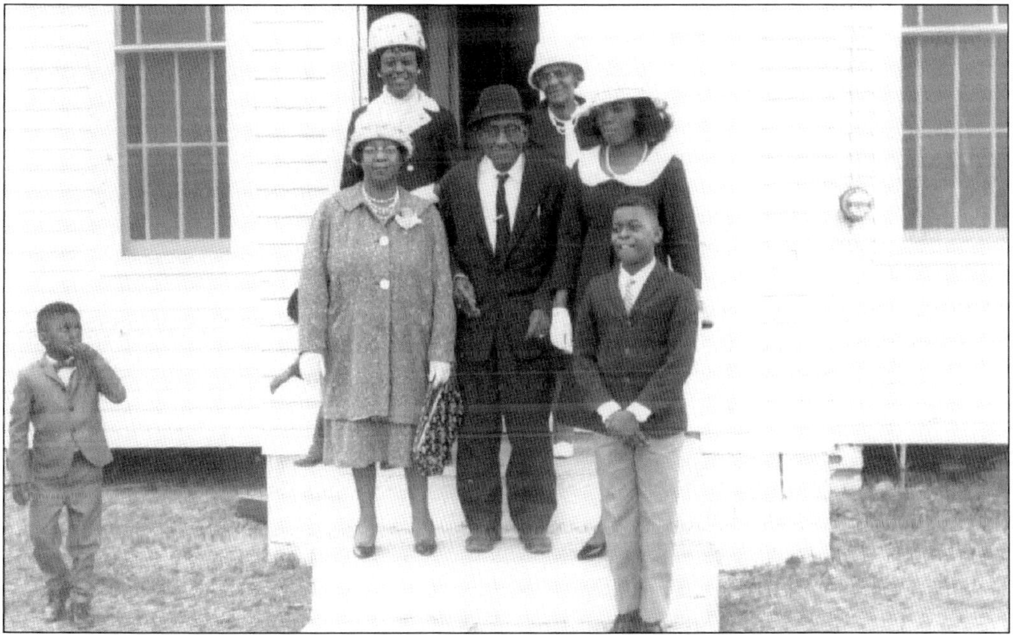

The origin of Thompsontown Chapel U. M. Church dates to 1878, when it included a primary school for African Americans. The ancestors of those pictured here donated labor and materials for erection of the present church building in 1909. This 1960s shot shows, from left to right (front row) Troy Camper and Gale Killette; (middle row) Mary L. Dockins, Archie Thomas, and Ann Dockins; (back row) Mary V. Thompson and Hattie S. Thompson.

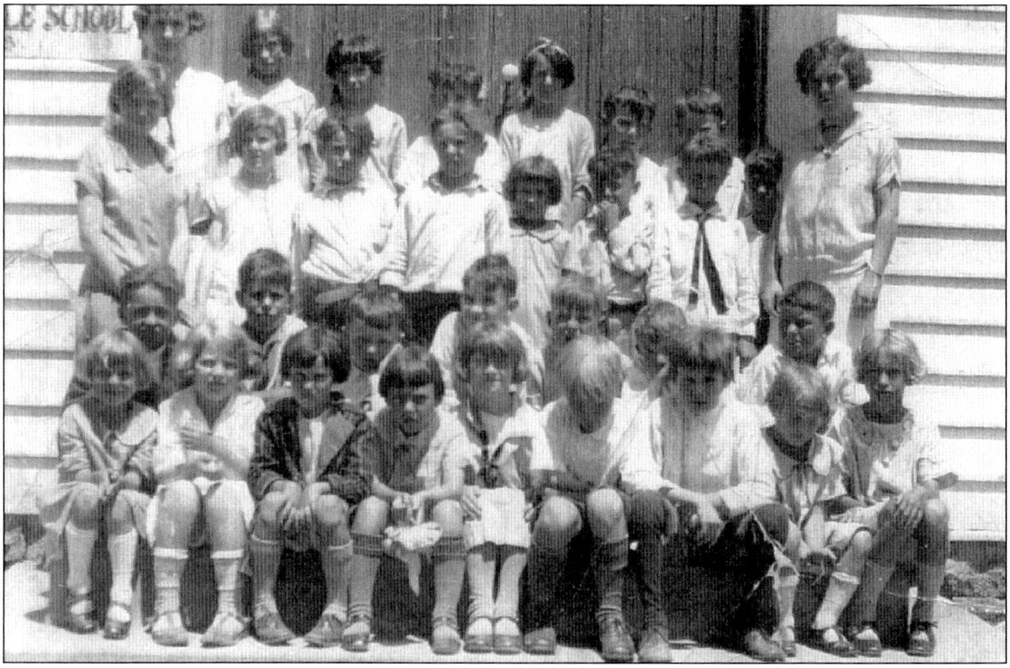

Neck District's 1925 Vacation Bible class included, from left to right, (first row) E. Brannock, Margaret Hastings, an unidentified student, Anna Thomas, Ruth Cannon, W. Wheatley, Leonard Hubbard, Naomi Hill, and Edith Seward; (second row) G. Spedden, Morgan Cook, Dick Marshall, C. Hubbard, Arthur Wheatley, N. Condon, and Paul Richardson; (third row) Dorothy Seward, G. Cook, Charles Hill, Thelma Cook, Billy Seward, Donald Spedden, and Herbert Dail; (fourth row) D. Condon, Edna Hill, Clarence Keyes, Anita Spedden, H. Seward, S. Keyes, and teacher Mary Frances Henry.

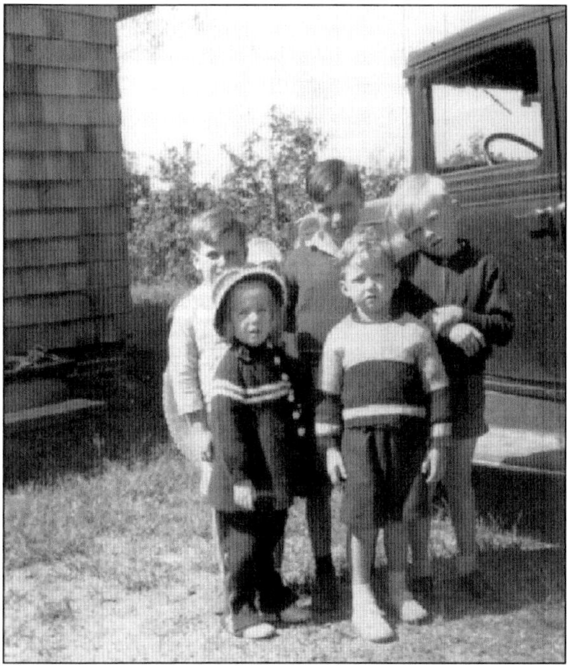

This Church of God Sunday school class in Puckum, c. 1940, was taught by Lola Payne Brinsfield of Eldorado. The young students are, from left to right, (front row) Norma Brinsfield and Leroy Andrew; (back row) Phillip McKelvey, Joseph McKelvey, and Melvin Marine. The church building now serves as a private residence.

Walter "Doll" Hurley, here with Alberta Langfitt Hurley, was born on Guinea Island. The couple lived in Steeles Neck and later Vienna. Speaking of Doll and Bertie and their 13 children, a neighbor recalled, "There was a whole lot of those Hurleys. They were all jolly. If you had a dollar, you could buy fish from Doll. And if you didn't have a dollar, you got your fish just the same."

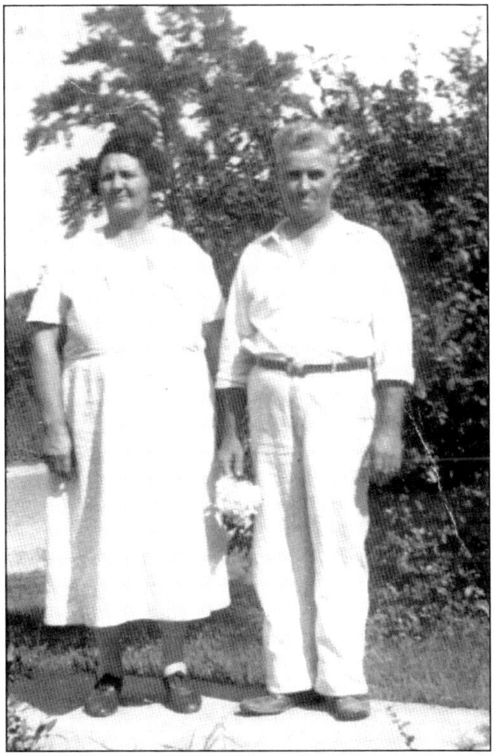

Four generations of Bromwells are pictured in June 1950 outside Joppa Church in Madison. From left to right they are Capt. Charles Bromwell Sr., Capt. Charles Bromwell Jr., Capt. Robert Bromwell Sr., and Robert Louis Bromwell Jr. In the rear is Joppa Church, now Madison U.M. Church.

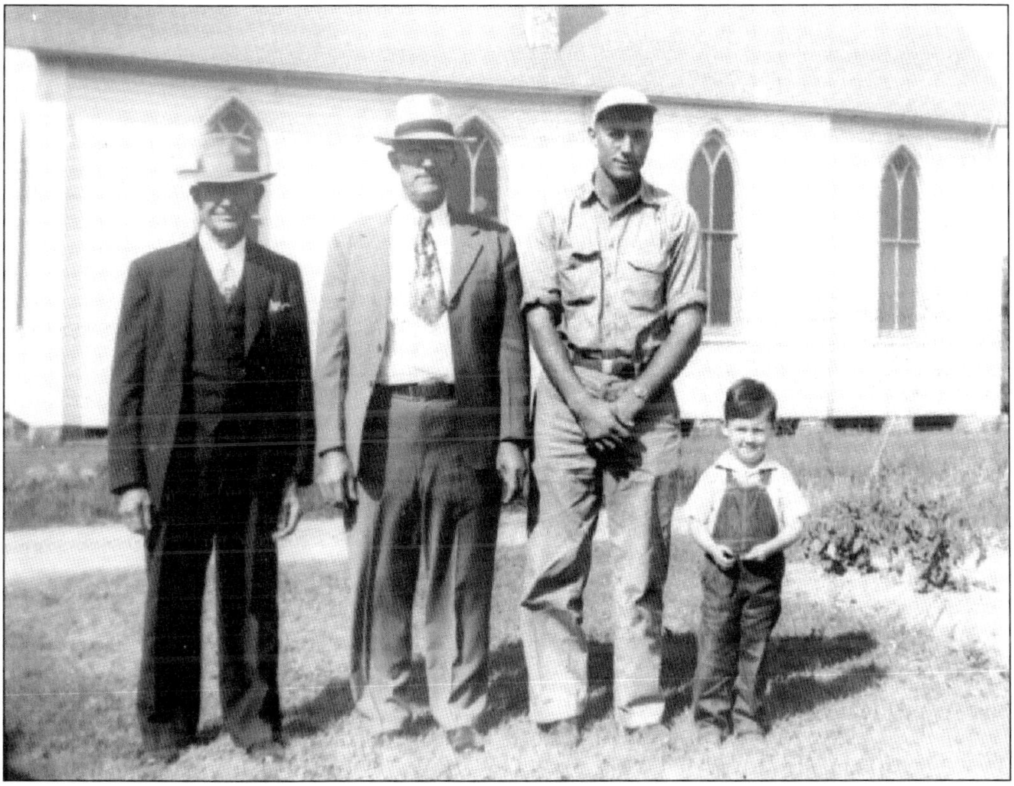

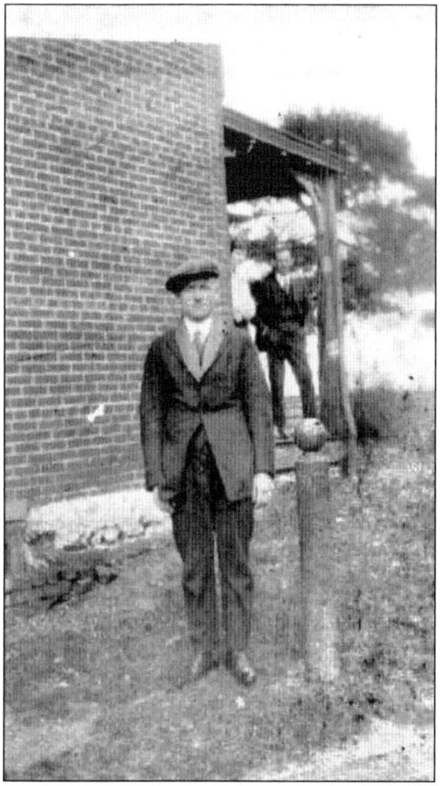

When Whitelaw Reed McCready of Henrys Crossroads was drafted, World War I inductees received rousing speeches and a parade before they left Cambridge by steamboat for Fort Meade. Whitey later led a quieter life, moored in Marshyhope Creek by the Brookview Bridge on a war-surplus barge. When he hadn't applied for Social Security at age 73, an agent tracked Whitey to his homemade floating cabin and delivered his first check.

North Dorchester might seem an unlikely location for a seafood market, but Elijah Wheedleton and wife Louise opened their Galestown store with that in mind. Elijah, a commercial fisherman, planned his house with enough length for hanging fishnets in the basement, an intricate job involving weights and floats and different sizes of mesh, variously configured to catch fish of different sizes, species, and feeding habits.

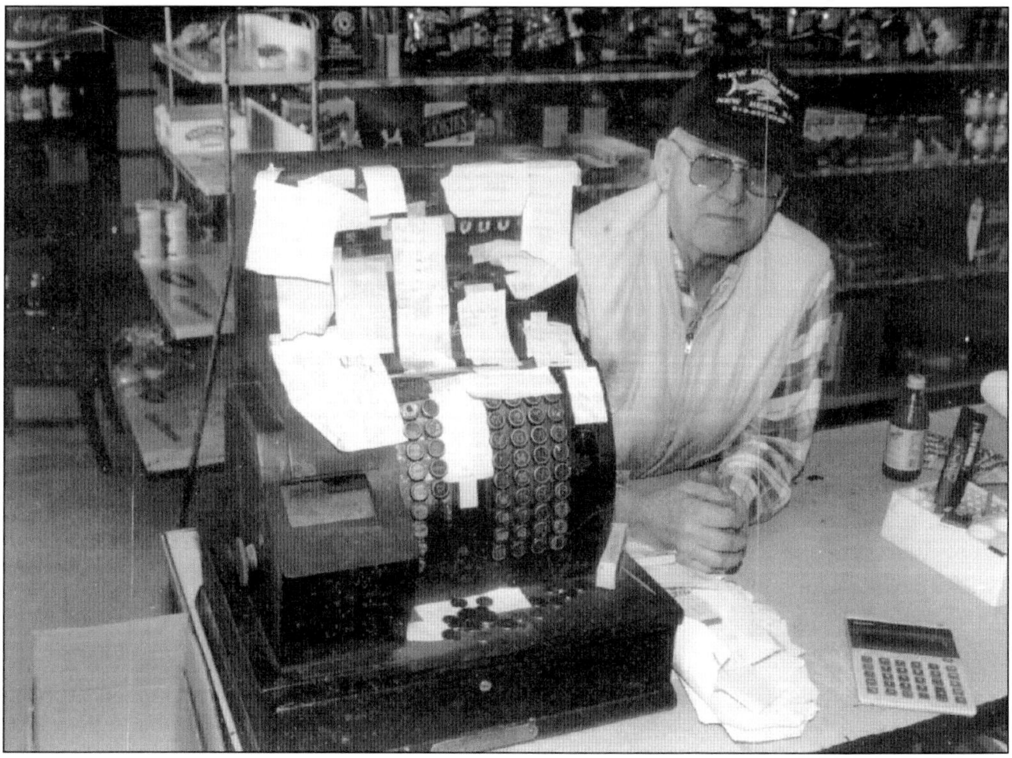

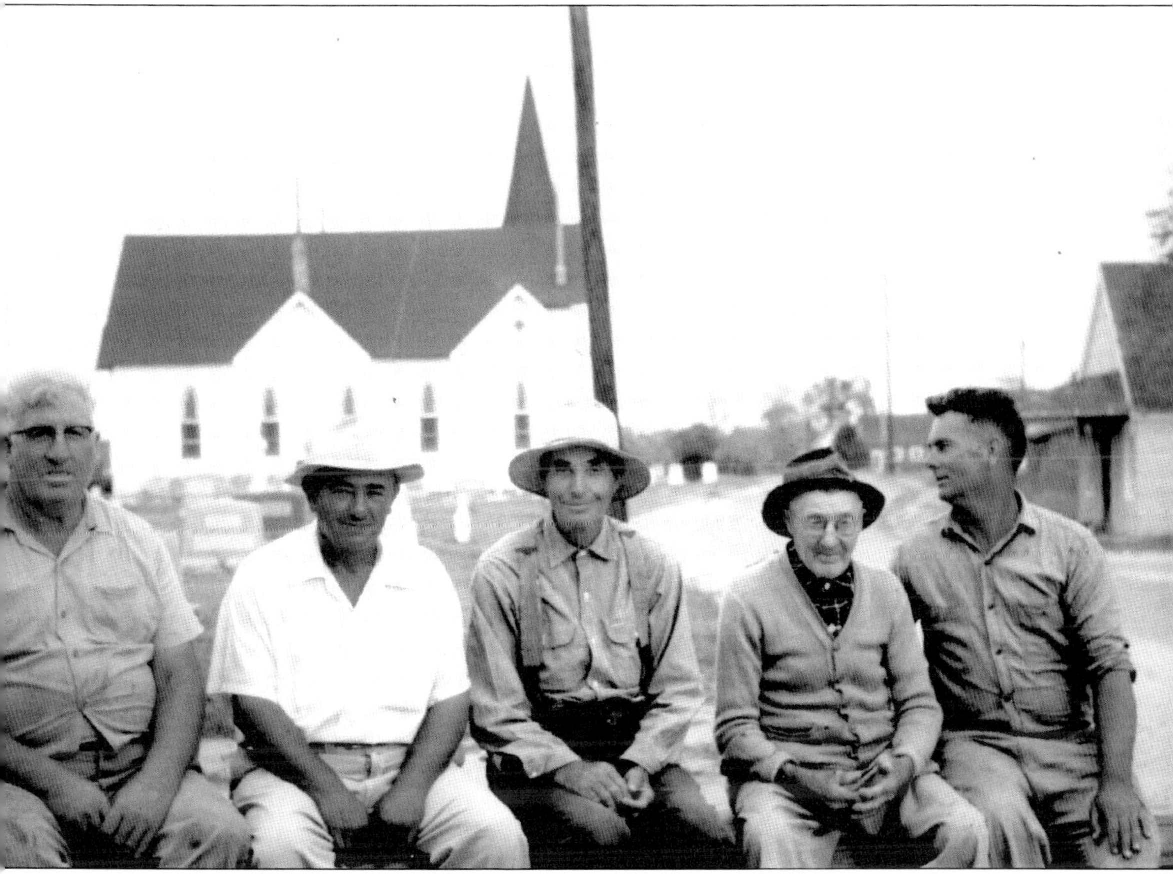

Before television, many began and ended their day with a visit to a general store to hear the news, local and national. Information available from the wise men seated around a pot-bellied stove including wind and tide estimates, weather forecasts, market prices, economic reports, political and sports updates, not to mention social tidbits. This group sitting on a bench outside Nora Foxwell's Elliott Island store in the 1950s is composed of, from left to right, Lennie "John Brown" Foxwell (Nora's husband), Hobson "Hobbie" Horseman, "Dickie" Melvin Thomas, Louis Gray, and Randall Lewis. Over Lewis's left shoulder is another store that belonged to Nora's brother William Ewell and nephew Howard Gray. It was later operated by Lawrence Gray, who introduced the island to television in this store. After this first brush with the new medium, "Miss Nora's Store" gained fame as a film by Oscar-winning filmmakers from the University of Maryland. It premiered in the community building at the church in the background and has since been shown on public television stations all over the country.

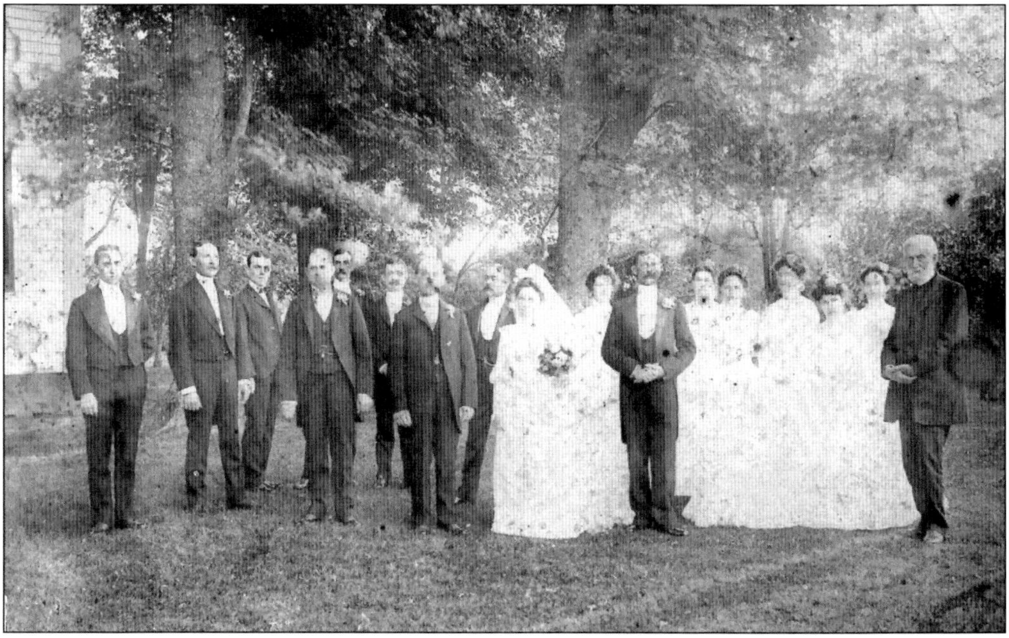

The inscription on this wedding photo records the marriage of Isabel Percy to Harry Franklin Bratten "on the lawn of The Woodlands, the old Percy homestead, June 3, 1901." A corner of the house called the Woodlands is visible on the left.

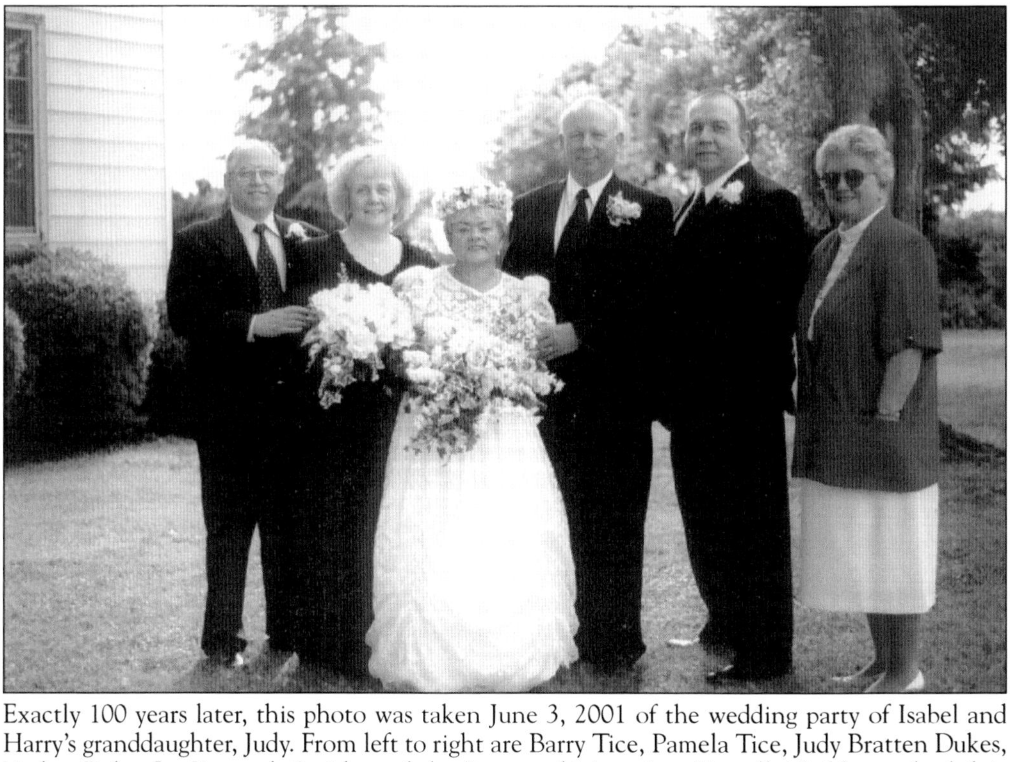

Exactly 100 years later, this photo was taken June 3, 2001 of the wedding party of Isabel and Harry's granddaughter, Judy. From left to right are Barry Tice, Pamela Tice, Judy Bratten Dukes, Verlon Dukes Jr., Kenneth Smith, and the Reverend Mary Ann Farnell. Visible on the left is the corner of the same house, now Woodlands Sporting Clays.

Six

JUST FOR THE FUN OF IT

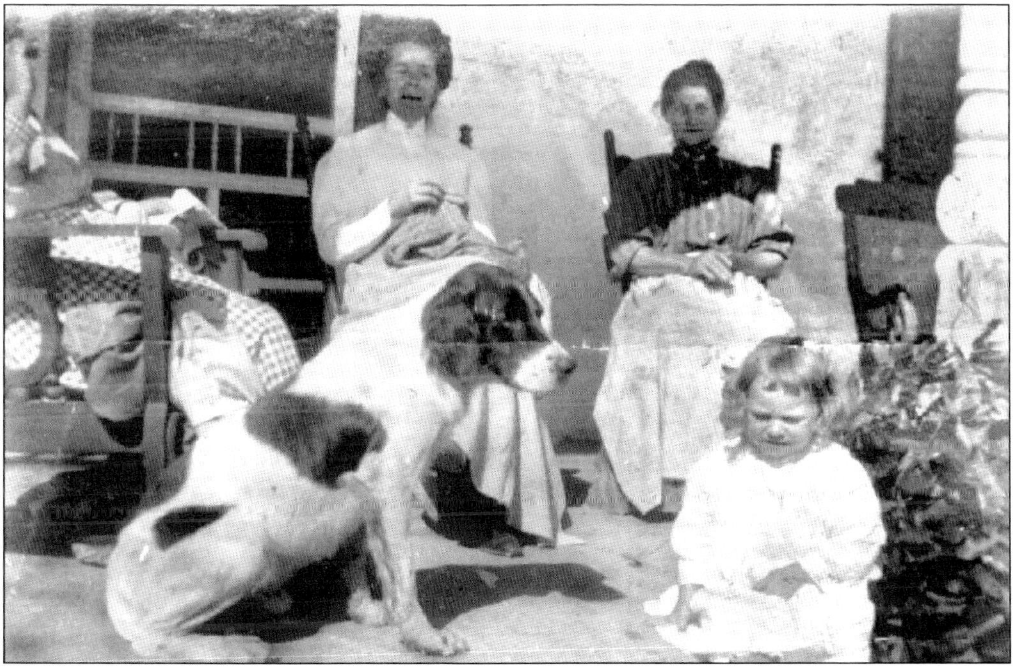

Before air conditioning, porch-sitting was a popular summer pastime. While hoping for a breeze to waft by, ladies could create their own breeze by gently rocking and doing needlework. On this porch, "Max and Elizabeth" are identified as the focus of attention.

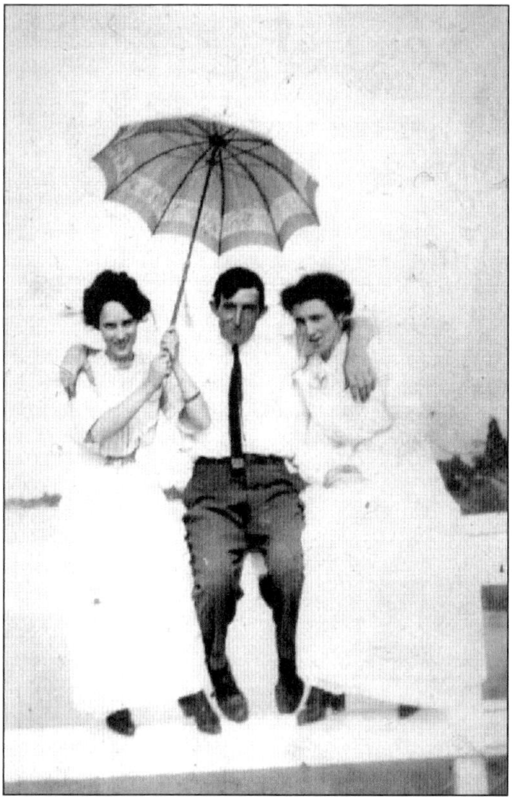

Cedar Grove, Greens Point, Beach Haven, and Oyster Shell Point were popular spots upriver from Cambridge where families and friends enjoyed summer outings. The heat must have been stifling when this photo was taken around 1910 at Oyster Shell Point. The gentleman has shed his jacket and one young lady has exposed her forearms. All the same, she keeps a grip on the parasol protecting her complexion.

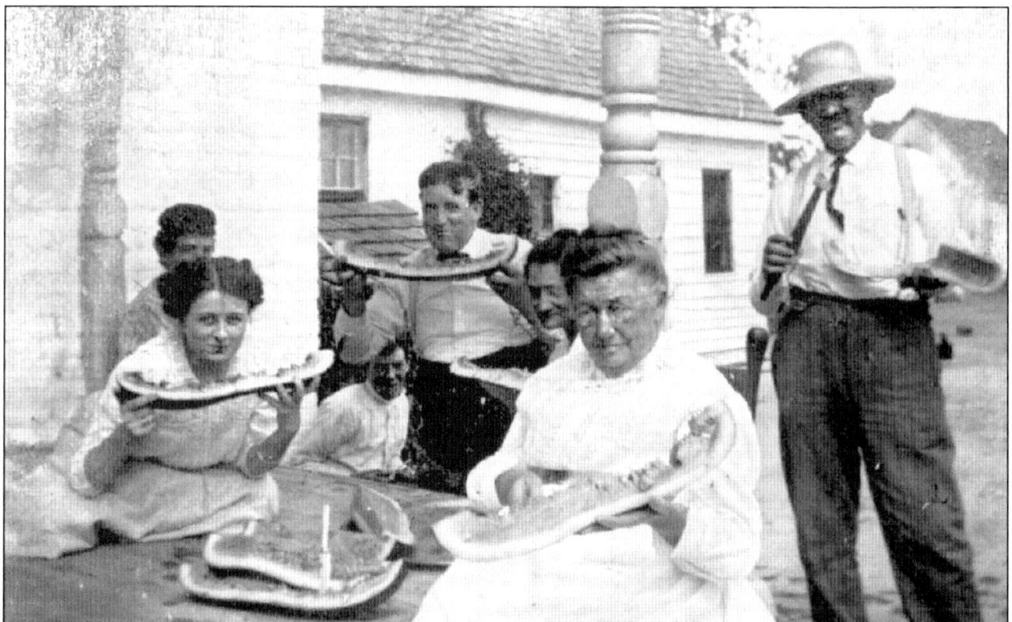

Watermelons have ever been a mid-summer delight. Around 1910, Mary Priscilla Higgins Handley and family enjoyed the seasonal treat. The locale was the Handley farm, formerly the Weir or Ware Neck farm on Hurst Creek, just upriver from Cambridge.

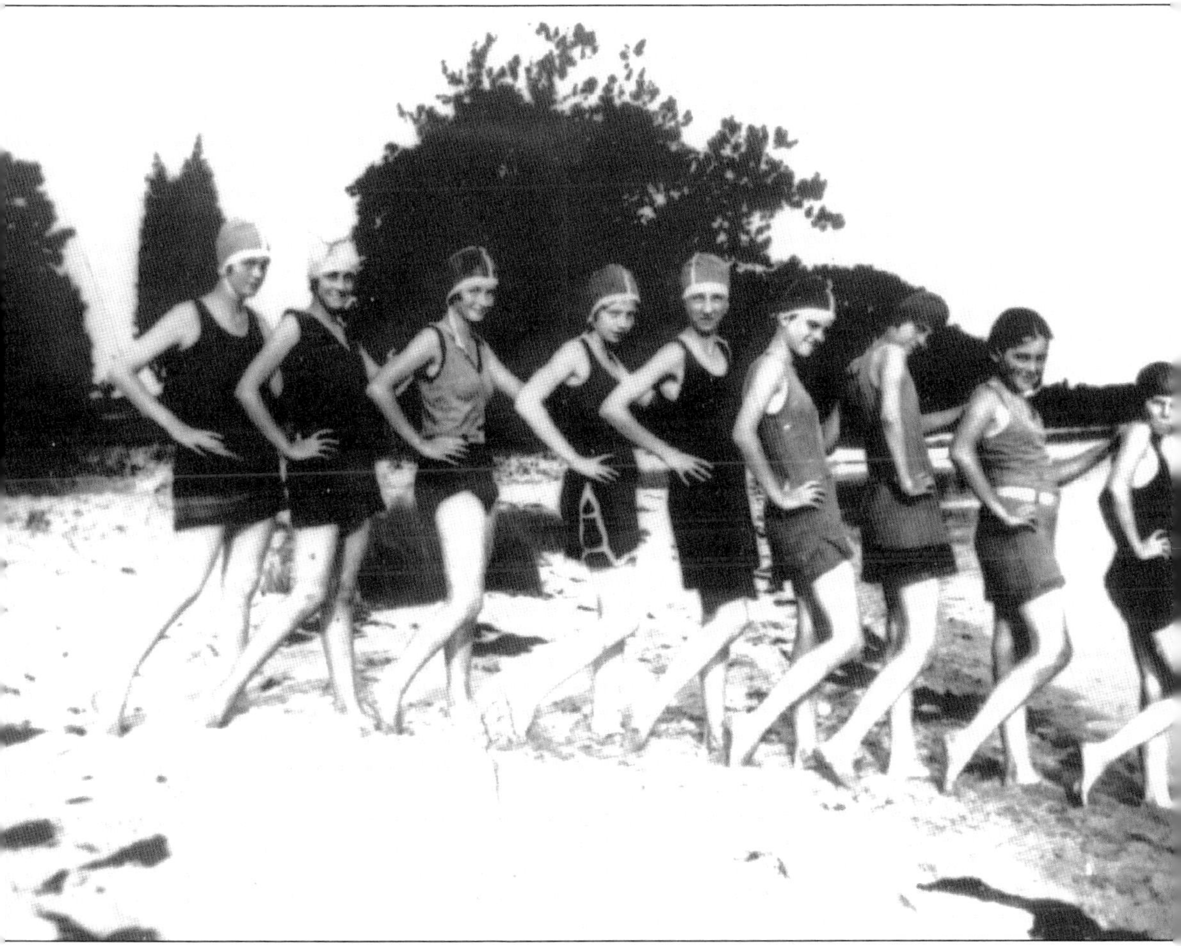

Nancy "Nanny" Bayly Waddell, with Margaret Small, organized a Girl Scout troop in Dorchester County in 1915. She was an avid sportswoman and a good friend of Annie Oakley. In 1925, under Capt. Ruth Phillips Meekins, the scouts all rode in the back of a truck to Beach Haven for a picnic and swim in the Choptank River. Pictured here, from left to right, are Hannah Mace, Lillian Bradshaw, Elizabeth Mace, Henrietta Jackson, Nancy Lanier, Mary Fletcher, an unidentified girl, Betty Hicks, and Beulah Fitzhugh. At that time, the troop met on Monday evenings and practiced signaling and flag-making. Good deeds, of course, were a regular part of their activities. Later, during the war, they took part in food drives and sold War Bonds.

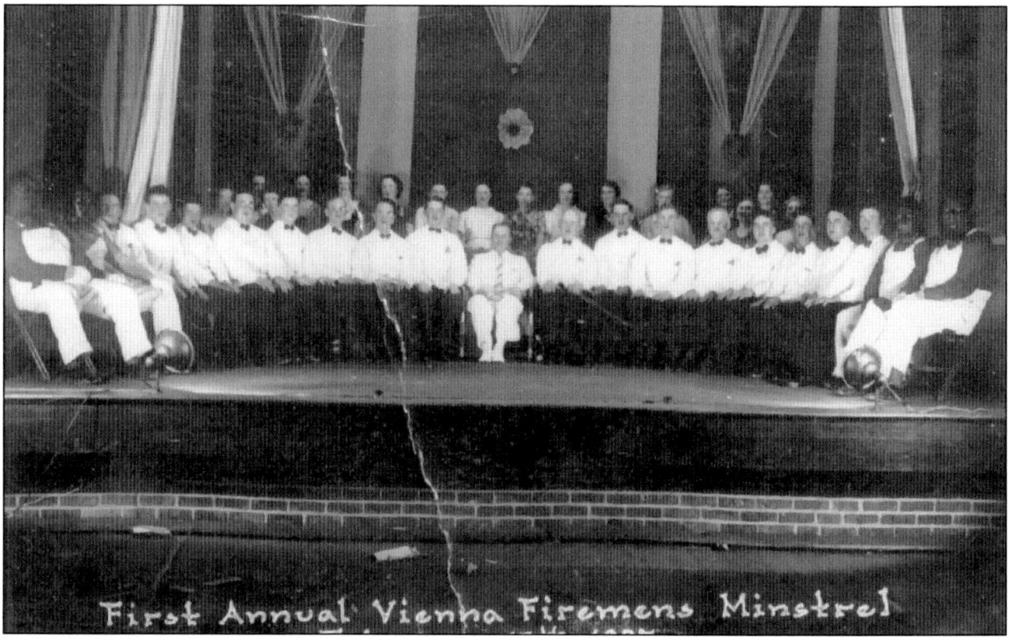

Though the stereotypes included in minstrel shows currently make them politically incorrect, they also portrayed obvious admiration for the African-American musical idiom. Some of America's greatest folk music was written specifically for minstrel shows by songwriters of the caliber of Stephen Foster. Minstrel shows were nationally popular for 100 years and locally lucrative as fund-raisers for various charities such as the Vienna Volunteer Fire Company.

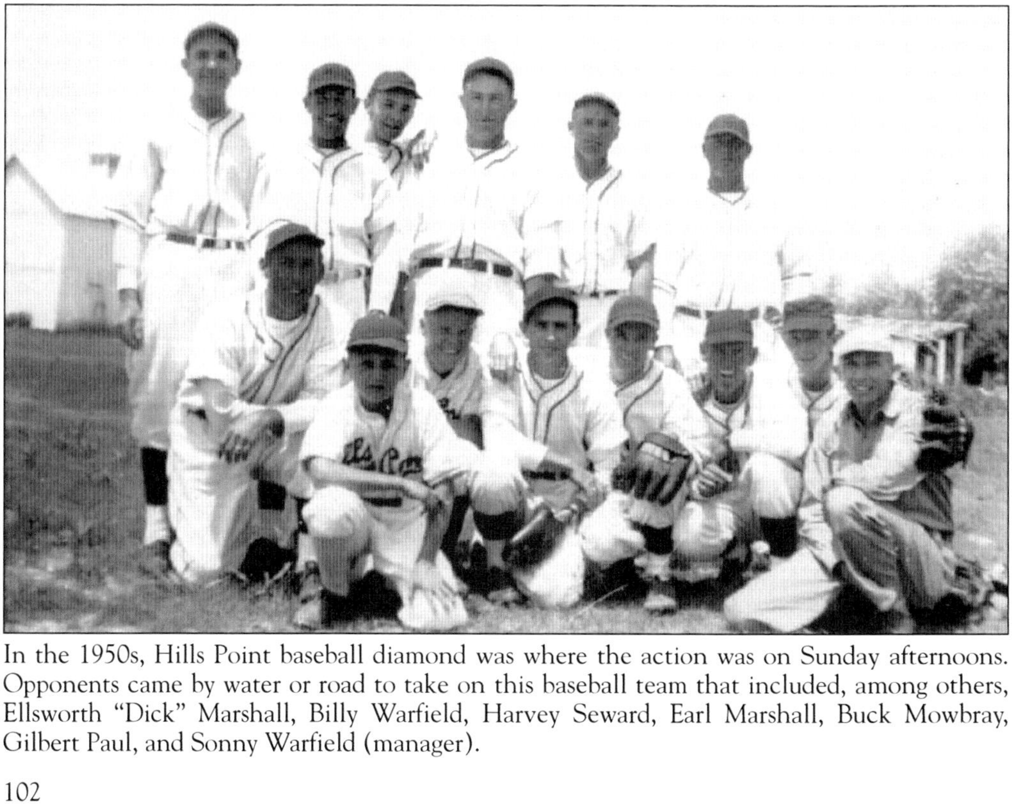

In the 1950s, Hills Point baseball diamond was where the action was on Sunday afternoons. Opponents came by water or road to take on this baseball team that included, among others, Ellsworth "Dick" Marshall, Billy Warfield, Harvey Seward, Earl Marshall, Buck Mowbray, Gilbert Paul, and Sonny Warfield (manager).

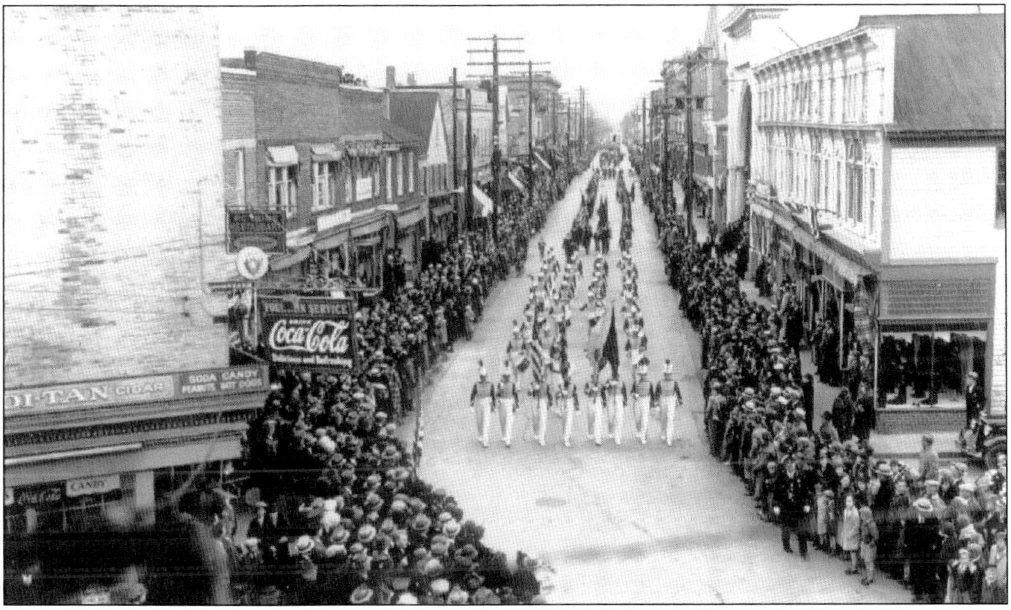

American Legion Post #91 boasted the Maryland state champion drum and bugle corps. In this photo from the 1930s by professional photographer George S. LeVarn, they lead off a parade down Race Street before a patiently waiting throng of spectators. Cambridge always loved a parade, a tradition that continues today, with the annual Christmas Parade drawing marchers from all over the Delmarva Peninsula.

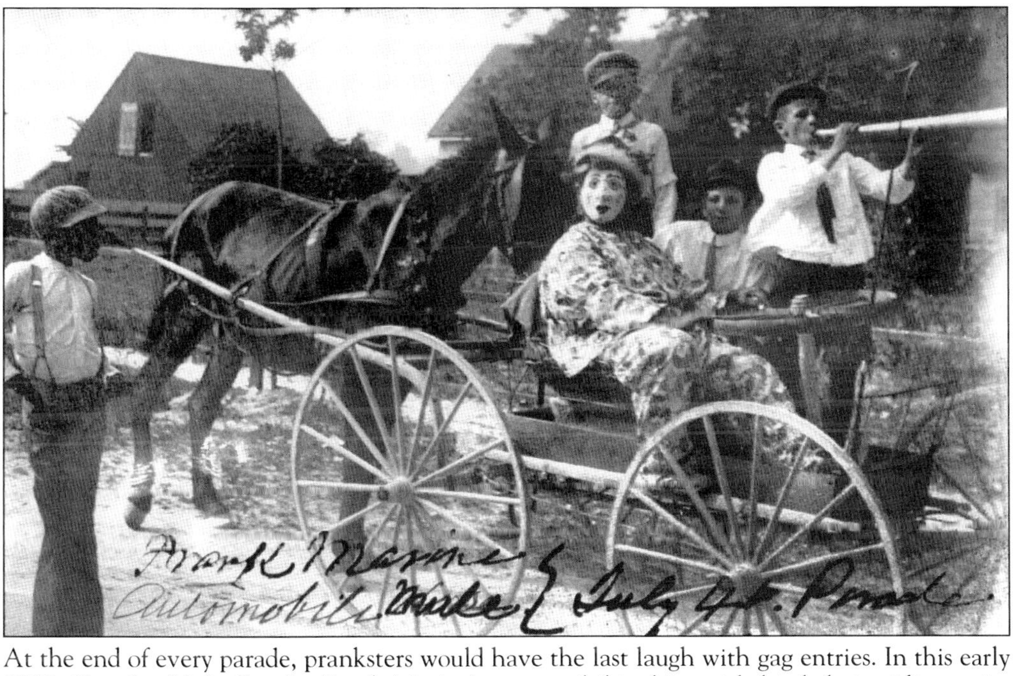

At the end of every parade, pranksters would have the last laugh with gag entries. In this early 1900s Fourth of July Parade, Frank Marine's entry exhibits him with his lady in riding attire driving out in their automobile with a one-mulepower engine. In the early days of horseless carriages, those with autos were often asked to fall in behind the marchers to show their machines to the crowd.

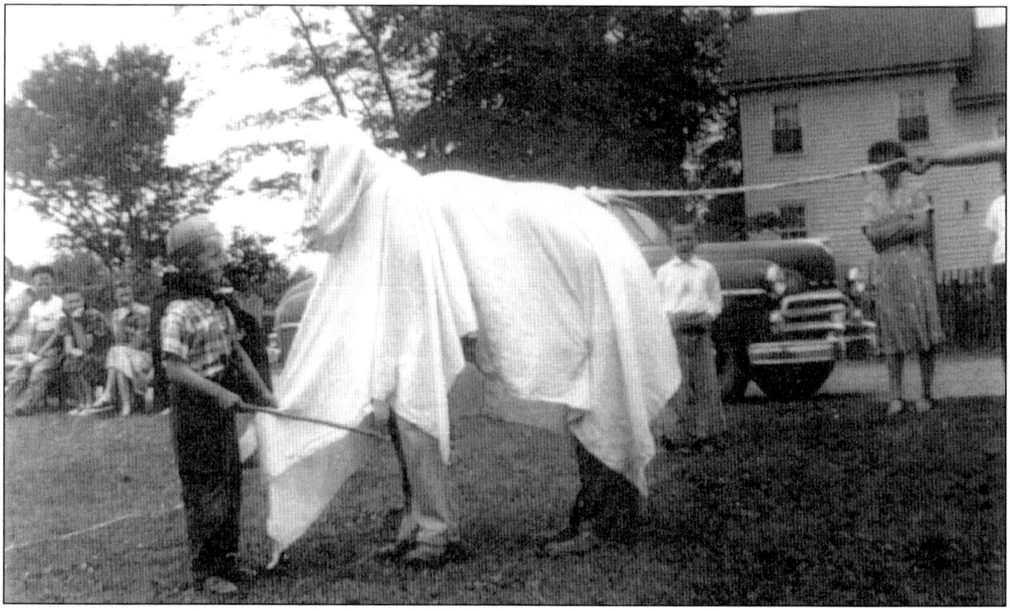

Teacher Minibel Butler Lankford may not have produced "The Greatest Show on Earth," but her May Day circus was the best show on Elliott Island in the 1950s. Dennis Ewell, ringmaster and animal tamer, put this show pony through its tricks, with the cooperation of sheeted cousins Delmus Bramble and Jimmy Jones. Jimmy's mother Delema on the right appears concerned about the tail being pulled, which may hint at his position.

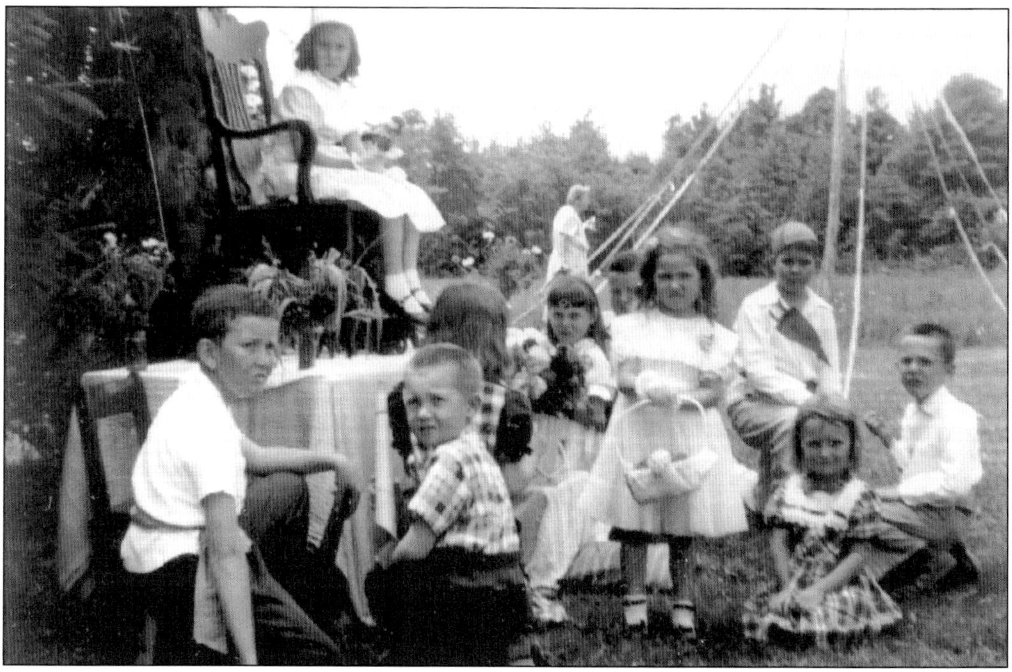

May Queen Mary Ellen Gray reigned over festivities at the Elliott Island School in 1954. Her court consists of, from left to right, Dennis Ewell, Harvey Waller, Joan Dayton, Linda Gray, Patricia Mae Palmer, John Gray, Dottie Ann Dayton, and Donald Gray. The Maypole can be seen to the right, ready for the young dancers.

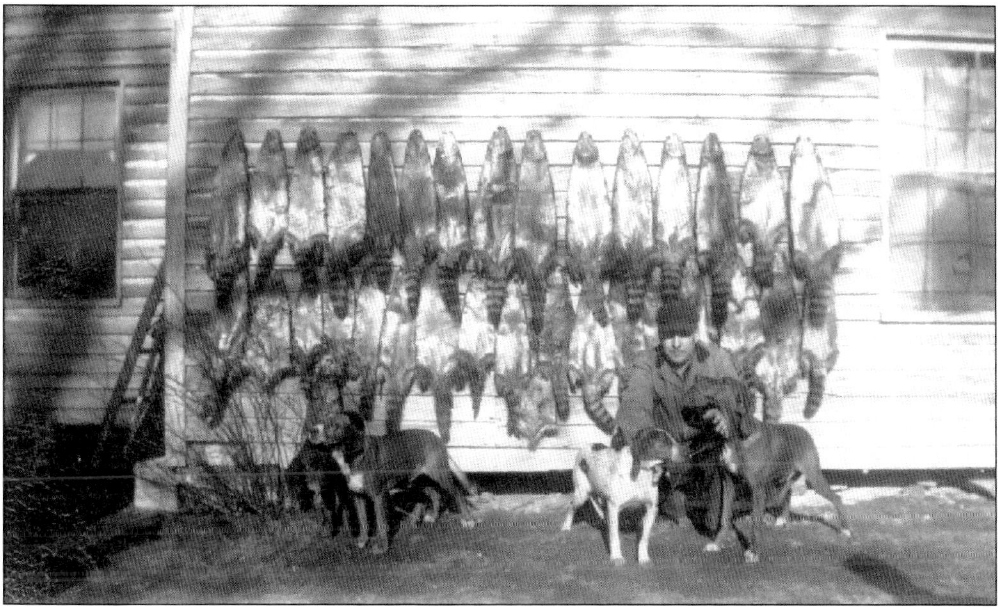

Coon hunting has a long tradition in Dorchester County, and practitioners have had many friendly competitions for the best coon hounds. Alton Hurley, pictured here in 1939, evidently had a right to be proud of his hounds. Alton and Nannie Mae Hurley kept store at Henrys Crossroads from 1942 to 1952. Nights when the men were hunting, the store stayed open all hours and folks sitting up could listen for the hounds.

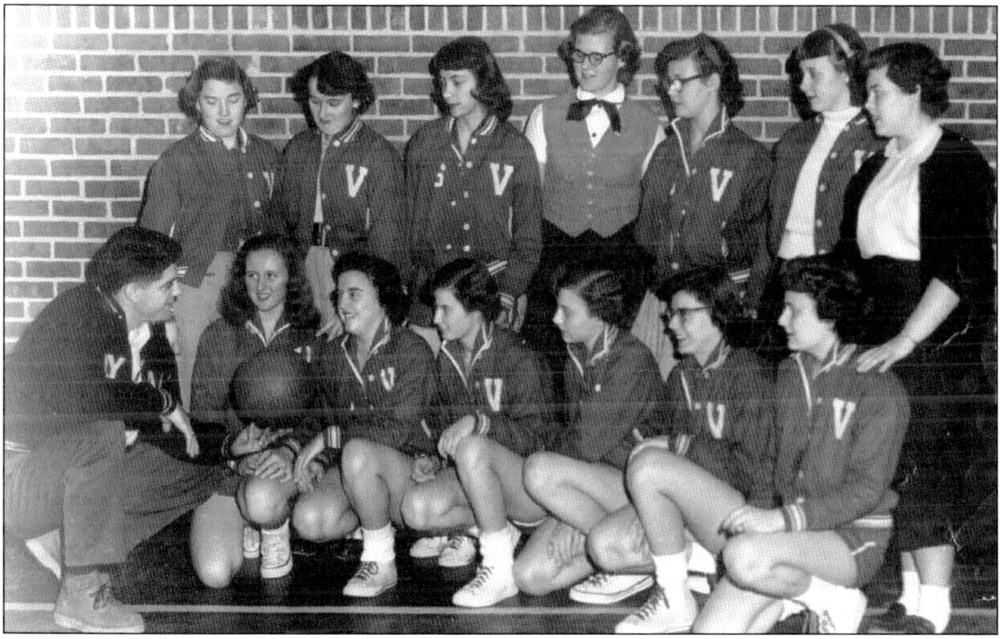

In their last season of play, the Vienna girls basketball team for the 1953–1954 season included, from left to right, (bottom row) Coach Hopkins, Brenda Foxwell, Shirley Dayton, Louise Johannsen, Jean Johannsen, Mary Agnes Bramble, and Carol Evans; (top row) Virgie Marine, Marlene Carneal, Fay Forester, Norma Baker, Eloise Willey, Jeanette Brinsfield, and Ruth Hurley.

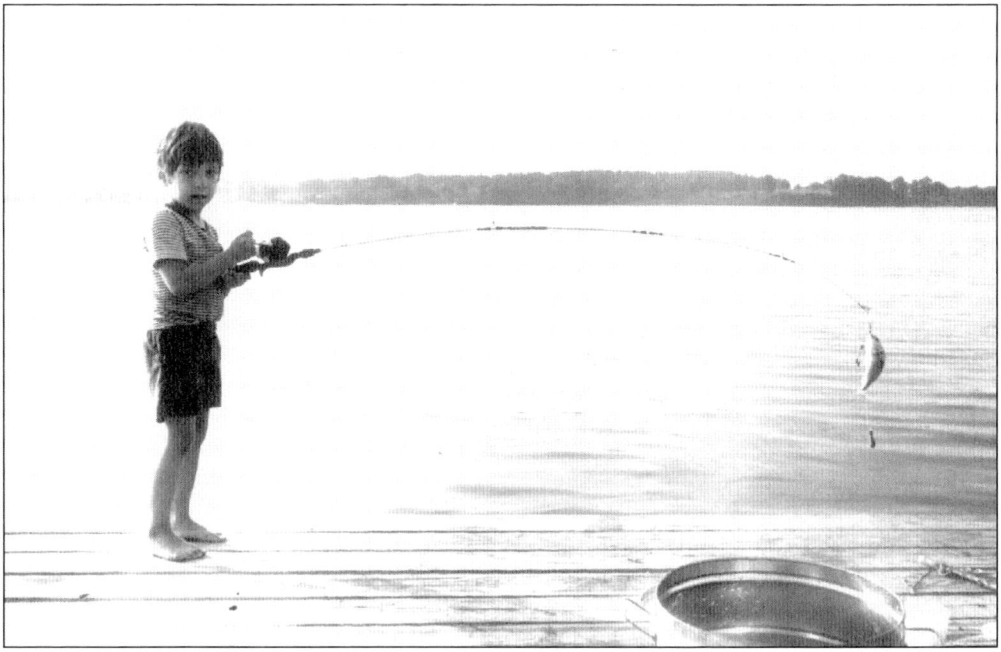

They start fishing young in Dorchester and never seem to recover. Before Malkus Bridge, Emerson Harrington Bridge crossed the Choptank and was the complete opposite of the idyllic spot shown above. Sidewalks on the old bridge were lined with fishermen angling for big ones lurking among bridge pilings. Men and women lined the rail shoulder to shoulder, lost in their watery sport and oblivious to beach-bound Route 50 traffic whizzing just behind.

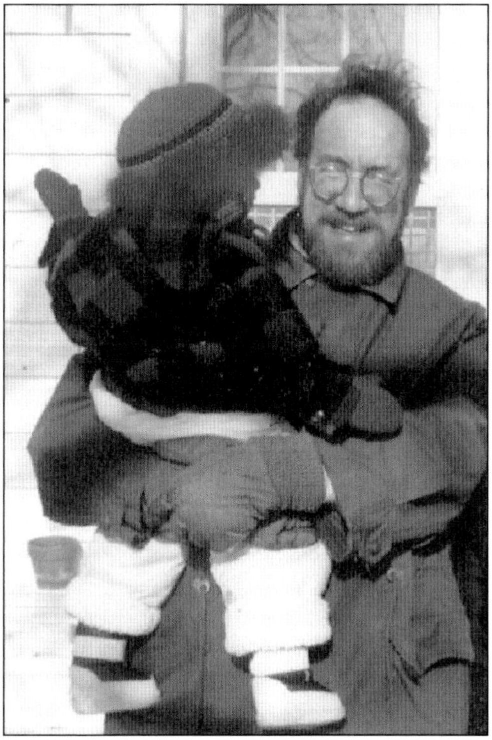

One blustery day on Horns Point, Richard Ben Cramer took a break to enjoy the snow with daughter Ruby. He was writing *What It Takes: The Way to the White House*, a chronicle of the 1988 presidential campaign. A second Pulitzer Prize–winning author, James Michener, also researched a bestseller in Dorchester County, but chose to relocate many local persons and events to a neighboring county in his novel, *Chesapeake*.

Seven

THOSE WHO SERVE

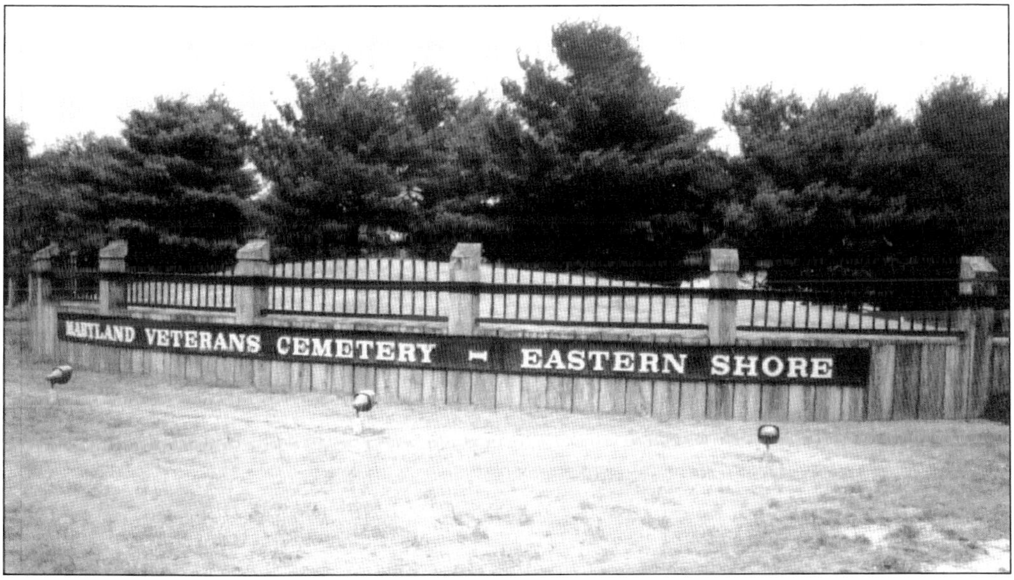

Many veterans of military service rest in the government cemetery at Beulah. Washington Cemetery at Hurlock features a statue of a "Doughboy," an affectionate term for World War I infantrymen equivalent to "GI" in World War II. The Italian-made marble Doughboy statue resulted from years of fund-raising efforts to honor those who served from the Hurlock area.

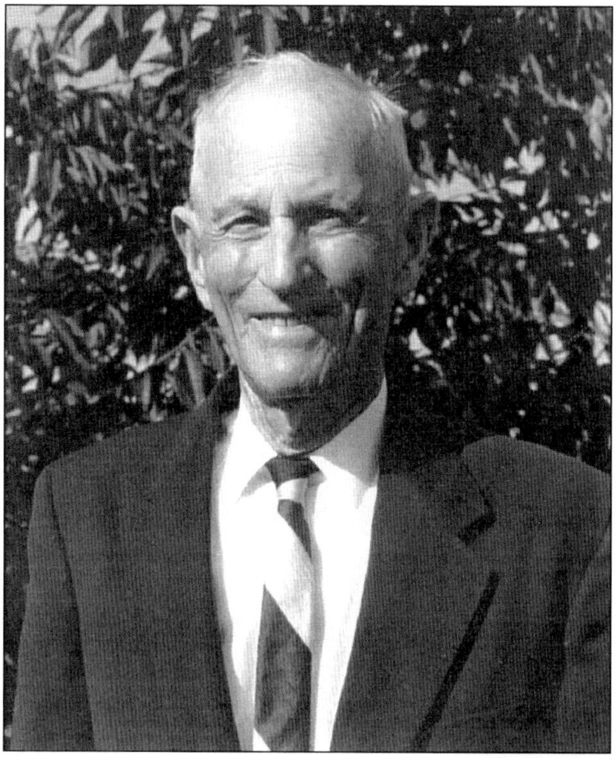

Ulysses Grant Murphy, born in Griffith Neck in 1868, sailed as a missionary to Japan at age 25. Mo Fu, as his name translated, inspired abolition of the then-legal practice of parents selling daughters into prostitution. An angry brothel-keeper once attacked the 5-foot-7-inch-tall preacher with a hammer. Looking back on the incident, 97-year-old Murphy said, "You can't hurt an Irishman hitting him on the head." Mo Fu in Japanese means Violet Wind.

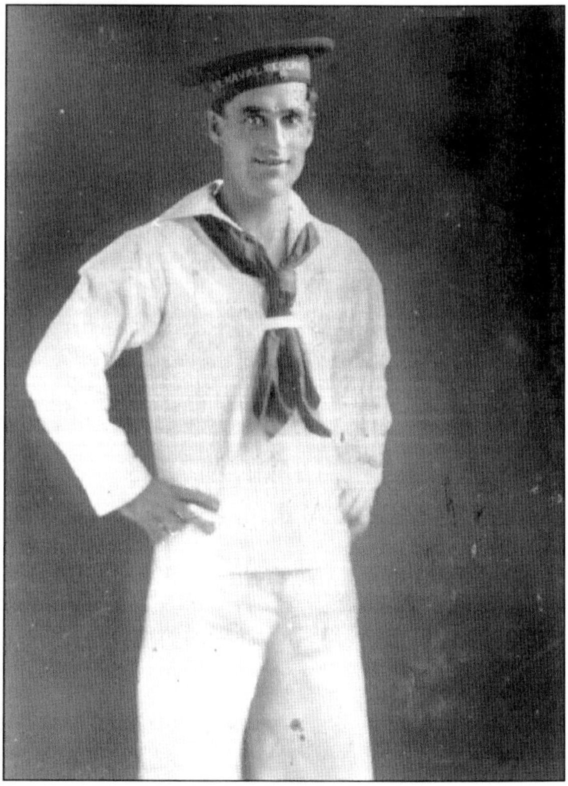

As a teenager, Robert Charles Casper of Ross Neck joined the Naval Reserve. He saw sea duty during World War I, sailing out of Norfolk, Virginia before returning to the Neck District. Mr. Casper loved people and loved ice-skating, so when the creek froze, youngsters knew who would get a party together. Another frozen treat often requested, homemade ice cream, started with Mr. Casper milking his own cow.

This 1943 photo shows World War II United States Army soldier Sidney English standing on the banks of Marshyhope Creek in his hometown of Brookview. Following the war, he worked at the Eastern Shore State Hospital. The cannery visible across the creek in Eldorado last belonged to Phillips Canning Company, but Zorah H. Brinsfield and Son had opened for business years before in 1908.

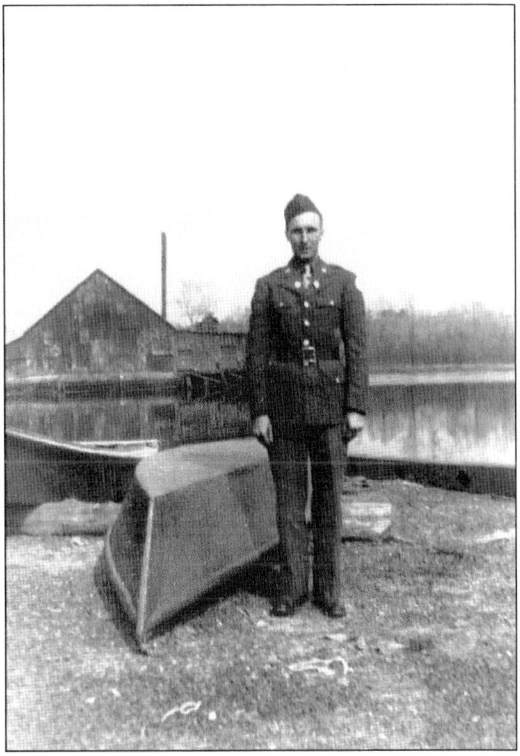

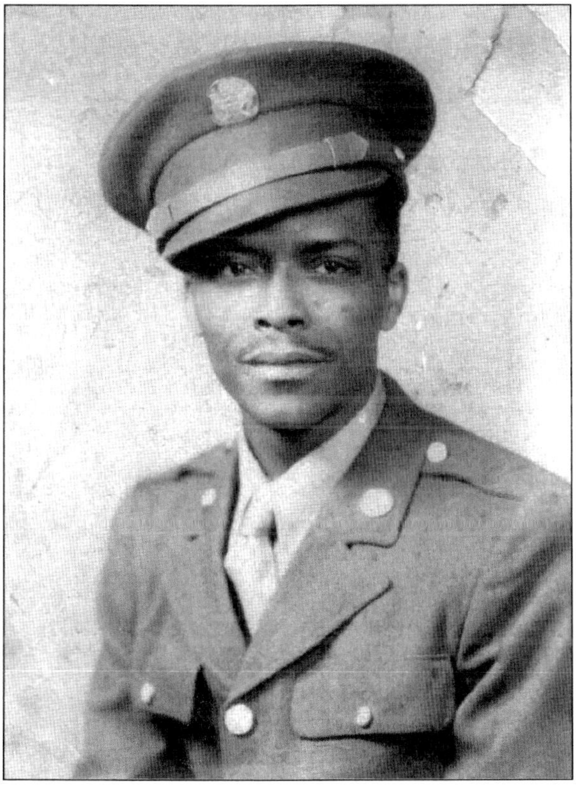

James Edward Cornish Sr. attended Frederick Douglass St. Clair High School in Cambridge, where he was a record-setting track star. After graduation, he served three years in the army during World War II. Returning home from Germany, he went to work for Phillips Packing Company and married Esther Marie Jackson. While raising six children, he retained his interest in youth sports and refereed basketball games at his alma mater.

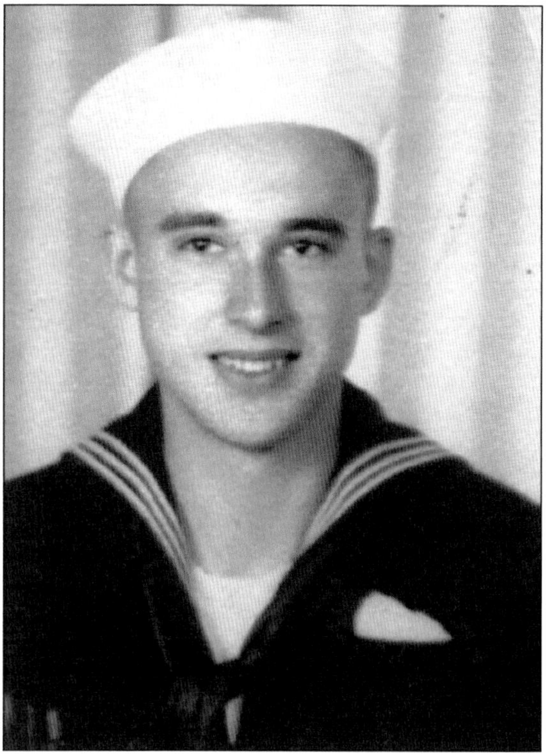

At dawn on June 6, 1944, Seabee Elijah Wheedleton of Galestown was coxswain of a rhino barge approaching Utah Beach behind the first wave of troops. Rhinos were merely two pontoon sections pinned together. Loaded with jeeps, trucks, anti-aircraft guns, and Cub reconnaissance planes, two outboard motors barely moved them. Armed with "my two fists," Elijah successfully discharged his cargo amid bursting artillery shells, but as he said, "There was something going on."

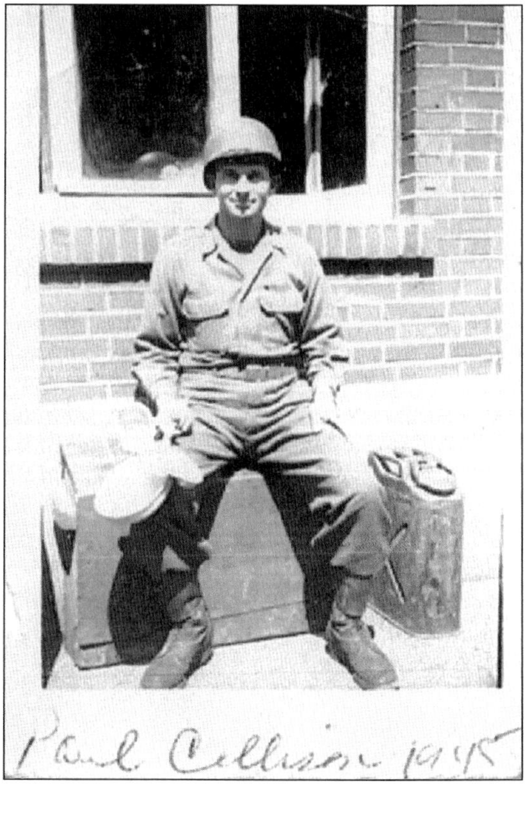

Paul R. Collison (1915–1969) served overseas during World War II with the 283rd Engineers Combat Battalion. He is pictured here in 1945, around the time he helped construct a bridge across the Rhine River that carried allied troops into Germany. He left a wife and three children at home when he was drafted and added one more child on his return. As promised, he built his mother a house in Brookview after discharge.

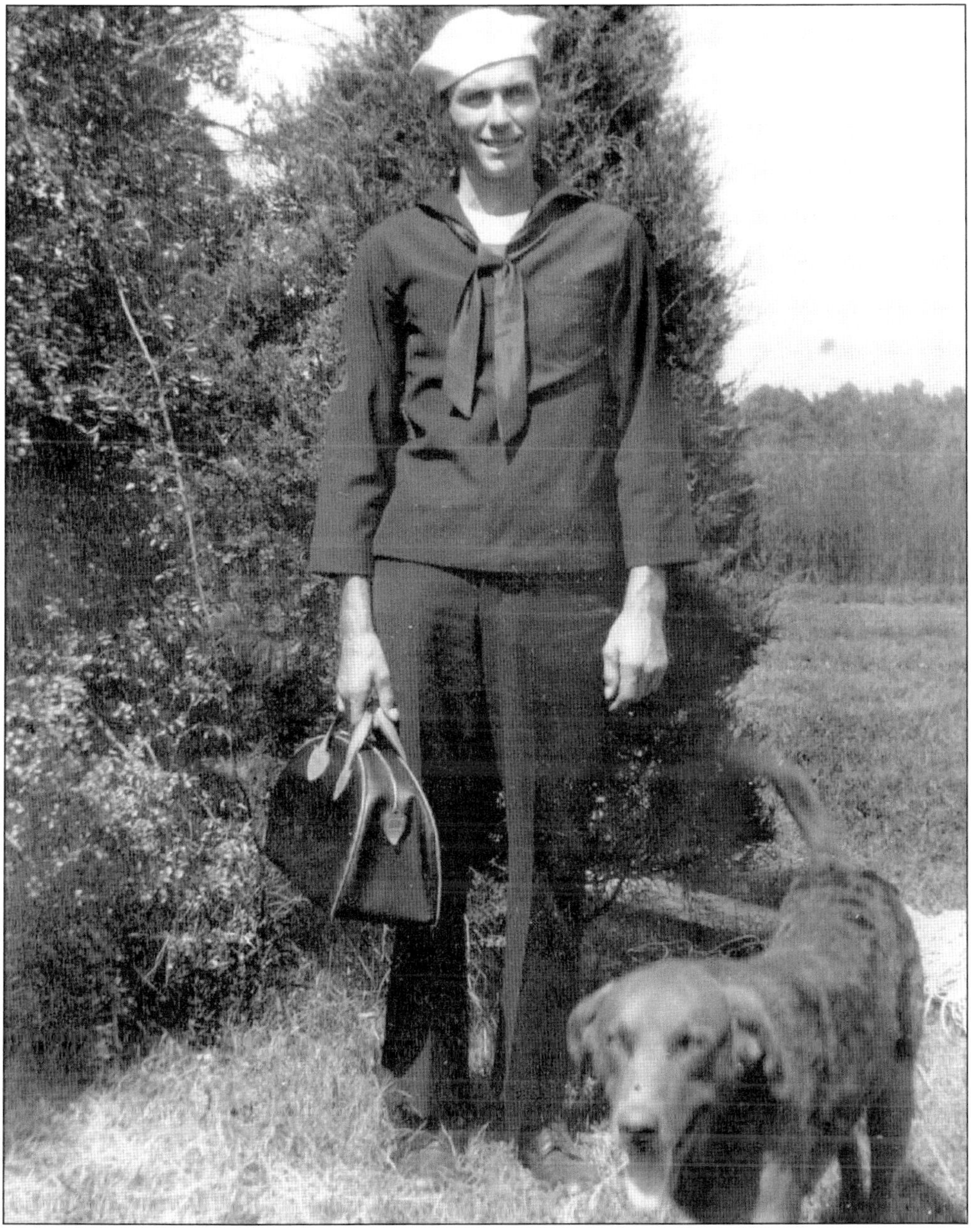

Leaving behind a good Chesapeake Bay Retriever like Plush was only one of the hardships of wartime duty. When Robert L. Bromwell Sr. left Madison to enter the United States Maritime Service during World War II, he also left behind his bride, the former Laura Ellen Sockriter. Before he was able to return home to Laura, his duties included transporting "war brides" to others. Their home in Madison was within sight of the former location of Joseph Brooks's famed boatyard and their house had been Brooks-built. When Robert returned from the service, he followed his father in making his living on the water. He had a boat, *The Princess*, built in Cambridge, earned a captain's license, and chartered fishing parties. Robert was a member of Gethsemane Methodist Church, the Madison Volunteer Fire Company, and the Dorchester Archery Club.

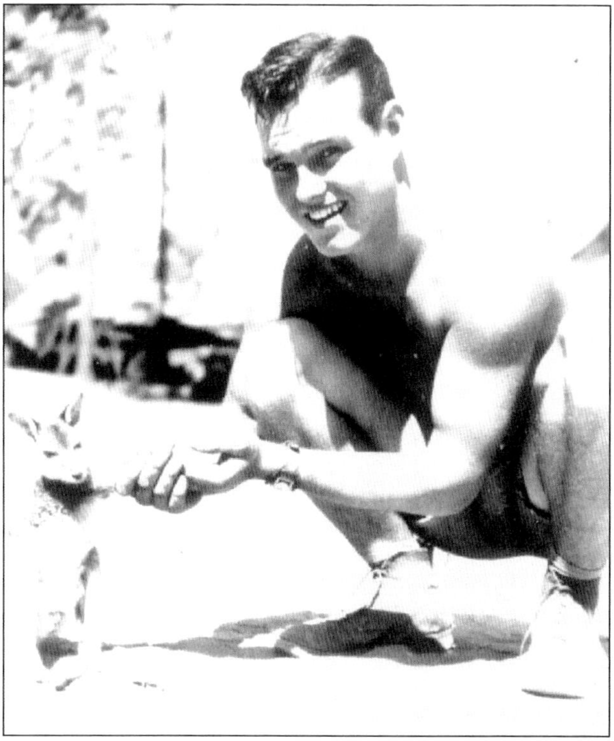

Sgt. Sam Roland Marshall of Eldorado poses in 1945 with a joey, a favorite pet among the GIs in Australia during World War II. Sam also served in the Philippines, while his twin, Robert, served with the Navy. For 35 years, Sam was employed as a technician with C&P Telephone Company in Cambridge, and also was Eldorado's constable in the early 1960s.

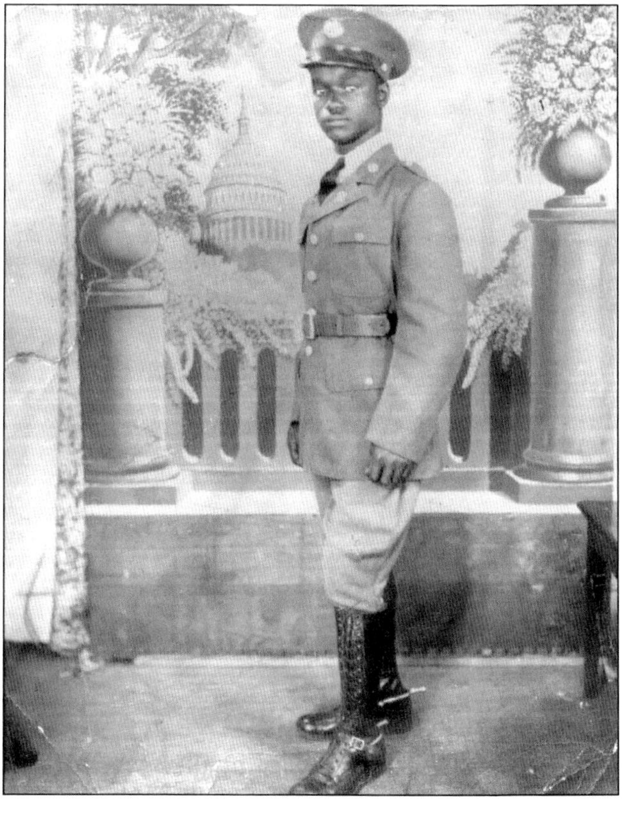

Orphaned, Albert Reginald Askins was raised at Railroad Hill in East New Market by his young sisters. Unaware that he was too young, he tagged along with school-age siblings, then passed to St. Clair High. After a stint with the Civilian Conservation Corps (CCC), in Buffalo Soldier tradition, he joined the army, serving through World War II and the Korean Conflict. Only after retiring, he found his birth certificate and discovered how young he was.

Enez Farrare was born at Railroad Hill outside of East New Market and educated at Frederick Douglass St. Clair High School, which was then the only secondary school in Dorchester County open to African Americans. In World War II, she served overseas as a WAC, a member of the Women's Army Corps. She returned to Railroad Hill after retiring from a career in federal service.

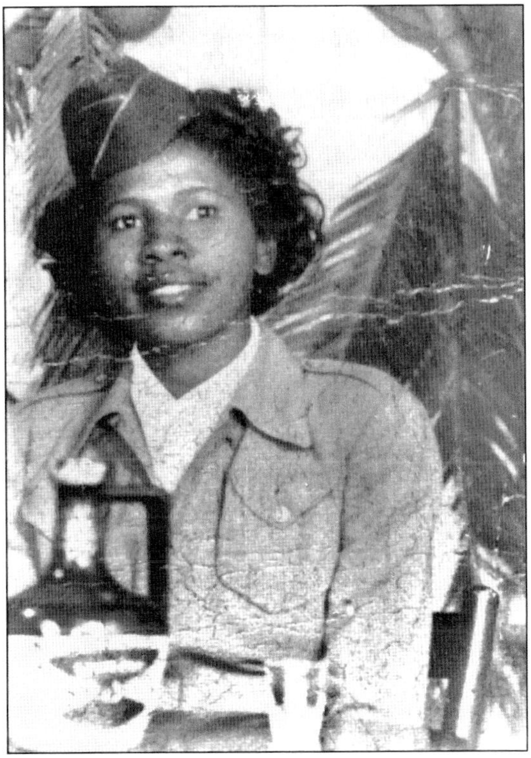

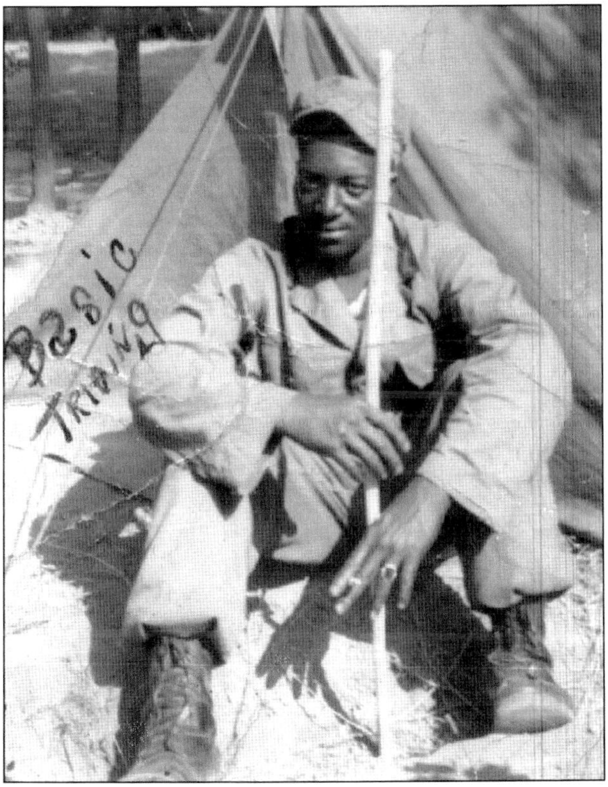

A corporal in the United States Army Franklin "Junebug" C. Conway Jr. (1932–1983) served in Germany during the Korean Conflict. Returning to his childhood home at Jones Village, he married Flossie Newcomb and together the couple raised 14 children. He was employed with Harper and Bateman Pickle Company as a truck driver and forklift operator for 30 years until Bloch and Guggenheimer took over the industry in 1982. He loved kids and was quick to smile or laugh.

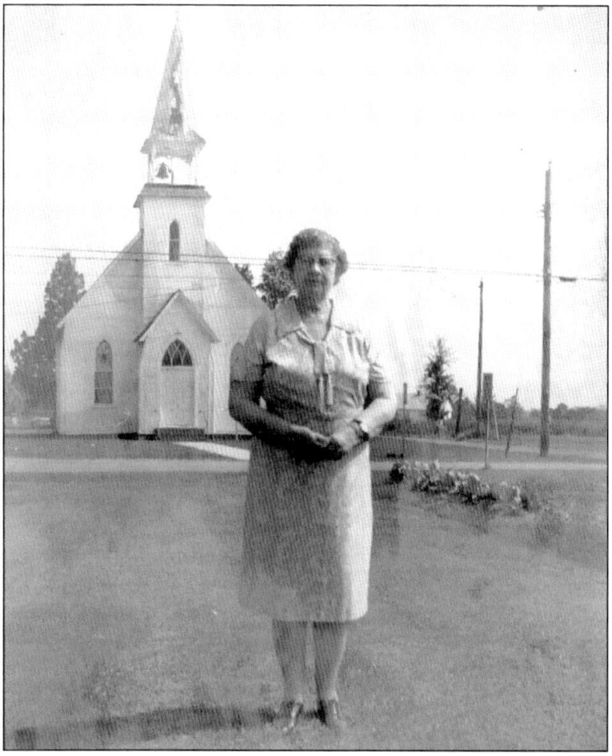

Amy Wroten Brittingham Christopher is remembered for having sheltered and raised a score of foster children that she took under her care at different times. There may have been one or two she had trouble handling, but many fine citizens were reared at Mrs. Christopher's home. Mrs. Christopher is pictured here outside Joppa Church in Madison.

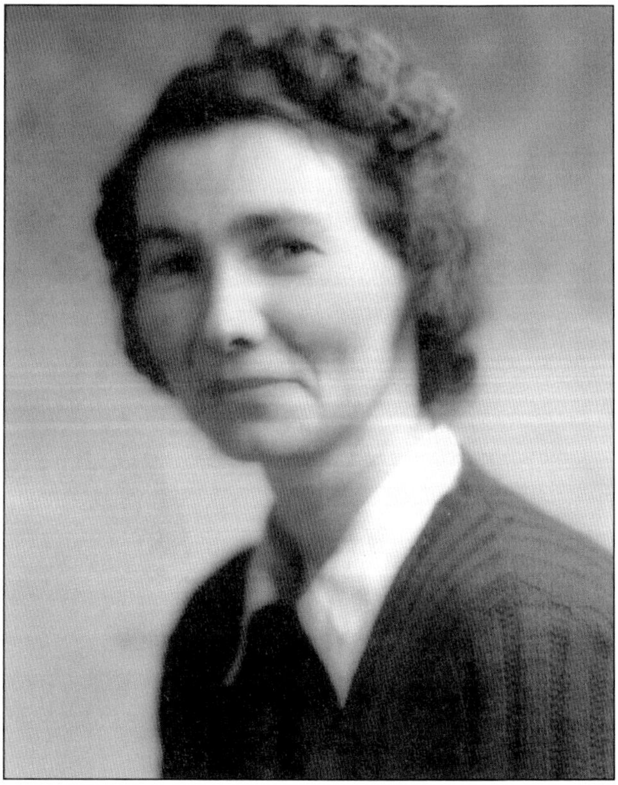

After teaching at Madison and at Hoopers Island High School, Louise Linthicum Bromwell turned to social work. Still interested in youth and active in church, she became especially recognized for assisting the elderly. The AARP honored her as Volunteer of the Year for lending her experience to several advisory boards, but she is probably best remembered by individuals who needed an advocate or a lift to the doctor.

Frederick C. Malkus Jr. grew up on the Little Blackwater River, financing a law degree by trapping and doing steelwork on Harrington Bridge. Hitting Normandy Beach D-Day plus one, his unit was to supply gasoline but the invasion stalled, so his men assumed the haunting necessity of burial duty. Senator Malkus served nearly 50 years as a legislator. His colleagues voted unanimously to name Harrison Bridge's replacement in his honor.

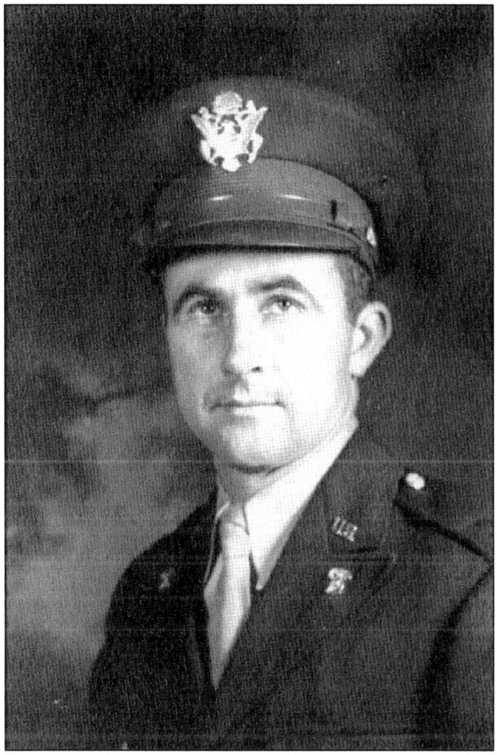

Capt. C. Calvert Evans called Elliott Island, Vienna, and Cambridge homeport at different times. As a boy, he sailed with his father aboard the schooner *Fannie Insley*, taking along a Brownie camera as well as a keen mind. In later years, he was a generous resource for Chesapeake Bay Maritime Museum historians and for authors of such books as *Chesapeake Bay Schooners* and *Elliott's Island: The Land That Time Forgot*.

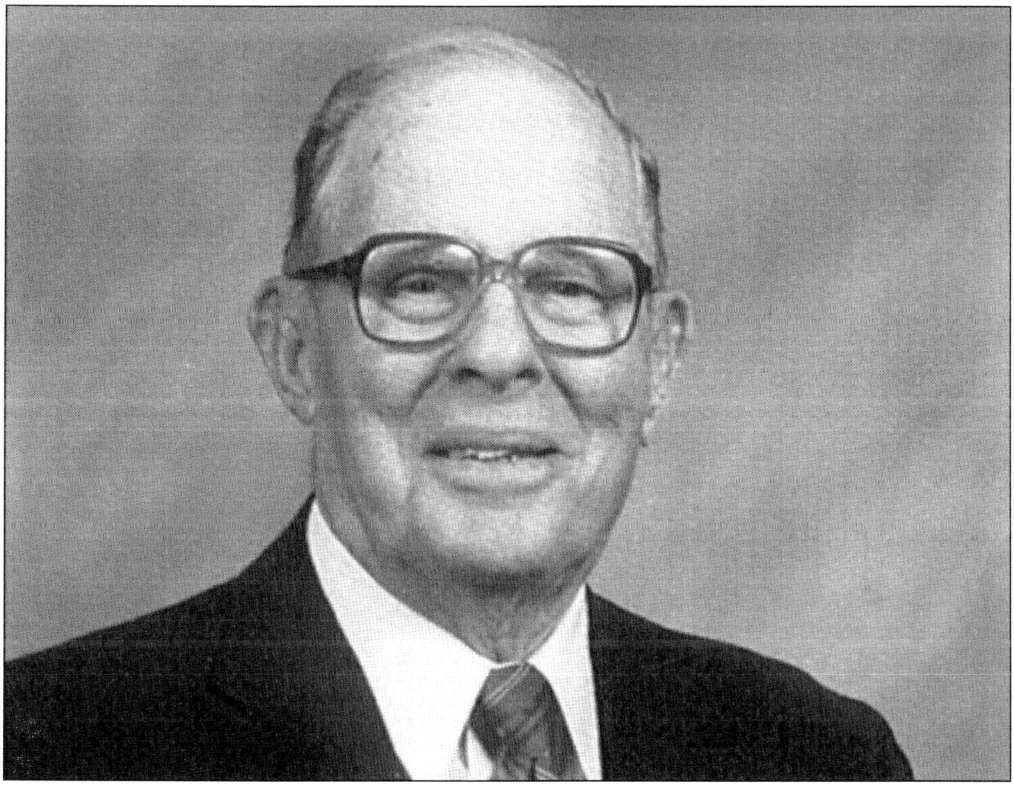

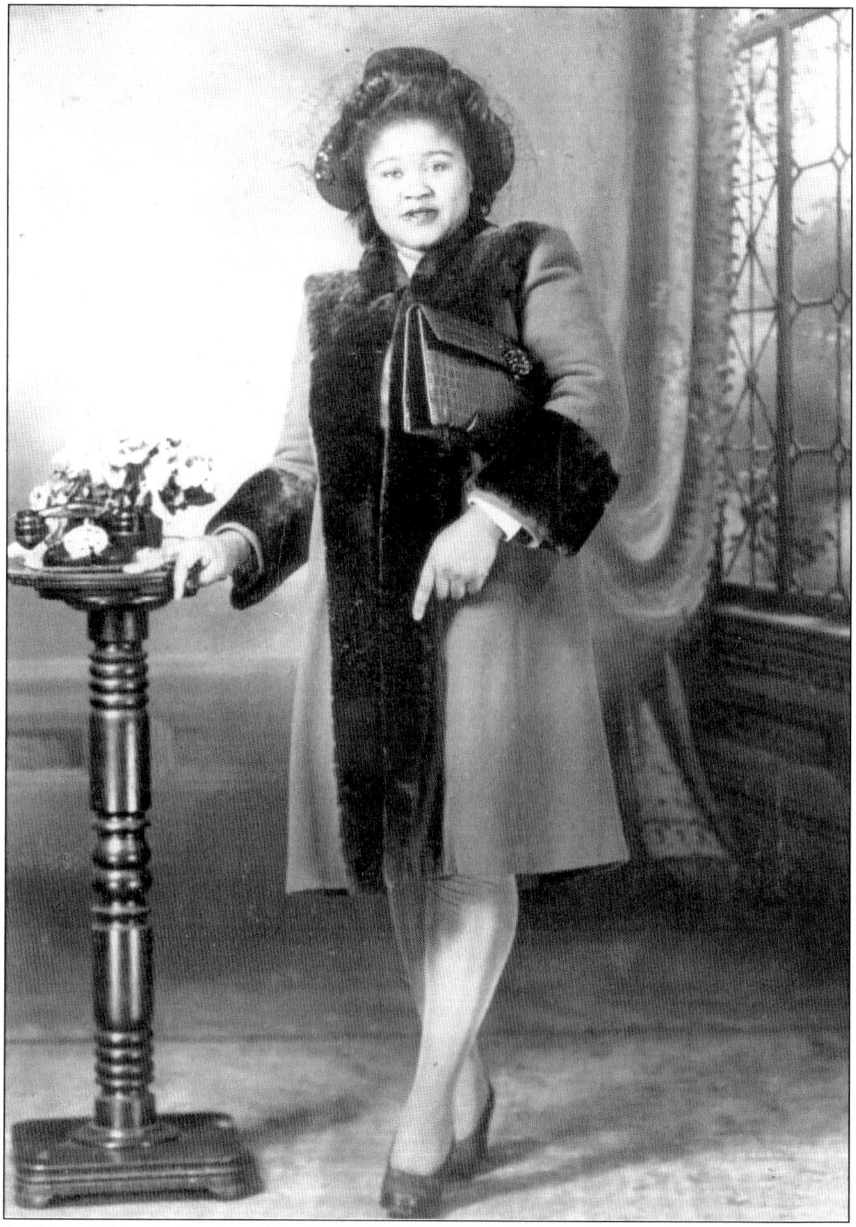

Elizabeth Carr Chase was raised in Steeles Neck outside of Vienna. She is pictured here in Philadelphia visiting an older sister, a teacher at Temple, who urged her to stay and attend college, but Liz wanted to return to Dorchester County. Her husband, Ike Chase, was employed by the Elliott family of Elliotts Island and the islanders grew very fond of Liz. She nursed several elderly islanders through their final days. When a new elementary school opened in Vienna, Liz was the first cook employed and fed the children for 10 years. From there she went to the Eastern Shore Hospital Center as a psychiatric aide. "You had to like it to be able to do it," she said. "Some of them were something. They'd spit in your face or anything, but Mrs. Albeitis the superintendent saw that no patient was mistreated." Liz still turns her hand to cooking for functions at her church, Wesley U. M. Church. For the past 17 years she has run a pantry called "Neighbors in Need" that supplements anyone in need of help with groceries.

Carlos F. Barroso, M.D. (1900–2001) practiced medicine in his native Cuba for 33 years. He fled with one suitcase on July 19, 1961 after the Bay of Pigs invasion failed, coming to Eastern Shore Hospital Center in 1963. Seeing North Dorchester in need of a doctor, he opened his Hurlock office and endeared himself to the community with his medical skill, sense of humor, and accessibility. He passed away on July 19, 2001, 40 years to the day after leaving Cuba.

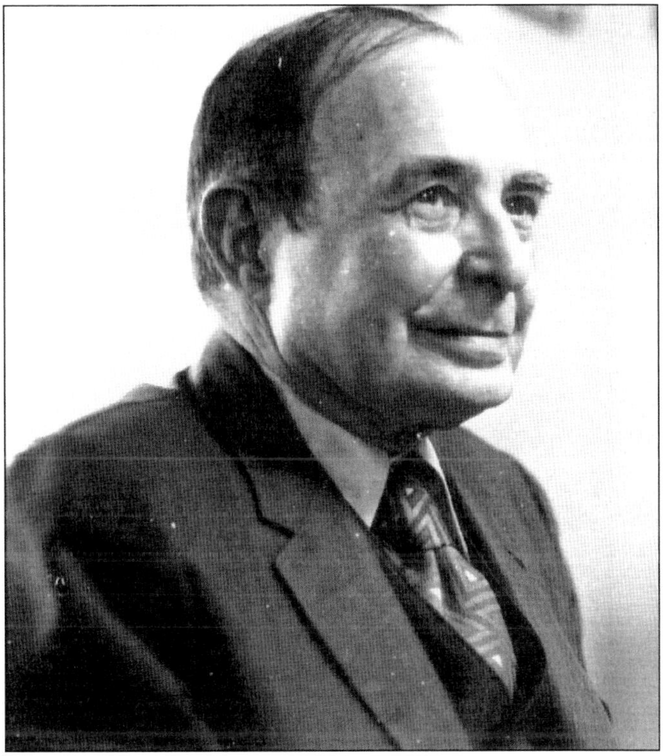

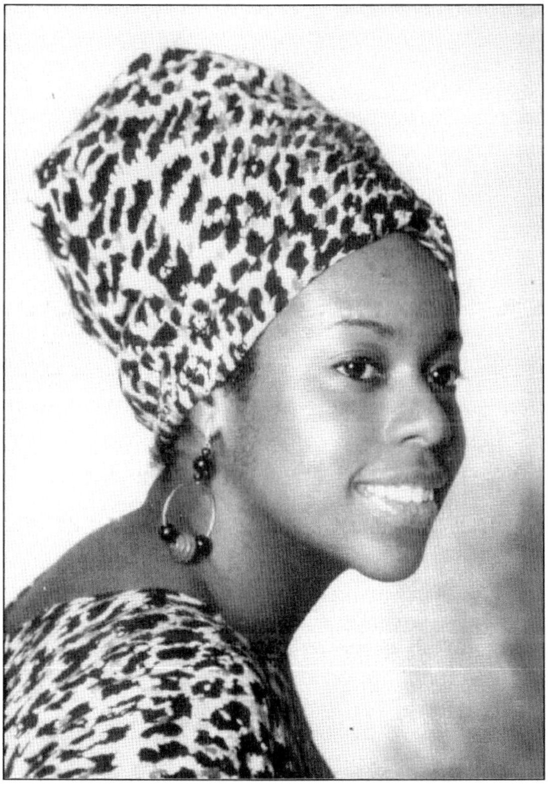

Kay Najiyyah McElvey, Ph.D., of Hurlock graduated Maces Lane High School as valedictorian. Returning from college to teach newly desegregated schools, she noted that black images had disappeared from classrooms. At North Dorchester High School, she taught Dorchester's first black literature class, then wrote *Early Black Dorchester* to document local heroes. Her docu-drama *The Message in the Song* will soon be available to schools.

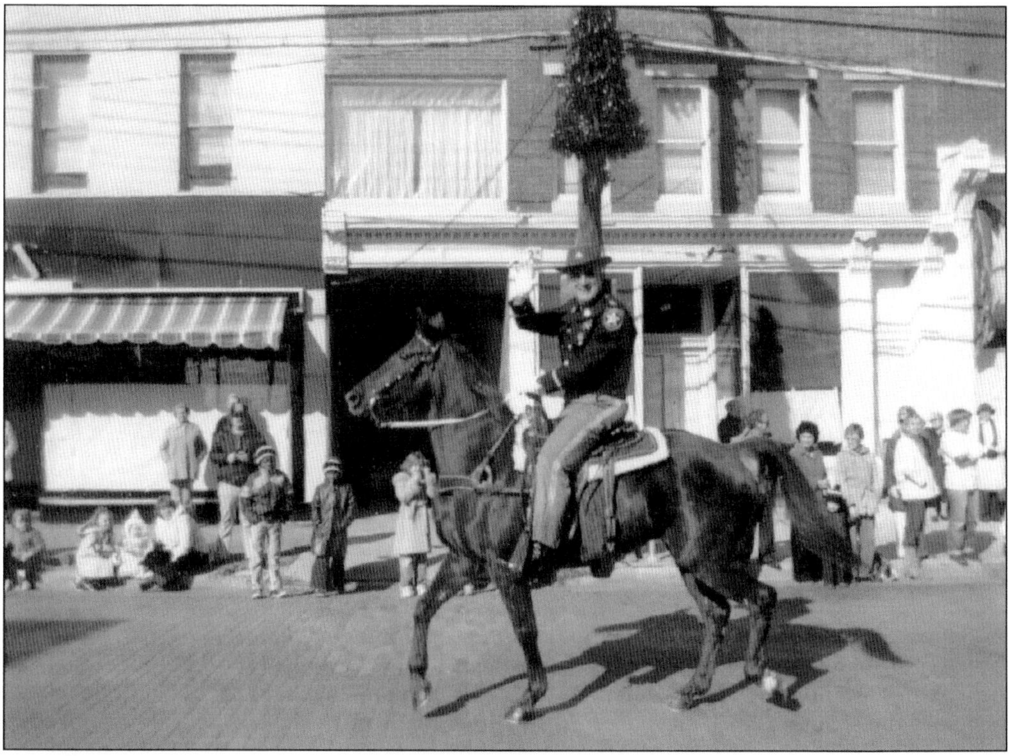

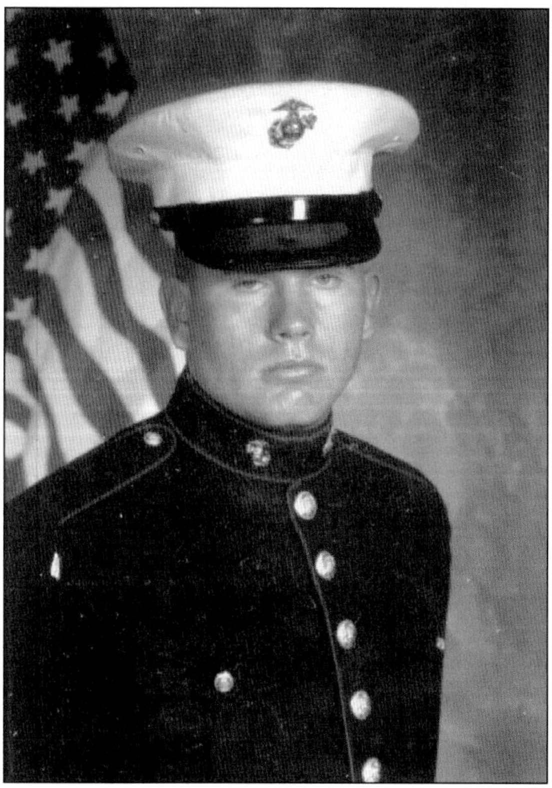

Phil McKelvey was sworn in as sheriff on December 1, 1978 and went on to be elected time and again, the longest serving holder of the county's oldest office. Dorchester County dates its history from the appointment of its first sheriff, Raymond Staplefort in 1669. A native of Harrison Ferry and graduate of Hurlock High School, Sheriff McKelvey is shown astride his Appaloosa, Krystl, in the annual Cambridge Christmas Parade.

Gregory Guy Collins (1969–2001) served in the Persian Gulf with the U.S. Marine Corps in 1991. He later served in the Navy Reserve, Army National Guard, and as a Correctional Officer at Eastern Correctional Institute. An outdoorsman and expert marksman, Greg grew up and lived near Marshyhope Creek. His wife Lena and daughter Sydney saw him honored in 2002 as the first Maryland officer recognized by the Correctional Peace Officers Foundation.

Eight

Worth a Visit

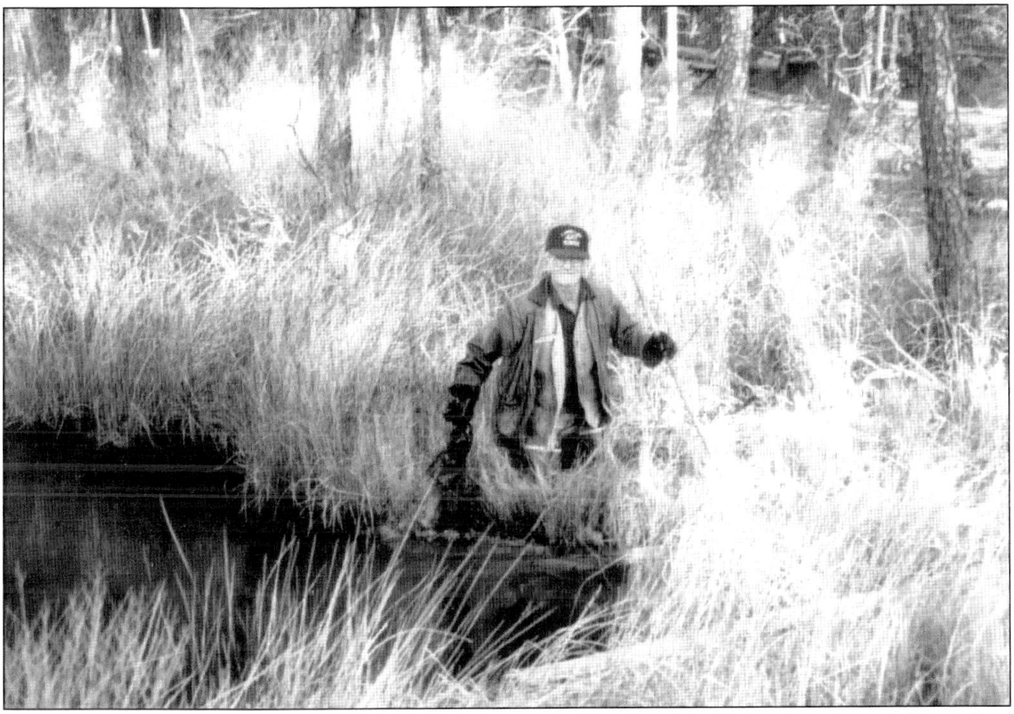

With Sen. Fred Malkus's passing, the sole surviving participant of the first National Outdoor Show was Shriver Mills, shown here walking his trap line. On the last weekend of February each year, the Outdoor Show is held at South Dorchester Elementary School. The show includes the World Champion Muskrat Skinning Contest, as wells as exhibits, craft sales, music, auctions, and various contests of cooking and outdoor skills.

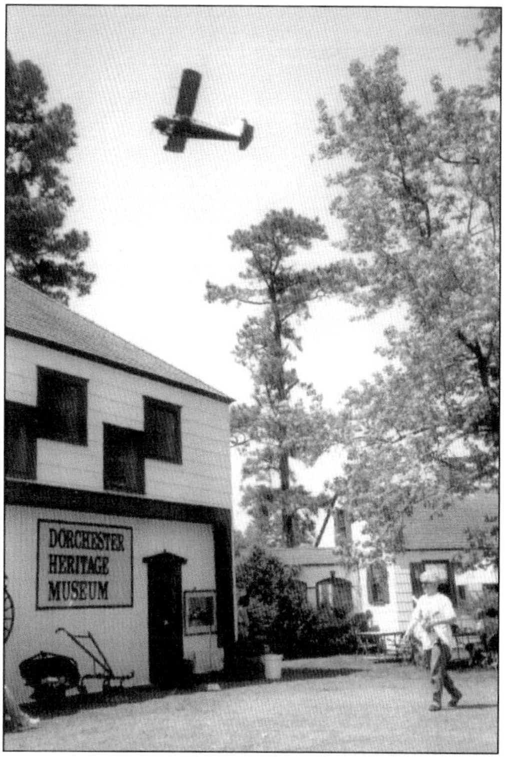

Dorchester Heritage Museum, formerly on the duPont's' Horn Point estate, occupies their pilot's house and hanger. Mr. duPont built the three-runway aerodrome in the 1920s, grass airstrips that now delight pilots of vintage aircraft. Museum exhibits, maintained by dedicated volunteers, span Dorchester life from Native Americans to early flight. Hundreds of aircraft, such as this 1940 Cessna, join an annual Fly-In on the third weekend of May, weather permitting.

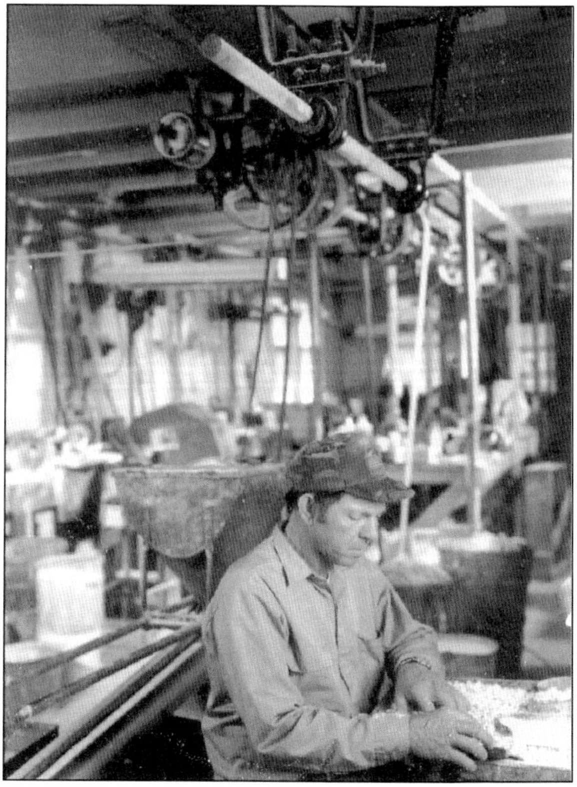

Among the exhibits at Vienna Heritage Museum is machinery from Martinek Button Factory, relocated from Elliott Island. Here, Daniel Martinek demonstrates cutting mother-of-pearl buttons, which plastic imitations gradually made obsolete. No plastic touched the vintage clothing nor the 1912 wedding gown, which are on display, along with farm equipment, British shot from the bombardment of Vienna, and other historic artifacts. The museum is open alternate Sunday afternoons or by appointment.

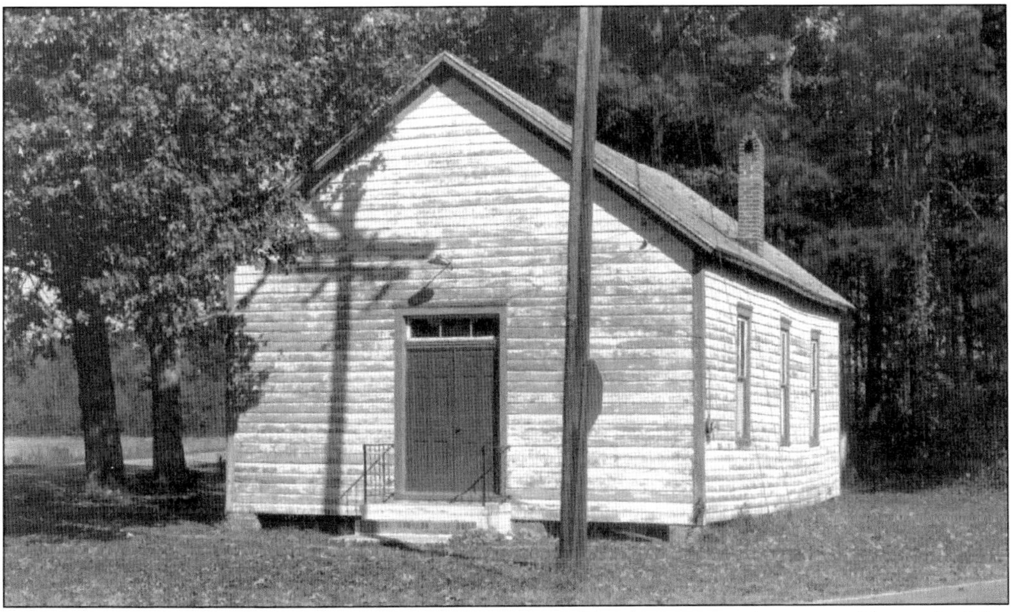

On the second weekend after Labor Day each September, the Native-American Festival of the Nause Waiwash Band of Indians is held at Sailwinds Park. The group traces ancestry to the original peoples of Dorchester County. Proceeds from their festival in recent years are restoring the former Hughes Chapel at the intersection of Maple Dam and Greenbriar Roads for use as a traditional longhouse. It is pictured here in the 1970s.

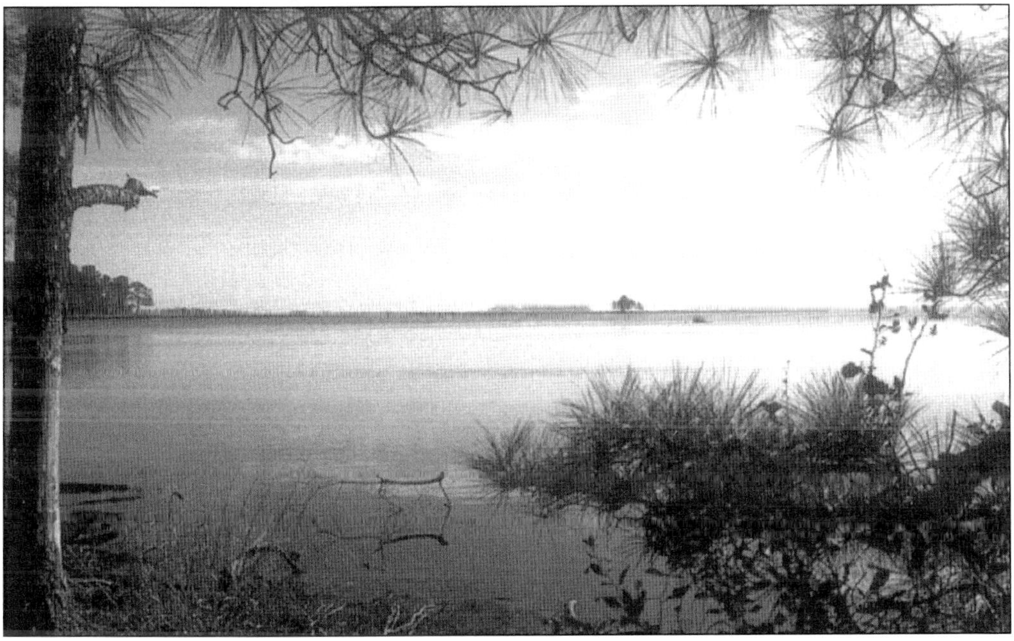

Blackwater National Wildlife Refuge draws visitors to scenes like this one—Marsh Edge Trail on Wildlife Drive—captured by Lisa Mayo. The refuge harbors waterfowl migrating along the Atlantic Flyway and provides habitat for bald eagles and the endangered Delmarva Fox Squirrel. A visitors' center and gift shop is open all year where special events are held, such as fall open houses and the Eagle Festival in the spring.

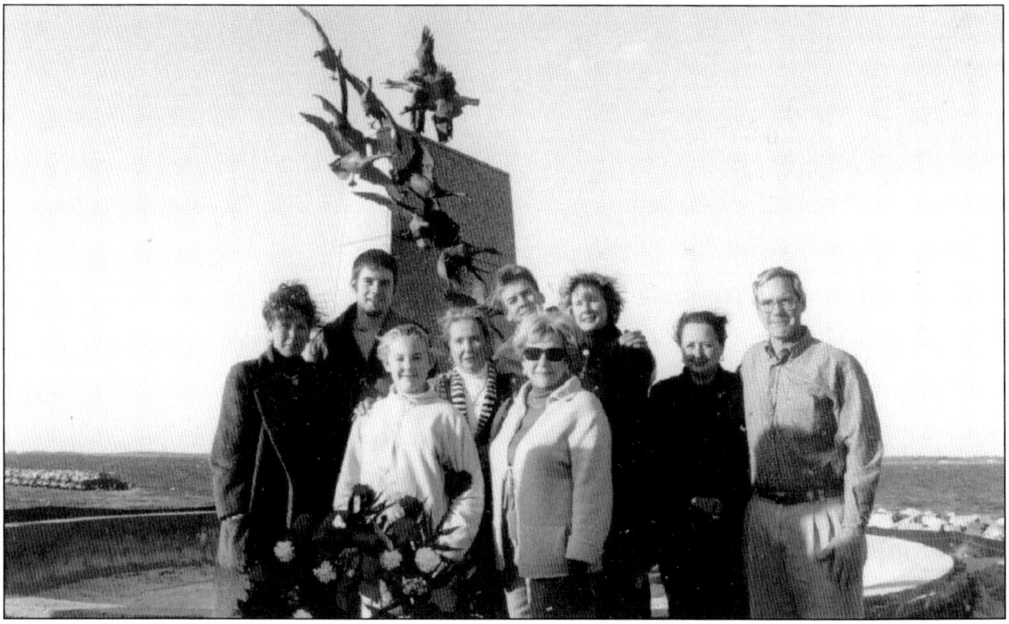

Wildfowl once arrived annually in such numbers as to block out the sun. Grand National Waterfowl Association strives to preserve this historic resource, as well as the sport of waterfowling. They invite the public to join each November at a traditional Eastern Shore Jamboree. GNWF sponsored the goose sculpture at the Visitors Center, erected *gratis* by Alan "Slim" Finchum, whose wife Ginny is surrounded here by their children and grandchildren.

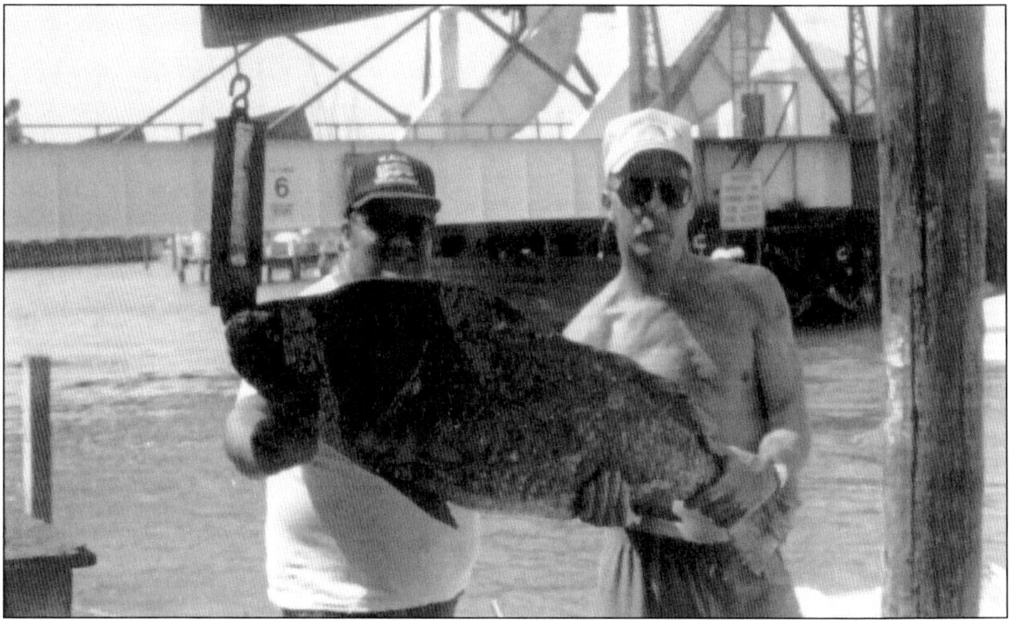

"I'd rather be fishing" is evident in this photo depicting a sample Choptank offering. Eldorado brothers Rick (left) and Allen Mansfield display Rick's 69-pound black drumfish. Several organizations sponsor fishing tournaments in South Dorchester each year, including Lakes and Straits Volunteer Fire Company, Hoopers Island Volunteer Fire Company, and the South Dorchester Community Center.

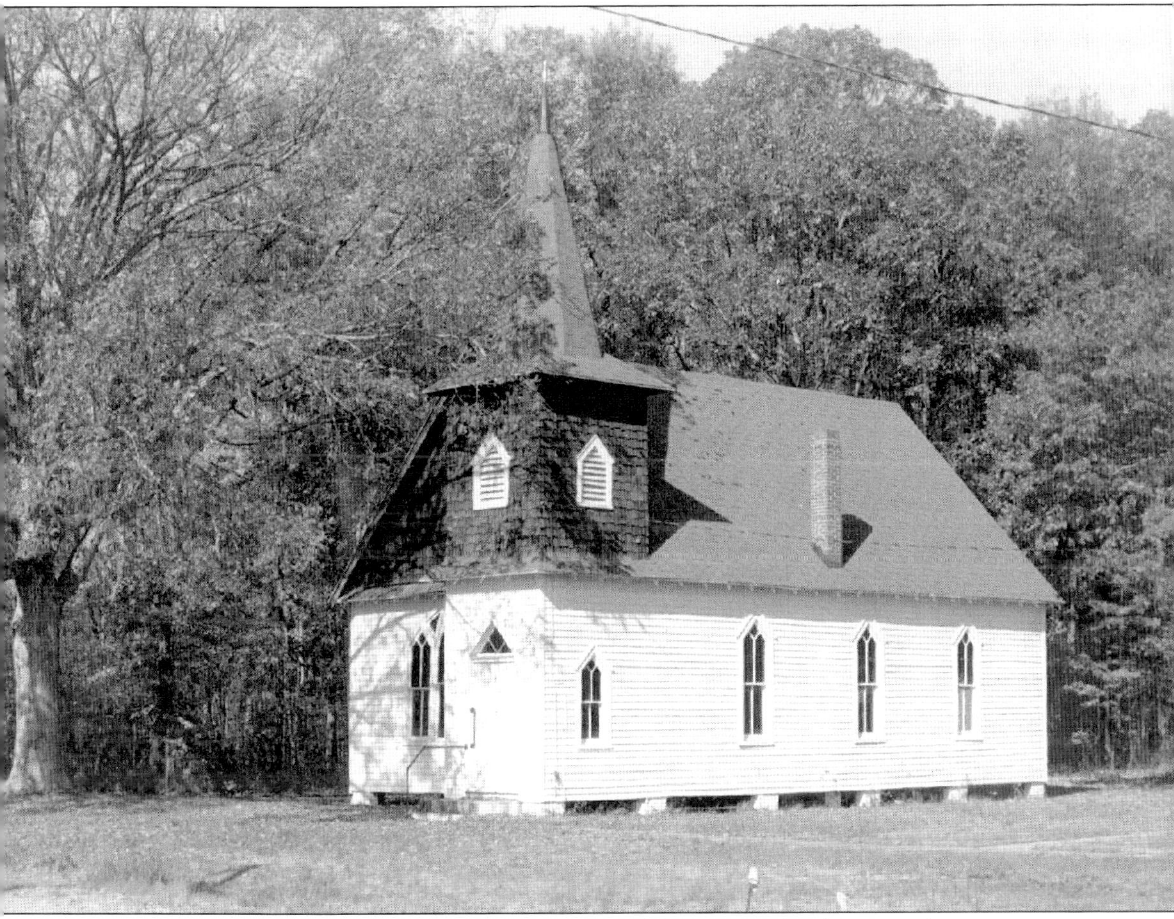

Built in 1894, Vaughn M.E. Chapel on Old Field Road drowses under the care of a community organization of church members and their descendants. A memorial service each spring honors loved ones in the nearby cemetery. Homecoming is the third Sunday in September at Old Field, and at various times at Harrisville, Taylors Island, and many other rural churches. Historically black rural churches that still hold old-time camp meetings are John Wesley U.M. Church on Liners Road and Jefferson U.M. Church at Smithville. In Cambridge, Bethel A.M.E. Church has a meeting and hosts the Poor Mans Supper on Martin Luther King's birthday, and in April hosts a Remember the Struggle Luncheon. Across Old Field Road from Vaughn M.E. Chapel once stood the Beverly School, founded in 1868 on land given by Daniel Orem. It is believed by many to have been the oldest Dorchester County school for black children. Established before the close of the Civil War, it was, of necessity, staffed initially by whites, two sisters who came to Old Field from Massachusetts.

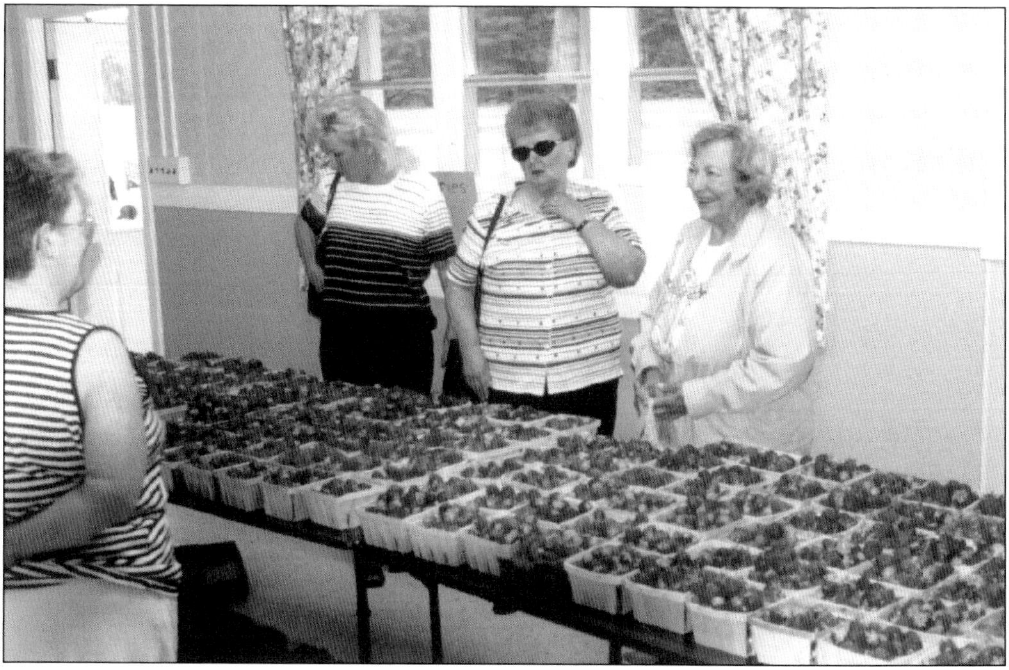

Visitors should follow locals flocking to Beckwith U.M. Church's spring Strawberry Festival and fall Apple Festival and Antioch U.M. Church's summer Peach Festival. Such events feature flea markets and fresh-picked fruit along with menus including sandwiches, fritters, fruit-filled dumplings, pies, homemade ice cream, and other devilish delights. Taking a break from assisting are Beckwith's Betty Wheatley, Paula Loque, Virginia Kupidlowski, and Rose Seward.

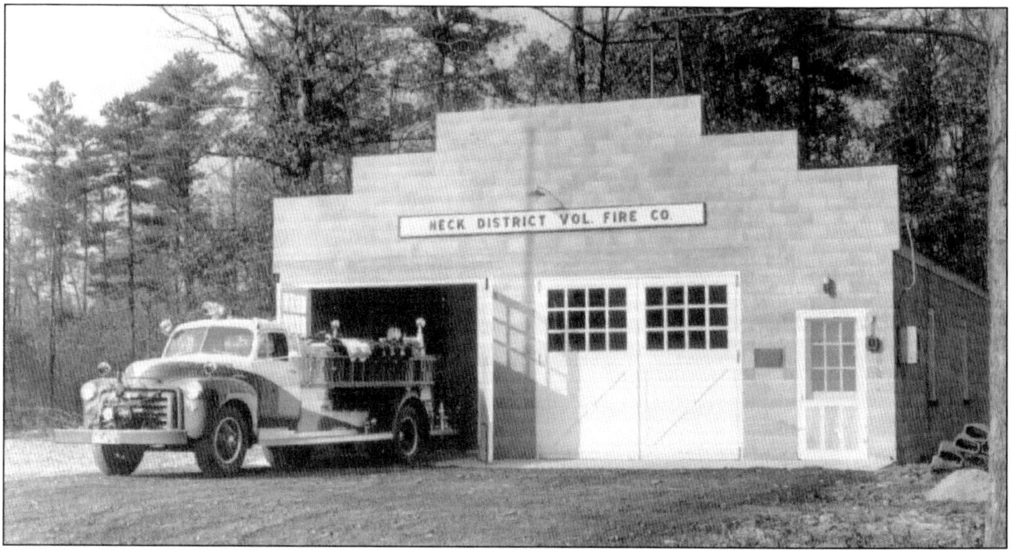

Neck District Volunteer Fire Company celebrated its 50th anniversary in 2002. At their initial fund-raiser, they netted 50¢ from a local girl charging contemporaries 5¢ to see her three-legged chicken. A popular modern activity is the Crab Cake and Ham Dinner Labor Day weekend. Visitors would do well to check for other fire companies regularly featuring home-cooked meals, such as oyster dinners at Linkwood, Hoopers Island, and Lakes and Straits.

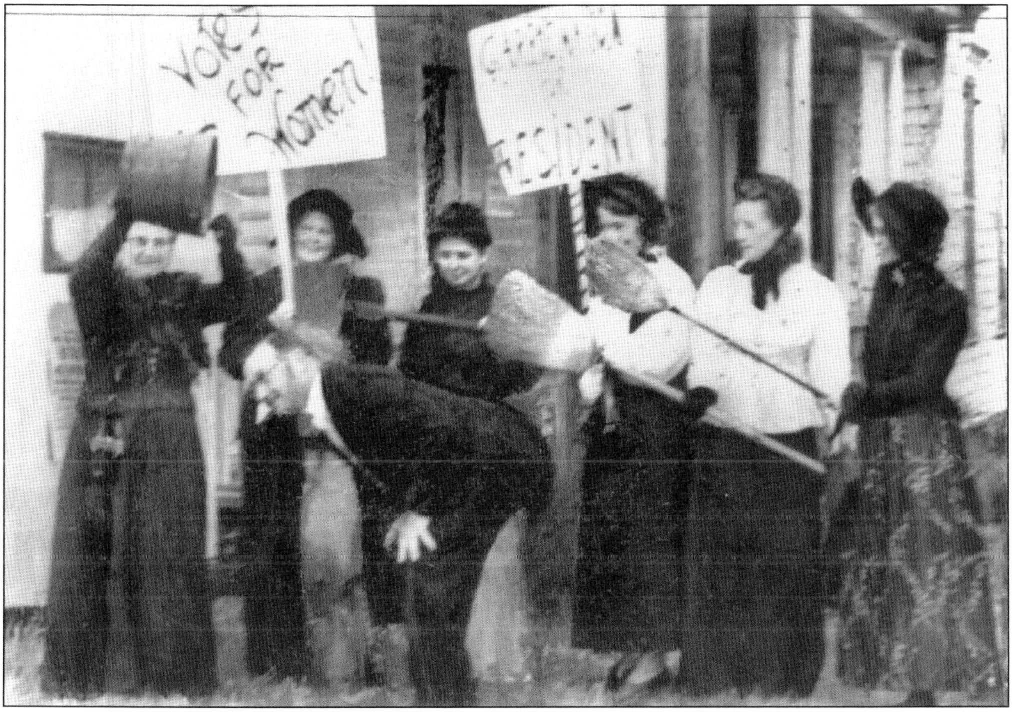

Each October the train rolls again carrying passengers from Hurlock as the Hurlock Fall Festival celebrates the town's history. These ladies attacking Alphonso Dean at the 1955 Hurlock Heritage Festival may joke about Suffragettes, but it's not likely they would forego the voting rights won for women just 35 years earlier. On the attack are, from left to right, Nellie Dean, Betty Wilder, Audrey Waldron, Bertha Stoker, Maude Venables, and Lula Powell.

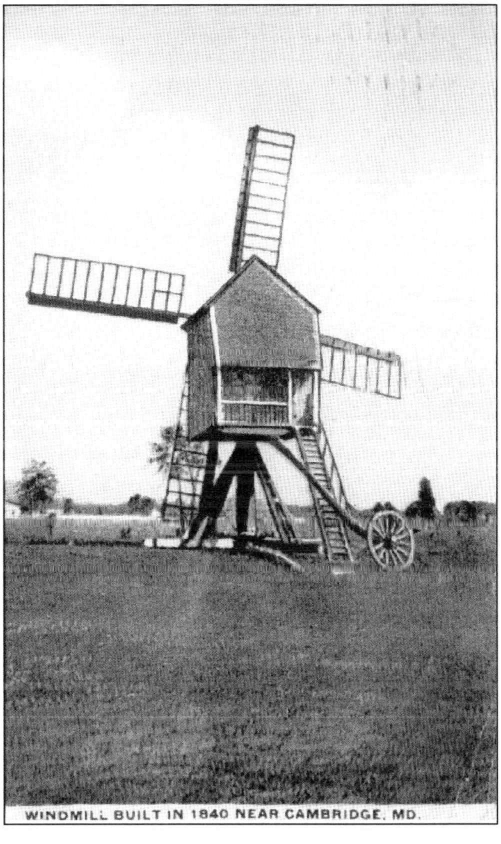

The Spocott Windmill in Lloyds is a reproduction post-type mill built in 1971 by premier boatbuilder James B. Richardson. Sen. George L. Radcliffe supplied millstones from a similar mill of his father's that was blown down in the Blizzard of 1888. Records indicate there were once 18 such windmills grinding grain in the county, including this one built in 1840. The Spocott complex includes a miller's house, a one-room schoolhouse, and a store.

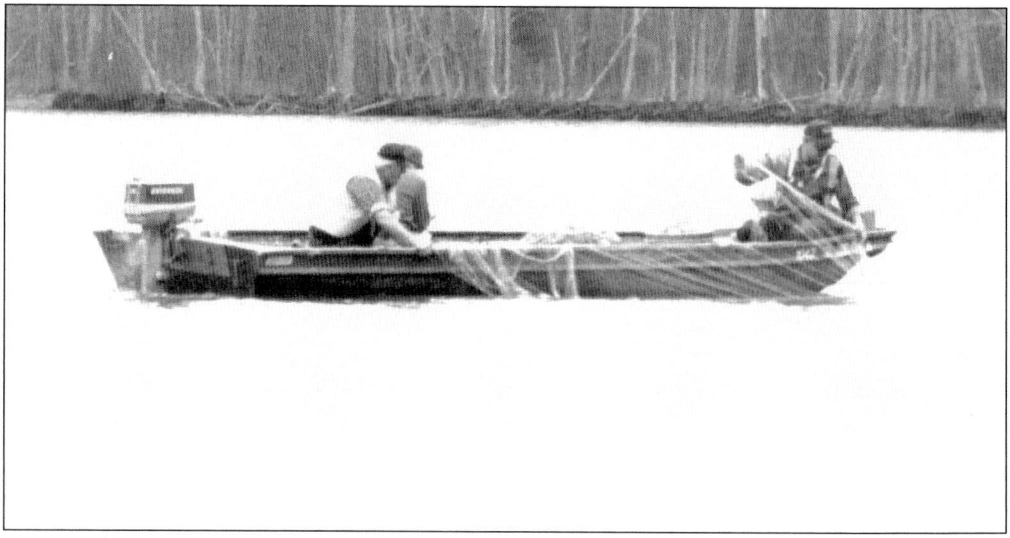

Elijah Wheedleton and Tommy Wheatley drift net for herring in Marshyhope Creek off the Nanticoke River, illustrating a fishing technique that has sustained the people of the watershed since time out of memory. In recent years, a Shad Festival has been celebrated on the last Saturday of April on the riverside in Vienna featuring traditional shad-planking and regional crafts. Another Vienna tradition is a Christmas Luminaria each December.

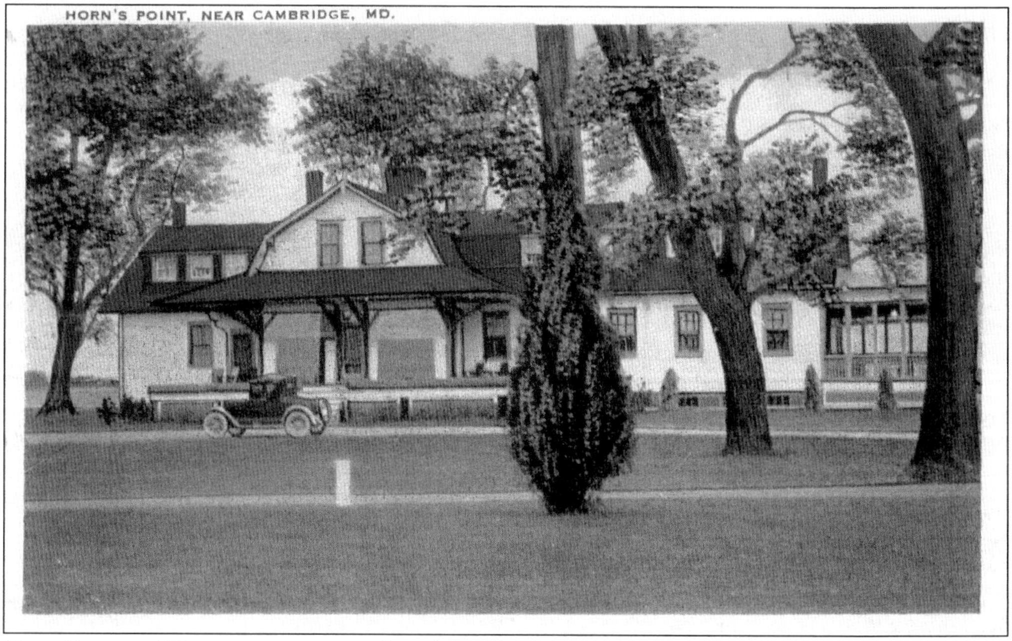

Horn Point, a 600-acre tract surveyed in the mid-1600s, in later years belonged to Sen. Coleman duPont. In 1930, his son Francis inherited the estate and in turn left it to the city of Cambridge. The original house had burned. The property now houses a laboratory of Maryland University's Center for Environmental Science. The public is invited every spring to attend an open house and view research in progress.

Nine

Then and Now

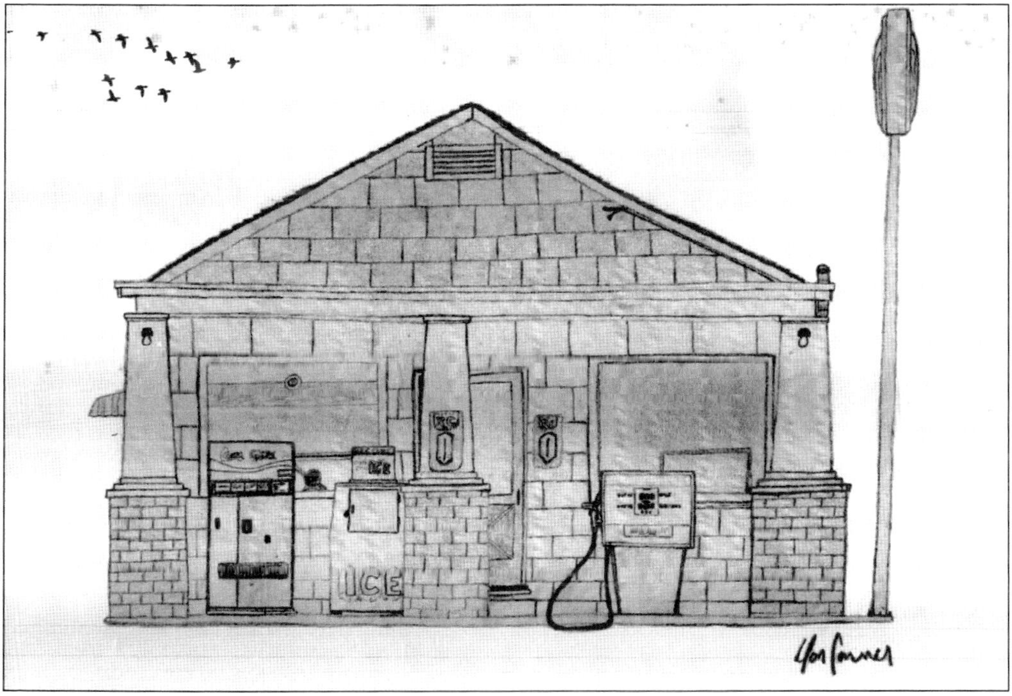

This sketch of Mutt's Place from a 1978 calendar rekindles memories of 10¢ crab cakes and 25¢ burgers that were the best around. Brothers William "Mutt" and George "Pete" Era bought the filling station outside Secretary from the Koskis in 1956 and renovated the rear living quarters into a kitchen. Mutt's kept customers happy until September of 1991. The calendar advertised crab cakes, oyster sandwiches, hard crabs, soft crabs, sandwiches, oyster stew, and hamburgers.

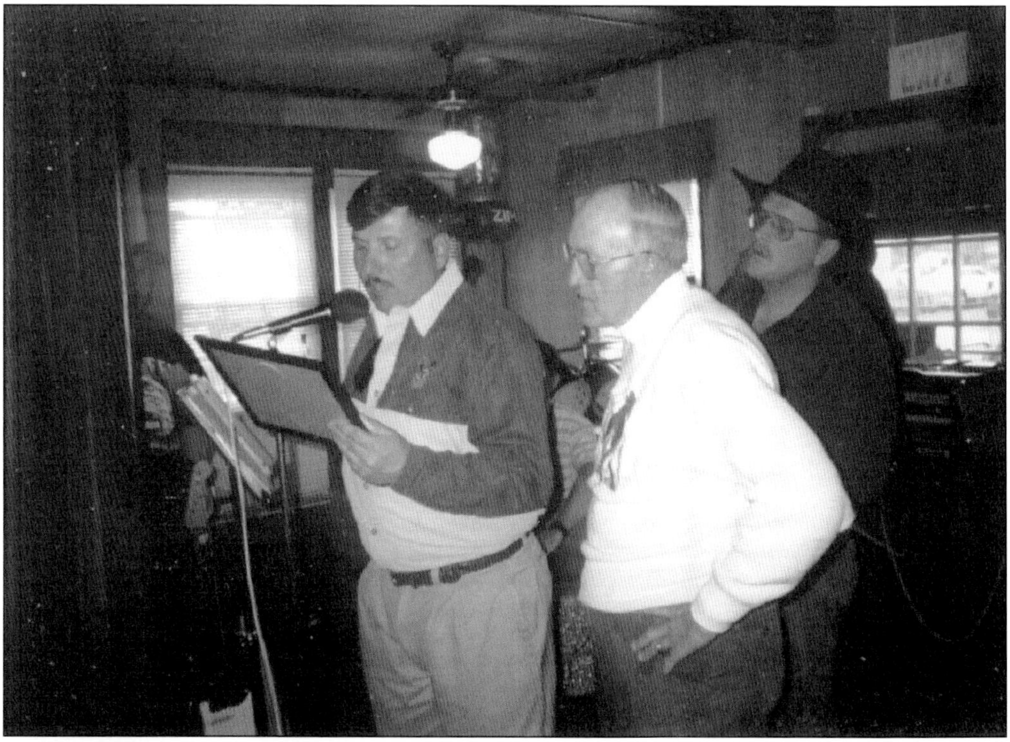

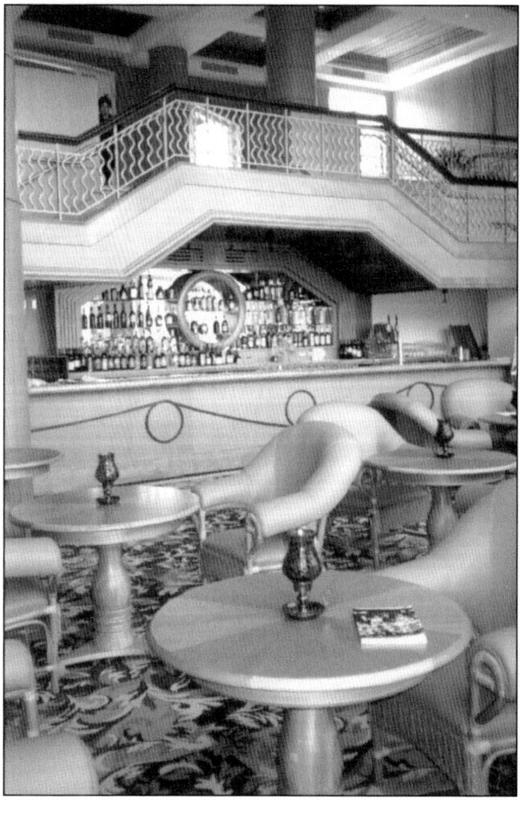

Nanticoke Inn provided room and meals to those working on the Vienna power plant constructed in the late 1920s. When it closed for gentrification and new management in 1996, generations of customers turned out for one last look at an authentic original. Wylie Abbott Jr. presented the final proprietor of the "Goat," Billy Dolby, (center) with a certificate honoring him as a worthy keeper of "the last great watering hole on the Eastern Shore."

Former customers of Mutt's and Nanticoke Inn can take solace at Hyatt Regency Chesapeake Bay Golf Resort, Spa, and Marina. The Hyatt menu in Michener's Library states, "We dedicate this to past, present and future watermen of the Chesapeake . . . quiet heroes dealing with blistering heat and furious cold whose companions were merely deer grazing on the hillsides of the Choptank River and the ritual visiting of geese from Canada."